The Tiffany Touch

RANDOM HOUSE ⌂ NEW YORK

THE
TIFFANY
TOUCH

BY
JOSEPH PURTELL

ACKNOWLEDGMENTS

For their help in the preparation of this manuscript I would like to thank Mrs. Hans Zinsser for her reminiscences about her father, Dr. George Frederick Kunz, and for her permission to quote from articles about his life printed in the Saturday Evening Post *in 1927-28; also the* Saturday Evening Post *for their permission; the American Museum of Natural History for permission to consult its archives; the New York Society Library; the New York Historical Society; the New York Botanical Gardens; the Museum of the City of New York; the Middleborough Historical Museum, at Middleboro, Massachusetts; Mr. and Mrs. Horace J. McAfee, who live in one of the old houses on Tiffany Acres and who graciously showed me their home; the Irvington-on-Hudson Public Library; the Morgan Library; and N. W. Ayer & Son, which made available to me full use of the De Beers archives; Leland A. Cook for supplying me with photographs; and permission to use the quote from Rudyard Kipling was granted by Mrs. George Bambridge.*

PICTURE CREDITS

*The author wishes to
acknowledge the following sources for
the pictures used in this volume:*

Acme, for the pictures on pages 172, 202.
N. W. Ayer & Son, for the picture on page 86.
Brown Brothers, for the pictures on pages 32, 39, 79.
Leland A. Cook, for the picture on page 146.
J. Clarence Davies Collection, Museum of the City of New York,
for the pictures on pages 4, 5, 8, 63.
Elite Camera House, Nairobi, Kenya, for the
picture on pages 302-303.
The Metropolitan Museum of Art, Bequest of
Michael Friedsam, 1932, for the picture on page 211.
Middleborough (Mass.) Historical Museum, for the picture on page 26.
Museum of the City of New York, for the pictures on
pages 6, 10, 11, 25, 31, 71, 88, 233.
Lillian Nassau, for the pictures on pages 120, 122, 126, 131.
The New York Public Library, for the picture on page 9.
Paramount Studios, for the picture on page 277.
U.P.I., for the pictures on pages 81, 166, 269.
Vogue magazine, for the photograph by Horst P. Horst,
Copyright © 1971 by The Condé Nast Publications, Inc., on page 263.
Ives Washburn, Inc., for the drawing on page 205.
Wide World Photos, *for the pictures on pages 167, 172.*
The Tiffany collection of photographs was used throughout.

Contents

THE
TIFFANY TOUCH

T

he 1830's in New York City rightly have been termed the Decade of Riots. They might better have been called the Decade of Disasters; fire followed fire; "cholera was endemic"; business failures spread like a plague.

A manic note was supplied by what the chroniclers of the day called *Moris multicaulis* fever. From 1832 through 1838 "the wildest speculation" centered on growing *Moris multicaulis,* the Chinese mulberry tree for feeding silkworms, as the first step in the establishment of a silk industry. On evidence no sounder than that which bankrupted their Dutch forebears during the tulip craze of the 1630's, New Yorkers lost fortunes before the scheme collapsed; flourishing businesses were ruined and "the affairs of others suffered greatly."

The riots were the most violent sign of the unrest which was begin-

(Above) Charles Lewis Tiffany at forty-one.

How the Panic of 1837 affected New Yorkers.

ning to trouble this overgrown country town, not quite ready to as-
similate the flood of immigrants—Irish, German, Welsh—changing
the manners and mores of New York and bringing with them new
problems, new politics. The poor had fled from the poverty of Europe
only to find misery, again, in the New World. More than half of the
population lived under incredibly wretched conditions—thousands occupied cellars which flooded at high tide. Homeless children roamed
and slept in the streets; more than a thousand under sixteen were arrested for drunkenness in 1837.

Despite these conditions, the well-to-do blamed the riots on inflam-
matory journalism and the revolutionary ideas of the immigrants.
In 1832, President Jackson had inaugurated the first era of the ''common man'' and when common men get together to protest, then as
now, the result is often violence. The decade opened with the ''mob
demonstrations'' of 1831. During the first open elections for mayor *
in New York in 1834, the Irish stormed through the streets and voted
their men into office. That year saw the first Abolition riots. The decade closed with anti-German riots and a bloody uprising of the Irish
workers who were building the Croton Aqueduct.

If the riots were alarming, the fires were an even greater source of
terror. The wooden buildings blazed like tinder. The Great Fire, to
distinguish it from the many lesser ones, burned for four days through

---

* Until 1834, New York's mayors were chosen by a committee of prominent citizens. One
of the results of Jackson's policies was the change to popular elections.

The Great Fire of 1835.

most of the business district in December 1835. More than fifty acres
of buildings and houses were destroyed. After the fire was finally out,
the ruin of many businesses was completed by the insurance companies' refusal to pay any claims.

Possibly nothing else so highlights the inadequacies of a town on
the verge of becoming a great city than did the Great Fire.* The firemen—all volunteers and fiercely competitive—arrived at the start of
the fire and, for once, did not take time out to argue as the flames shot
up. But the day was unusually cold—ten below zero—and the water
froze in the leather hoses. Soon the pumping engines themselves froze.
The firemen forgot the fire and pitched in to help save furnishings and
store goods. In the excitement, as the fire spread out of control, one
unnamed ''military man'' offered to blow up City Hall (with himself
inside) to stop the conflagration. Cooler heads prevailed and the gun-
powder was used instead to knock down the buildings to the east of
Broad Street. Firemen came to help from as far away as Philadelphia,
hampered by the fact that the new railroad between the cities had not
been completed. They had to haul their equipment ''by horse and foot
over six miles of the Jersey sand hills.''

---

* The Great Fire caused the city to become concerned about its water system. Work was
rushed on the Croton Aqueduct, to fill the great reservoir uptown on "fifth avenue" (not
yet important enough to be capitalized) where the Public Library now stands. The system
was made operative in 1842 amid much civic rejoicing. There was little private sanitation
and no running water; hence, there were no plumbers. "Billiard hall attendants and barbers"
set themselves up as "practical" plumbers. Results: never have so many ceilings fallen on
dining room tables, so many sleeping tycoons been drenched in their beds.

In all, some 674 buildings burned, and a contemporary account put the losses at twenty million dollars. The writer also noted that other fires that same year did another three million dollars in damage and that every day "New York is on the verge of conflagration."

Of all the bad years, the worst was 1837. New York was but partially recovered from the fire, inflation was rampant, the mob on edge. The year opened on the financial Panic of 1837, in many ways the worst until the Great Depression of the 1930's.

The panic, like the recession of 1970, was brought on in part by the federal government. The crisis, smoldering since the beginning of the decade, was fed by speculation in the sale of government-held Western lands, abetted by other policies of President Jackson, who believed that the common man could best be helped by "easy money." He was prejudiced against the hard (coin-backed) money of the Bank of the United States, in which the federal government deposited its funds. In 1834 Jackson broke the bank by withdrawing all federal funds and depositing them in small banks. This, naturally, brought a great increase in the number of banks—from 329 to 1788—founded solely to obtain federal deposits and to qualify for the right to issue their own currency. The flood of easy money brought about such an increase in speculation that even Jackson finally became alarmed.

Too late, he ruled that government lands must thereafter be paid for in gold or silver, a very scarce commodity in the new banks. Most of them collapsed—and the panic was on.

The diarists of the time—such as Philip Hone, former mayor of New York; Asa Greene, successful merchant and traveler; and Charles H. Haswell, naval architect and man about town—write about little else except the panic that year.

On New Year's Day, usurers were already "fattening on their 2½

Philip Hone.

and 3% a month.'' The well-to-do were property-poor, notes Hone, who "like other poor devils must bow and scrape to men with money in their hands; I am a proud man and not used to it.''

In the following months, more and more rich men went bankrupt; by May "the number of failures today are not worth recording, as there have been so many this year it ceases to be worthy of remark.''

The same month saw the beginning of the bank failures in New York. On May 8 the Bank for Savings and the Dry Dock suspended payments. On May 10 all New York banks stopped specie payments. Hone describes the last day at the Bank for Savings: "It could not close at the usual hour of 6 P.M. It was still paying out at 9 P.M., the people mad, the women nearly pressed to death and exhausted, but still with the strength to keep up their chant of 'Pay! Pay! Pay!' ''

As in many recessions, tight money was accompanied by inflationary prices. Hone noted that brooms "25¢ since time out of mind, are now 50¢. Poor New York!'' The prices of rent, food and fuel had risen even more sharply. It was said that no working man could eat and still pay his rent.

This state of affairs led to the Great Flour Riot in February. The price of flour had risen from ten dollars to about fifteen dollars a barrel, and a head of cabbage, once almost free, cost thirty-one and a quarter cents. The mutterings grew louder. During the month the rumor spread that speculators had cornered the market in wheat, and that even further price rises were ahead. Handbills were distributed around the city on the afternoon of February 10 proclaiming, "Bread, meat, rent, fuel—the voice of the people shall be heard.'' The mob converged on City Hall Park, then as now the scene of city protests. Word spread that the culprit was the firm of Eli Hart & Co., on Washington Street, and the crowd surged toward the warehouse. The firm hastily barred doors and windows, but to no avail. The rioters emptied five hundred barrels of flour and as much wheat into the street by the time the mayor and his constables arrived. The mayor tried to tell the mob that it was destroying its own food. In reply, the rioters filled the mayor's mouth with flour, nearly choking him, and broke the constables' long pine sticks, their badge of office. The police retreated and the crowd reenacted the scene at the warehouse of Herrick & Co., in Coenties Slip. It was not until darkness fell that the mob broke up to go home, conscious of a day well spent.

The poor were not the only ones grumbling about prices. Newspapers carried a cost-of-living index, which showed that since the turn of the century, the price of a hundred oysters had risen from one pence (one penny) to some twenty shillings (about two dollars and fifty

Pigs scavenging at City Hall Park in 1819.

cents); beef from three pence (three cents) a pound to a shilling (twelve and a half cents) and a hen turkey from four shillings to sixteen. Diarist Greene was certain that such inflation would automatically check the growth of the population; celibacy, he noted, was growing more popular as "bachelors could not take on the expense of a family."

In March and April of 1837 alone, two hundred and sixty businesses with liabilities exceeding a hundred million dollars closed their doors. It was being said that William Astor laid the foundation of his millions as a result of the fire and panic, when he foreclosed on ninety establishments. August Belmont, who arrived in New York in 1836 to be the American representative of the Rothschilds, also was said to have done so well picking up bargains in real estate and businesses that he was able to open his own investment firm in 1838.

Added to the poverty and starvation of the poor were innumerable hardships and accepted conditions of everyday life that knew no discrimination. New York had no official department of sanitation. The city's doughty garbage collectors were her pigs. In 1829 they numbered twenty thousand, but by 1837, after many grisly accidents, the force had been cut in half. No matter: the city depended on these free-roaming beasts to take care of its waste until well into the 1840's.

Dickens, in his *American Notes,* gives an account of a stroll up Broadway in the Day of the Pig: "These are real republican pigs. They mingle with the best of society, go where they please, on equal if not superior terms with everyone—who make room for him. For they are the City's scavengers, ugly brutes with scanty brown backs with unwholesome black patches and long, gaunt legs . . . Be careful! here come two portly sows trotting behind a carriage . . .

"Never attended, fed, driven or caught, they all know their own homes, and as evening comes they start for home, eating as they go with perfect self-possession and immoveable composure."

New York pigs were competent indeed, but one letter to the editor complained that "Cincinnati has pigs which are both larger and more efficient."

Household filth, pigs and a constant stream of horses were only part of the hazards confronting a shopper. Diarist Greene gives these directions for crossing Broadway: "The attempt is as much as your life is worth. To perform the feat, button your coat tightly, see that your shoes are secure at the heels, set your hat firmly on your head, look up and down the streets at the same moment to see what carts and carriages are upon you—and run for your life."

In many ways the village aspect was apparent. Along the dirty, cobbled streets, wooden water pumps were set every four blocks. The famous tea-water pump, so called because the water was thought to add a certain delicate flavor, was situated on Chatham Street. Despite the dirty town, the water surrounding Manhattan in the 1830's was so clean the ships' slips were filled with fish, and porgies were hawked through the streets at one cent apiece.

The first houses to be built for those other than the owners were

Raiding party seizes pigs concealed under bed
after they were banned as New York's garbage collectors.

*Huge sleeves
were all the rage.*

going up: houses for tenants, hence, tenements. They were marvels of shoddy construction, as were many commercial buildings. In 1837 the large store of Phelps and Peck collapsed, crushing five people. Philip Hone complained that most houses stood up only because they leaned against each other—and often as not, both fell down.

Good news or bad, New York liked to read about itself. There were fourteen daily papers and eight semiweeklies. There was no society news as such, and New Yorkers were proud that "no namby-pamby trash of fashionable movements finds its way into American papers." Eating habits remained of the frontier variety. *Lady's Magazine* championed them: "It is an effete affectation to put every morsel of food into the mouth with a fork. If you think as we do that Americans have a right to eat in their own fashion, you may choose the convenience of feeding yourself with your right hand armed with a steel blade. However, do not close your lips tightly over the blade." Fortunately for the budding luxury trade, 1837 saw the introduction of dining *à la française* in the more fashionable homes—which meant that knives, forks and spoons were used and the food served in courses, with the plates changed in between.

And luxuries there were. Visitors, then as now, could not believe the love of extravagance and show, the spending on frivolity and fripperies, which distinguished the rich New York native. No disaster seemed great enough to deprive the privileged few of any new luxury.

Women's clothes were brighter, in richer materials, and hung with more trimming than the dresses in London and Paris. Women still

*Young dandies
fancied
tasseled canes.*

wore enormous bonnets, with huge colored bows tied under the chin.
Cloaks were brightly lined, and silks and satins *de rigueur* for afternoon wear. Low necklines were appearing, both for evening and
afternoon. Sleeves were enormous; an etiquette book published in 1837
advised that "the better hostesses serve pin cushions with the soup
to enable the ladies to keep [sleeves] out of same." *Lady's Magazine*
compared sleeves to balloons filled with air. "In case of shipwreck, the
sleeves would serve nicely as life buoys."

Young men, for the most part, were clean-shaven. Facial hair for
men was so rare that the Egyptian consul, who arrived late in 1837,
was insulted for wearing a mustache. There was a considerable market
for slender canes, with a golden eye or carved ivory at the tip. In-
serted in this was a tassel of silk, which the young dandies constantly
switched around their heads, possibly to keep away the swarms of
flies, another of the unsung hallmarks of New York.

This was the scene: growth, panic, change; tight money and a desire for show and pleasure; opportunity, if only one had a little cash
and an abundance of ambition and imagination.

This was the city in which Charles Lewis Tiffany founded his
store in the fall of 1837. To the ordinary person, this period of gloom
and disaster would have seemed to be the worst time to start a business, but Tiffany was not an ordinary young man. His business, born
during crisis, has seemed to thrive on disaster; during panics, wars,
revolutions and riots in the 135 years of its existence, Tiffany & Co.
has gone its serene way, often doing better during a storm than when

all was calm.

Charles Tiffany was an upright man; he would never have planned deliberately to profit from the bad fortunes of others. But he was a Yankee and schooled in the Puritan ethic. If the Lord let disaster strike, there was no reason why a wise man should not benefit—if he could do so without harming others. His attitude was a far cry from the ethic of American capitalism in the nineteenth century. Never once was Tiffany associated with the shameful tactics of the Robber Barons—Jim Fisk, Jay Gould, Drew, Vanderbilt and the others who made their fortunes out of financial machinations which ruined their investors. Charles Tiffany went his own way, minding his store, and doing it so well that he became an American legend, his name a part of the language as a synonym for the best.

In the Middle Ages, Tiffany was a popular Norman name, derived from Theophania, a name brought to Gaul by the colonizing Greeks in the pre-Christian era. Theophania was the Greek mid-winter festival of the epiphany in honor of Apollo; the Normans corrupted the name but kept the original religious connotation, albeit in a different religion. Babies born on the Christian feast of the Epiphany were often named Tiffany.

Members of the Tiffany family came to England soon after the Norman conquest. They settled in Richmondshire and their progress has been preserved in historical annals in the following doggerel.

> *William de Coninsby*
> *Came out of Brittany*
> *With his wife Tiffany*
> *And his maid Manfrass*
> *And his dog Mardigrass.*

The first Tiffany in American history was Squire Humphrey Tiffany, who joined the Massachusetts Bay Colony in 1660.

The squire's life came to a sudden and tragic end. Samuel Sewall's diary for July 15, 1685, preserved in the records of the Massachusetts Bay Colony, notes that the day was "very dark, with great thunder and lightning. One Humphrey Tiffany and Frances Low were slain by thunder [sic] and one horse was slain. An attending maid was 'stounded' but not slain." Records also note that Frances Low's father caused a metal tablet to be affixed to a nearby tree reading:

> *Squire Humphrey Tiffany And Mistress Low*
> *By a stroke of lightning Into eternity go.*

The copperplate script of Charles Tiffany,
a model for the store's correspondence for years.

One of the squire's sons was drowned; among the five surviving children was James, who settled in Attleboro, Mass., in 1688. He was the grandfather of Charles. A painting of his farmhouse shows it to have been quite handsome and substantial, set in well-kept gardens.

James's son, Comfort, was born on the farm on February 14, 1777, the eighth of nine children. As a fairly young man, he decided to start a textile mill, and finding Attleboro too far removed from active business, Comfort and his bride, Chloe, an Attleboro girl whom he married in 1803, moved to Killingly, Conn. It was there that Charles Lewis was born on February 15, 1812.

Comfort's textile mill prospered and Charles went to the typical small grade school of those days; later, he spent two years at Plainfield Academy, a private school some ten miles from home. His father formed a new company to expand his textile business and, with a new partner, built a new mill.

Just as there are prodigies in the arts, so are there prodigies in business. Comfort Tiffany recognized these talents in his son and began to train him. He opened a country store and sent for Charles to come home to take charge of it. At fifteen, Charles was the store's entire staff, doing everything from selling goods to keeping the books and making buying trips to New York to restock his shelves. Within a year he had increased business to the point where he could hire help to run the store for him and could return to Plainfield Academy to finish his education.

In the meantime, Comfort Tiffany had bought out his partner and

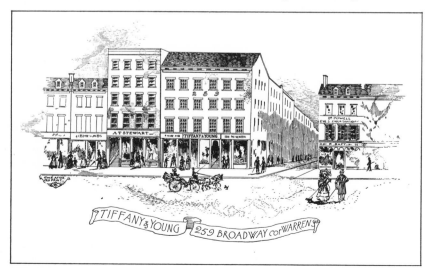

The first store of Tiffany and Young.

hopefully renamed the company Tiffany & Son. But Charles had other ideas. He did not especially take to the textile business, and the small Connecticut town seemed too limited to him. He had been to New York enough times to decide that it might be as easy to be a big fish in a big pond as to remain a big fish in a small pond.

He was encouraged to make the jump by his one-time neighbor and schoolmate, John P. Young, who had been in New York for six months working in a stationery and "fancy goods" store (a term which covered almost everything that could be sold). Since Tiffany knew how to run a store and Young knew about stationery and fancy goods, the young men decided to open this type of business. Tiffany, Sr., agreed to lend them five hundred apiece and they set out to conquer New York.

After the fact, it is easy to endow the young men with more acumen and daring in the face of the panic than they probably possessed. They had the bright enthusiasm (and ignorance) of youth, and the knowledge that the worst that could happen would be that Charles would have to go back to Tiffany & Son.

So many businesses had failed in New York that there was no difficulty in finding quarters for the store. Downtown on Broadway, within a block or two of Wall Street, was the fashionable shopping district. However, it had been burned out and the new brick buildings were renting at three thousand to five thousand dollars a year.

"Uptown" meant above Canal Street, but ladies refused to cross Canal Street. A theater which had opened just north of it that year had closed for lack of patronage. Another curious fact was that the ladies would not step one foot off Broadway to do their shopping—a pity for merchants, since space adjacent to the best locations could be had on the side streets for six hundred dollars.

However, on Broadway facing City Hall Park was a small area, still a fashionable residential district, just being taken over by business. A. T. Stewart had his department store there, at 259 Broadway, between Warren and Chambers streets. Stewart, who had begun in the smallest way twelve years before, was rapidly becoming New York's most successful merchant, attracting the wealthier people, the same customers who might be lured to Tiffany and Young's store. The two young men must have counted on curiosity, if nothing else, to make the Stewart patrons look in on the new establishment.

Just south of Stewart's was a small two-family dwelling. One half was occupied by a fashionable modiste, Mme. N. Scheltema, another attraction which might bring in the ladies. The other half supplied the vital frontage on Broadway—fifteen feet—which Tiffany and Young knew they must have. Quite as important, since the neighborhood was still semiresidential, the rent was the same as for quarters on a side street—six hundred dollars per year.

Years later, Charles Tiffany recalled how he and Young sat on the newly installed fence around City Hall Park, glancing nervously across the street at what they hoped was to be their new business premises, worrying whether their decision was a wise one, on the one hand, and afraid, on the other, that their offer might be turned down. The offer was accepted, and the young men assembled their stock. Considering the small capital, there was an impressive variety: bric-a-brac; Chinese goods, which were then very popular; papier mâché articles from Japan, terra-cotta ware, umbrellas, walking sticks for the young dandies, desks, dressing cases, and—most of all—stationery.

The store was opened on September 18, 1837, and went unnoticed by competitors as well as by most shoppers. Sales that first day were exactly $4.98. The second day was even more disappointing; only $2.17 was added to the cashbook. Then business boomed; the third-day sales shot up to $24.31. The next day they fell again and the last day of the month, twelve days after opening, sales were only $1.50. Cash on hand at this point was exactly $152.57. Advertising expenses for the first week had been $1.40 and the printing bill was $4.25. Despite the tiny sales, according to the old cashbook, the store seems to have been in the black that first week to the amount of thirty-three cents.

The partners apparently paid themselves a base salary of $10 a week, but had drawing privileges when that was not enough. Sometimes they drew as little as fifty cents a week, but every cent taken in, spent or drawn was meticulously noted. The cash on hand dropped to a low of $84 during those first weeks. In fact, it is incredible how little cash was needed to keep the store going for the first year. The money on hand was never more than a few hundred dollars. But sales increased, as Charles had hoped; customers of Stewart's and the dressmaker could not resist a look into the store next door, and they often bought. On the eve of New Year's Day, which, rather than Christmas, was the day New Yorkers then exchanged presents, sales rose to $679.

It was Charles Tiffany who first realized the opportunity offered by the popularity of Chinese and Japanese goods. He worked out an ingenious method of being first with the newest articles from the Orient, and at little outlay of cash. He would walk around the docks, making friends with the ship captains who had just come in from the Far East. Most of them brought back a personal stock of novelties to sell in order to add to their salaries. Tiffany made arrangements with

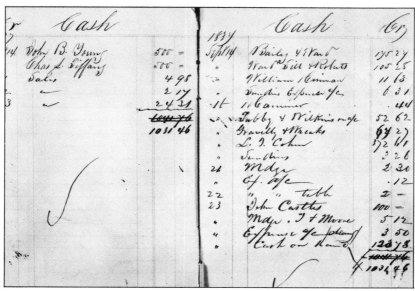

The first entry in the cash book and the first days' sales.

many of these seamen to handle their goods on a consignment basis so that he did not have to tie up cash. The plan did not always work, and then Tiffany had to scratch for money.

On the fiftieth anniversary of the founding of the store Charles recalled in a contemporary news story the difficulties of those early days.

I remember as though it was yesterday the first inkstand we sold. It was a bronze inkstand, imported, as most of those things were. I sold it to a fashionable society woman, who resided down in Cliff Street, which at that time was an aristocratic part of the city. Our entire force in those days consisted of my partner, an errand boy and myself. The boy had gone for the day, so when we closed up the shop I wrapped up the inkstand and carried it down to Cliff Street myself.

I shall never forget one of my first big purchases, two or three years later. Word reached the city that a consignment of fine Japanese goods had arrived in Boston. It occurred to me that this was a fine opportunity of getting some choice new things for our stock; but we had no ready cash and practically no financial standing. How to raise the money was the problem. I went down to Killingly, my old Connecticut home, and tried to get one of my associates, who was considered to be a pretty well-to-do farmer in those parts, to endorse a note for $300 for me. He would do almost anything else for me, with this exception. This rebuff, however, only made me more determined,

*and I finally found someone with enough confidence in me to endorse
the note, which I quickly discounted, and with the money started off
to Boston. I invested half of the entire amount in two articles—a mar-
velously beautiful Japanese writing desk and an ornamental table;
they each cost $75, and both pieces attracted so much attention, and
sold so quickly, that I was sorry there were not more of them.*

A present-day analyst can read into this simple story the reasons
for Tiffany's phenomenal success. He was not afraid to assume the
most menial tasks; even when he counted his money in millions he
remained remarkably available; if he really needed something—like a
loan—nothing could stop him; and already, at twenty-seven, he
evinced a love and appreciation of beautiful things, a talent for good
taste.

Through Charles' shrewd picking and choosing, the store expanded
steadily during 1838, but, the birth pangs over, the baby almost died.
On January 1, 1839, robbers broke in and took everything movable
out of the store. The loss was nearly four thousand dollars. Fortunately, the cautious young men had taken all the cash home with them,
and since the robbery came at the end of the New Year's Eve shopping
season, there was enough money to restock. Soon, they were happily
expanding, renting space next door, on the corner of Broadway and
Warren. This not only gave them forty-five feet more on Broadway
but a window on Warren Street.

Now, for the first time, the partners added paste, or costume
jewelry, imported from Hanau, Germany. In these early days, Tiffany & Young made no pretense of being jewelers, and years later
Tiffany recalled that the paste from Hanau was not only cheap, it
was garish, in poor taste and badly made. It is probable that neither
young man had even seen a diamond when they invaded New York.
Real gems were rare in the United States; garnets and turquoises
were regarded as fine jewels. Cameos were the fashionable ornament
of the day, caricatured in cartoons and verse as being of such enormous size that it was impossible to see the wearer behind them.

At this time the store set up a price policy so revolutionary that it
made headlines all over the country. Charles decided that every article
in the store must be plainly marked with the selling price, and that
the price on the Tiffany tag would be *the* price. During this period
merchandise in most stores was not marked at all, or had only a theo-
retical price, the point at which customer and seller would begin haggling. After Tiffany's tagged its merchandise there was no price cutting at the store. The policy was not only reassuring to the timid
customer, but it often led to lower prices at Tiffany & Young than at

their competitors. The aggressive customer at another store might get the price down as low as Tiffany's but the timid shopper paid more. The policy, which paid off handsomely, is still adhered to, even on $100,000 necklaces. The only discounts are to employees and to corporations which buy trophies and gifts through the Contract Department.

By 1840, New York had begun to recover from the money panic. The Henry Brevoorts felt secure enough that year to revive a favorite old pastime when they gave a costume ball at their elegant home on Fifth Avenue and Ninth Street. This was the first private party covered by a reporter, a man from James Gordon Bennett's *Herald*, who prudently hid his identity with a full suit of armor. The story covered, among other things, the ladies' jewels, and when it appeared, the reaction was predictable. Philip Hone ranted against the "shame of penny dreadfuls which report on the innocent and refined amusements [of their betters] striving to sow seeds of discontent in an unruly population." The diarist adds: "Bennett had better not show his ugly face in Wall Street."

All this was good for Tiffany & Young; business was growing so fast that by the spring of 1841 they took in another partner, J. L. Ellis, and the name of the store was lengthened to Tiffany, Young & Ellis. The new partner provided the capital to make possible a long-considered plan to send a buyer to Europe and to make Tiffany's "the only store in New York with a representative abroad." The gamble in cash would be sizable, but a European buyer could supply the latest in novelties and merchandise which would not be available in other New York stores. The partners chose John Young to go abroad. Although they could not have foreseen it at the time, this decision was to prove a turning point for the firm.

The year 1841 marked a milestone for Charles Tiffany in another way. On November 30 he married Harriet Olivia Young, sister of his partner, and daughter of Judge Ebenezer Young, of Killingly. Charles took his bride to a home at 125 Chambers Street, a respectable neighborhood, but too far from Broadway to be fashionable. As soon as he was able, in 1847, Charles moved his family, which now included a baby daughter, to a more correct address, 57 Warren Street. As was proper for a Victorian lady, Mrs. Tiffany was rarely mentioned in the news of the day, although as Charles Tiffany rose in the business world the Tiffanys were included in the guest lists of balls and other social events. The one time Mrs. Tiffany was mentioned in the press, she was described as "a woman of exceptional beauty and admirable character" with an erect carriage and curling brown hair.

When Young arrived in Paris in 1841, his first discovery was a line of paste called Palais Royale. The diamonds were false but the settings were carefully made, even elegant—there was no comparison with the vulgar baubles from Hanau.

As soon as Charles Tiffany saw them, he was excited by the possibilities of the Palais Royale line. The line became an instant success; women flocked into the store to buy the jewelry, proving that New York women did have taste, if given the chance to show it.

The success of the Palais Royale convinced Charles Tiffany that the store should import real diamonds in real gold settings. By 1845, the store had discontinued all paste and was selling only brooches and bracelets and scarf pins from the goldsmiths of Paris and London and, eventually, Rome and Florence. By the time the store celebrated its tenth anniversary in 1847, it had become necessary to move into larger quarters farther "uptown," even if the move was only a block to 271 Broadway, north of Chambers Street.

The larger store enabled the firm to add watches, clocks and bronzes, and to expand the silverware department. In fact, the stock became so large that Charles decided to publish an annual catalog, great-grandmother of the famous Tiffany Blue Book. There is only one mention of jewelry in the catalog: "Tiffany, Young & Ellis have determined to pay special attention so that they will receive by the French steamers and packets a limited number of every new style of bracelets, hairpins, dress combs, head ornaments, chatelaines, scarf pins, brooches and shawl pins, in fine gold only."

Other paragraphs list a bewildering number of articles. There were more than seventeen preparations for the hair, an equal number for the skin and shaving, scores of perfumes, and such "sundry items for the toilet as tongue scrapers and mouth mirrors." There were horse whips and dog whips, Chinese goods, chessmen, "seegar" boxes and "seegar" cases, tea sets, dinner sets and cuspidors, bronze curiosities from "ancient Indian temples," moccasins, belts, American Indian artifacts of birch bark embroidered with moose hair, "suitable for friends on the other side of the water."

For the home there was French fancy furniture, Swiss osier work, silver and vermeil ware, sets of napkin rings—"a most rich and elegant gift"—and the largest and most complete line of stationery in the city.

The catalog also contained a discreet swipe at competitors: "As many of the parasols and sun shades sold in the City are called 'French,' Tiffany, Young & Ellis desires to say that all theirs are made to order *IN PARIS* and are guaranteed to be not only more tasteful in style but more nicely finished than any made in this country, while the price is but a trifle higher." The daring could purchase a pair of ne plus ultras (garters), pic-nic boxes and a mysterious item called "railroad eyes."

This wide variety made it plain that there was still no focus to Tiffany's: it was a fancy-goods store, getting fancier, but noted for no one category of merchandise. The importation of gold jewelry was a step toward catering to the increasing wealth in New York, but not enough to give the store a personality.

In 1848 the store established its proper niche in the merchandising world. Tiffany's, founded during a year of disaster and mob demonstrations, came into its own in the midst of revolution and disaster, and as a direct result of further mob demonstrations. In France the regime of Louis Philippe was faltering, and revolution broke out suddenly, just as Young and his assistant, Thomas Banks, landed on their annual buying trip. When they reached Paris, the barricades were up, the city was in turmoil and the supporters of the regime had but one thought—to get out of France. As often happens, the gentry was short of ready cash but well supplied with diamonds, if anyone would buy them. There were few takers. Overnight the price of diamonds fell 50 percent. Young was on the spot, to come to the aid of the distracted court—though not exactly out of the goodness of his Yankee heart.

His buying schedule had called for investing in diamonds and "novelties"; but he threw away the schedule for novelties (a tactic which Charles had always advised if better purchasing opportunities turned up on the spot), and decided to spend every penny on diamonds—hoping he would stay out of jail long enough to do so. Shopping in Paris was dangerous. Young was arrested and threatened with the firing squad before he convinced the revolutionists that he really was only a simple New York merchant, not a royalist conspirator in disguise. Banks, his assistant, was not so lucky. He was arrested and impressed into a street-cleaning gang; fortunately Young saw him and got him released.

It was at this time that Tiffany's, somewhat mysteriously, came into possession of its first French crown jewels. Louis Philippe and Queen Amélie had escaped from the Tuileries in such haste that they left behind the jewels in the vaults beneath the palace. The mob broke in and sacked the Tuileries, but in the cellar, along with the jewels, were ten thousand bottles of wine which set the insurrectionists off on a glorious drunk. They staggered out the next day with no idea of the riches that could have been theirs for the taking. Quickly the harassed police moved the treasure via underground passages to the nearest prefecture. For several days the jewels lay in a corner, covered with an old tablecloth. When order was restored, the jewels were removed to the nation's vaults for safekeeping, but—a number of pieces were missing.

No official suggestion has ever been made as to precisely what happened to them, but a few discreet lines in a Paris newspaper of the times record that Tiffany's had acquired a store of diamonds during a buying trip to Paris—including some of the French crown jewels.

Tiffany's, like every other diamond fancier from the Shahs of Persia and Cardinal Mazarin to the bidders at Parke-Bernet today, could be hazy about when and where jewels were bought. Many years later, when Marie Antoinette's zone (the Victorian word for girdle) was first mentioned as being owned by Tiffany's, the date of acquisition was given as "about 1850." It could only have been acquired earlier in the confusion of the revolution. Tiffany's did not sell the zone whole, but broke it up into several pieces of jewelry because it said it could not "prove" that the girdle had belonged to Marie Antoinette. Probably the store did not want to prove this; the zone had been the property of the government of France, and the sale to Tiffany's, whether by a revolutionist or a fleeing royalist, was technically illegal. Whether or not it was the zone, the fact is that Marie Antoinette did have one, and no other one was ever found, and when Tiffany's felt it safe to say so, it did claim—and still does—that the zone had been Marie Antoinette's.

In any case, when Young and Banks arrived in New York, Charles Tiffany saw to it that the diamond coup went far beyond those few lines in a Paris newspaper. Charles dwelt on the perils the store's agents had gone through and embellished the beauties of the treasures bought. Charles, with his inclination to leadership, his natural liking for people, his friendship with reporters and his talent for furnishing them with news, always was regarded as the most important figure in the firm. Besides, his father's money had founded it. Since the press prefers heroes to amorphous "spokesmen," it was natural that Charles Tiffany, the friend of the reporters, should turn out to be the hero of the diamond coup, rather than John Young, who had bought the gems. The whole affair was neatly summed up when the press crowned Charles Tiffany "the King of Diamonds."

T he diamond coup had come at precisely the right time. Money was once more pouring into New York from many sources, some of which were deplored by Philip Hone, who wrote that "men grow rich supplying the starving population of Ireland [following the potato famine]. Palaces are being erected out of the freight of a shilling sterling on flour."

That year, the glitter of diamonds was first talked about when the great Rackets (tennis) Ball was given, "old money and new lavishing it on extravagances and love of show, to which New Yorkers are prone."

Neither amateur diarists nor the press tired of berating the city for its vulgarity and "love of show." In a year or so, cheating the Irish

(*Above*) *Gideon F. T. Reed, a new partner.*

was forgotten, and the villain was said to be the wealth pouring in from the California Gold Rush. The press pretended sympathy for the plight of the Eastern businessman whose wife felt compelled to compete with the Western nabobs. The ladies ''dress with more magnificence than ever, with no taste, too many brilliant colors and too many jewels and gold ornaments. Thus do they support the luxury stores, but beggar husbands, as it takes a Croesus to maintain a woman of fashion.''

The 1848 coup in France had another effect on the future of the New York store. Tiffany's decided it would be profitable to open a Paris branch, to take advantage of any more sudden fluctuations in prices, and Gideon F. T. Reed, a new partner who was formerly a member of a leading Boston jewelry firm, was made head of the Paris office. Tiffany's selling methods worked as well abroad as at home, and soon this branch, too, was moving to larger quarters. Along with European royalty, nobility and merely rich, many Americans traveling abroad felt it was cozier—and more reliable—to pick up their more expensive mementos from a firm they knew and could trust.

Meanwhile Charles Tiffany was developing his superb talent for publicity. In the process, he came to know P. T. Barnum, whose museum of freaks and genuine marvels was only six blocks away, down Broadway, at Ann Street. While Barnum played upon the unflagging desire of people to be entertained and amazed by something new and different, Tiffany strummed a variation on the same theme—the primitive desire of people to own something new and more splendid than others of their tribe. Tiffany and Barnum joined their talents several times, to their mutual benefit.

When Barnum brought Jenny Lind to the United States for her first grand tour in 1850, she was scarcely ashore before she visited Tiffany's, already one of the sights of New York. Delighted with the work of these New World craftsmen, she commissioned the firm to make her a memorial of the voyage to present to the captain of the ship—one of the first of the endless memorials Tiffany's was to make.

Contrary to the rococo taste of the time, the design for the silver tankard was a marvel of restraint. The motif was nautical: the curving handle, a mermaid rising from the sea, while Triton, suitably armed, emerged from the cover. The carving on the sides showed a rainbow, an incident of the trip which the singer wanted to include. When the tankard was completed, both Barnum and Jenny Lind were so delighted that they asked Tiffany's to make several duplicates for presents to other friends.

On another occasion, when one of Barnum's elephants was sentenced to death, Charles Tiffany saw a chance to cut himself in on the publicity. The elephant, Mr. Forepaugh, had killed ten men—or possibly only eight, depending on which paper you read—and he was to be strangled to death. (How do you go about strangling an elephant?) When the sentence was carried out, Tiffany bought the body, had it skinned and the hide tanned. The trophy was exhibited in the window while the store advertised that leather articles would be made from the hide of the celebrated killer.

When the articles were put on sale, the store was mobbed, and the police had to be called in to control the crowds.

And then there were the midgets, Barnum's most celebrated attraction: General Tom Thumb, Commodore Nutt and Lavinia Warren. According to Barnum, there was a fierce rivalry between the general

Jenny Lind.

and the commodore to win the fair, if tiny, hand of Lavinia. When interest was at its height, Barnum announced that Lavinia had been won by the general.

The wedding, an event of almost civic importance, took place in Grace Episcopal Church, the most fashionable house of worship in New York (it still stands at the corner of Broadway and Tenth Street). It was impossible to move through the streets, let alone get into the church. Displayed in the most conspicuous place among the wedding presents was a silver horse and carriage Charles Tiffany had made for the little couple. Naturally, as a public service for those who had no entrée to the reception, the carriage had been on view in Tiffany's window for several weeks before the ceremony.

These first successes convinced Charles Tiffany that there was a large market for silver of all kinds in America. The new rich were

The wedding party of Gen. Tom Thumb and Lavinia Warren (in center).

replacing crockery and tin with solid-silver services. The old rich were
playing all sorts of new games—tennis, golf—and indulging in other
new sports—racing yachts and horses—all of which required suitable
trophies for the winners. For these sporting bloods, Tiffany's had been
importing English silverware, but in 1844, a protective tariff of 30
percent had been passed on imports which made it possible for American firms to undersell foreign goods. Charles Tiffany was prepared
to take full advantage of this situation. For some time, he had admired
the silverware of John C. Moore, who supplied the top jewelry stores
and was considered the best silver craftsman in the country. Tiffany
contracted with Moore to supply Tiffany's exclusively and instructed
Moore to make the silverware as pure as possible—a standard of 925

John C. Moore,
the master silver
craftsman.

parts silver out of 1,000, the same as English sterling. (The other 75
parts were needed to harden the metal). This put Tiffany's ware on a
par with the British and well above the standards of most American
smiths.

The general practice among silver manufacturers had been to melt
down metal from Mexican and Spanish coins, whose purity varied
widely. To compete with Tiffany's, all silver makers were forced to up-
grade their metal and eventually the Tiffany standard for sterling
was written into United States law, the same law that is in effect
today.

While Charles, now a robust forty-one, was just hitting his stride,
Young and Ellis, who both were older, thought only about retiring.
Each had made a considerable fortune out of the firm and, in addition,
the company was in a position to buy them out. Gideon Reed had put
a sizable sum into the company when he became a partner, and with
the store's ample earnings there was no lack of cash. The details of
the buy-out are not known, nor was much ever written about Young

and Ellis. Charles Tiffany, as the firm's name indicates, was the dominant figure. What history there is of the early days revolved around him; he was the man with the dreams. The store was not only his business; more important, it was his hobby and his fun. He liked to meet people and made friends with everyone he met. To quote from a newspaper of the period: "Mr. Tiffany is a man from New England with the heart of a gentleman from Kentucky." No customer was surprised to walk into the store on a busy day, and find Charles behind the counter, and many a woman shopper, waited on by Charles Tiffany in the afternoon, was his hostess at dinner that night.

After Young and Ellis left the firm in 1853—under the friendliest circumstances, for Charles later bought a house from Ellis—the name of the firm was changed to Tiffany & Co., which it has remained to this day. The departure of the partners caused no change in Charles' plans for expansion. It was time again to move, not only farther "uptown" but to much larger quarters, a four-story building at 550 Broadway, between Prince and Spring streets. Here it was that Tiffany installed Atlas, bowed under his clock, which has become a familiar figure to generations of New Yorkers. It can be seen now over the Fifth Avenue door of the present austerely elegant Tiffany building. Darkened to a fine green shade that resembles the patina on bronze, Atlas is actually carved from wood. The carver was Henry Frederick Metzler, a friend of Charles' who made figureheads for sailing ships. (His other claim to fame is that he invented the four-wheeled baby carriage.)

The figure of Atlas is almost nine feet tall, high enough so that the man who cleans the face of the clock can stand almost upright inside. When the clock was first installed between the windows on the

*Atlas clock
got the clerks
to work on time.*

Catalogue cover.

second floor of the building, the works, made by Tiffany's, were not in the clock, as they are now. They were in a glass case on the third floor and so ingeniously constructed that they not only ran Atlas' burden but several other clocks in the store.

One legend of the 1860's, which has been repeated many times since, is that the clock stopped at the exact hour of Lincoln's death at 7:22 A.M. on April 15, 1865. True or not, it is the kind of interesting tidbit that Charles Tiffany would drop in the course of a talk with reporters. Ever since the clock was mounted, it has been noted for its accurate time. *Leslie's Weekly* ran a well-illustrated feature story in the 1860's on how clerks and messengers, too poor to own pocket watches, depended on the Atlas clock to get them to their jobs on time. The illustrations show the boys and young men thrusting their way through the crowds, with apprehensive glances over their shoulder at the clock, as they scurried up and down Broadway.

Along with the expanding store, Charles' family also grew. Charles, Jr., was born on October 7, 1842, but he died in March of 1847. Annie Olivia came next, in November 1844. Louis Comfort Tiffany was born on February 18, 1848, and Louise Harriet on December 18, 1856. Another Charles, born in 1858, lived only a year. Possibly discouraged by the fate which seemed to overtake his namesakes, Charles named his last child, a boy, Burnett Young (after his wife's family name and his first partner) when he was born on April 12, 1860.

Charles moved his family out of Manhattan, briefly, for sentimental reasons. During the winter of 1851 the Tiffanys went to live in Brooklyn, in the home of Charles' sister, Eliza, who had married Nathan B. Morse, a substantial citizen in his own right, a judge both of the circuit and supreme courts of the state, treasurer of the City of Brooklyn (not yet a part of New York) and president of the Brooklyn Ferry Co. Charles' widowed mother made her home with Eliza Morse,

and Charles moved to Brooklyn to be close to her during her declining
days. She died in 1852; after that, Charles moved his family back to
the Warren Street house.

If there was one custom indigenous to New Yorkers, until rent con-
trols and the lure of the suburbs changed the pattern of years, it was
the annual move, so puzzling to outsiders. A year after the move back
to New York, the Tiffanys were uptown on Tenth Street, in the area
made fashionable after the Astors had built on Astor Place. The
Tiffanys moved twice on Tenth Street, until 1860, when their address
is given as Madison Avenue "between 38th and 39th Street." There
was a reason for this vagueness; although Madison had been laid out
north to Forty-second Street, no numbers had as yet been assigned.
Here Charles Tiffany lived out his life.

Madison Avenue at that time was far removed from the fears which
already enveloped the busier parts of the city. The *Strangers' Guide
To New York* for 1853 sounded a warning for the out-of-town visitors
to Tiffany's, Lord and Taylor, Stewart's et al. "Well might [the
visitor] be alarmed by the many tongues on Broadway," cautioned the
Guide. "It is feared that the foreigners will get together, rise en
masse, and send back to Europe for a king."

Despite such warnings, visitors and native New Yorkers poured
through Tiffany's to be thrilled by a variety of new jewels. Charles
the First, King of Diamonds, did not disappoint them; like other
kings, he looked for new worlds to conquer and became fascinated
with pearls. The Oriental pearl, before the days of the cultured variety, was the favorite of both royalty and the wealthy. Queens and
duchesses, shahs and rajahs filled their coffers with diamonds, rubies
and emeralds, but they wore—and valued—pearls more than any other
jewel. Oriental pearls were not only more expensive than diamonds,
but lacking their cold gleam they were vastly more becoming. Mrs.
William and Mrs. John Jacob Astor, Mrs. August Belmont, Mrs.
Willie Vanderbilt all wore ropes of pearls which fell to the waist.

Before the era of the Oriental pearl ended, Tiffany's sold millions
of dollars' worth of strands. The necklace they assembled for Mrs.
George Gould was worth over a million dollars. Ropes of pearls costing three hundred thousand and more were a popular size with the
rich—worn in many cases in sets of three.

Mingled with the fabulous story of the Oriental pearl is the nearly
forgotten American saga of the great fresh-water pearl hunt, as
frantic as the gold rush of '49. Like many other incidents concerning
jewels, the story began in the office of Charles Tiffany.

One day in the early 1850's a pair of oxen, yoked to a rude cart,

Mrs. William K. Vanderbilt.

Mrs. George Gould
wearing her million-dollar rope of pearls.

was driven up to the store and the animals hitched to the nearest post. Out of the cart piled a roughly dressed man with his wife and daughter. They marched into Tiffany's, past the startled clerks, past the smiles of the customers, right into the office of Charles himself at the back of the store.

The man handed Tiffany something wrapped in a soiled piece of paper. It was a lustrous, perfect, rare pink pearl, over 100 grains in weight. Tiffany turned it over a few times, carefully, and then quietly asked the man how he had come by it. The night before, the farmer said, he had been musseling in Notch Brook,* off the Jersey shore, a scant seventeen miles from Manhattan. The family opened the mussels for dinner, and they came upon the pearl. Even these unsophisticated farm people knew that it might be valuable. They agreed that the only person to approach was Mr. Tiffany. Before dawn they hitched up their oxen and set off on their first venture into the big city.

In recalling the incident to an associate Tiffany remembered that as he examined the pearl, the man shuffled his feet and looked up slyly, "My wife and girl here want to trade this thing for some jewelry."

Tiffany remained silent for some moments, his mind racing. At once he saw the pearl both as a promise and a threat. If the pearl was unique, it was worth a deal of money. If, on the other hand, it was typical of what might be found in the unexplored country and its uncharted streams, it might be one of hundreds of thousands. Pearls might become so common that the whole market would collapse. Obviously the farmer had no idea of the real value of his find; in fact, he seemed to find it less appealing than a handful of trinkets. On the other hand, the pearl was an exceptionally fine one, and Tiffany hoped he was an honest man. A nice problem, both in finance and ethics. Tiffany made his decision: "Suppose I give you twelve hundred and fifty dollars in cash and two hundred and fifty dollars in trade—would that please you?"

The man was quite overcome by what he considered an overly generous offer. Quickly, before Tiffany could change his mind, his wife and daughter picked up handfuls of the brightest lockets and pins; the farmer clutched the cash in his fist, and the family left.

Tiffany's found a buyer at once in the Empress Eugénie; the gem became known in Europe as the Queen Pearl. After the fall of the Second Empire, Tiffany's bought the pearl back, and sold it to a wealthy German industrialist, Hänsel von Donwermark. In the man-

---

* Eventually, pearls valued at three hundred thousand dollars were taken from Notch Brook, but none either as large or as fine as Tiffany's was found. Notch Brook has since disappeared in the development of the shore.

ner of great jewels, its history became clouded. Somehow, it became a part of the crown jewels of the House of Saxony, and its last recorded appearance was just before World War I when the Grand Duchess was seen wearing it as a pendant. In 1970 Tiffany's was still hoping for word of what had happened to its pearl.

Charles' concern with publicity remained keen, and his most successful stunt took place a few years later. It was tied in with the laying of the Atlantic cable at the end of the 1850's. After several years of failure, Cyrus Field was finally close to linking America to Europe telegraphically. In 1858 the cable, for once unbroken, stretched to the sea just off Ireland, and the public interest was aroused. As the cable crawled slowly to its ultimate destination on land, the national excitement rose—comparable to the fever over Lindbergh's flight. At last the great news came; the final stretch of cable was in place.

Charles Tiffany was in Europe at the time. There were miles of unused cable left, and Tiffany shrewdly discerned a chance to cash in on the fever. He made a deal with Field to not only buy the left-over cable, but to receive a letter as well, stating that bits of Atlantic cable sold by any one but Tiffany were fakes—only Tiffany had the real stuff.

Tiffany proceeded to have this "wonderful mechanical curiosity," as he called the cable in his ads, cut into four-inch lengths, each fastened with a brass ferrule. Enclosed with each piece went "a copywrighted facsimile certificate of Cyrus W. Field, Esq.," guaranteeing that the piece was indeed cut from the original cable. Since Field had apparently overshot his mark, "twenty miles of it have actually been submerged and taken up from the bottom of the ocean. This will be the first sold, in precisely the condition in which the great cable now lies in the bed of the Atlantic." (Presumably, since it had been covered with mud, this saved the cost of a cleaning.) The price of this wonderful curiosity: fifty cents. Other parts of the cable were made into paperweights, canes, umbrella handles, seals, watch charms and "coils for ornamenting parlors and offices." As usual when Charles Tiffany staged a promotion, the crowds were so great when the souvenirs were put on sale that the constabulary had to be called.

Meanwhile, back at the cable, Field was busy installing the telegraphic equipment to make transmission possible. In June, transmission started, then failed; the same thing happened in July. But on August 6 the cable was finally declared to be an unqualified success.

The climax of the cable fever was to be an enormous banquet at which the elite would fete Field and pay proper tribute to his genius. Unfortunately, at the precise time when the banquet was in progress,

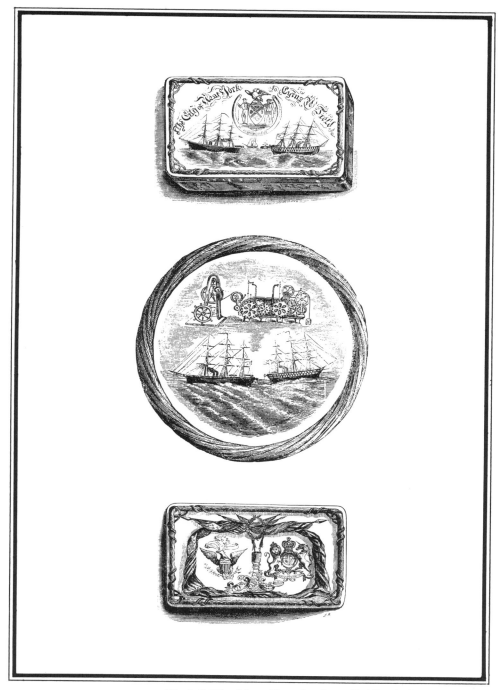

(Top) Solid-gold snuffbox showing mid-Atlantic joining of cable.
(Bottom) Reverse of snuffbox. (Center) Gold testimonial medal.

the cable broke down completely. The Civil War intervened and the cable was not put into operation until 1866. Diarist James Haswell, no admirer of Field, noted: "The only enduring manifestation of the enterprise was that the Cupola of City Hall caught fire during the illuminations [fireworks] and the whole upper story suffered considerable damage, which went unrepaired for a long time."

Ignoring this embarrassing fiasco, the City of New York went right ahead and commissioned Tiffany's to commemorate the great event with "solid gold snuff boxes ornamented with a scene showing the laying of the cable." Naturally, in the weeks before the presentation, the works of art were on view in Tiffany's windows, along with the testimonial medals. At times it seemed hard to tell from the stories in the press who had really laid the cable—Field or Tiffany.

When the Civil War began three years later, many firms found themselves in deep trouble because many an owner could not decide which side to be on, or having decided, what to do about it. Not Charles Tiffany; his uncomplicated New England soul never faltered. He was for the Union, body, soul and business, and he did something about it immediately.

Through the Paris office, Tiffany was able to order models of all the armaments of the French army, as well as those of the leading arms manufacturers of Europe. While waiting for their arrival, he took additional space next door, almost doubling the size of his store. When the models arrived, the elegant showroom which had once held diamond necklaces and ropes of pearls now displayed army shoes, caps, and swords, "warranted to cut wrought iron," as the ad stated, and rifles —not to mention gold epaulettes, cap ornaments and navy laces: "Goods forwarded to all parts of Loyal States."

Since Tiffany's was the first to assemble such a depot and to submit to the quartermaster general a complete list of the equipment of the French army, the orders were enormous. (It must be remembered that the United States had no armament industry at this time). Besides the orders for swords and guns, other sundries were supplied by Tiffany's. Ohio alone ordered twenty thousand badges for her soldiers.

"Business in the diamond department is very slow," one salesman of the period noted, "but we are very busy in gold braid and cutlery."

One customer was no less a person than Abraham Lincoln. The President might have been an austere person, but Mrs. Lincoln was not, and the President himself purchased a string of pearls, earrings and other jewelry which amounted to some twenty-six hundred dollars in two years.

Tiffany was personally involved in the draft riots which shook New York for four days in 1863. The Civil War, like the Vietnam war, was far from popular and the Union was so short of troops that Congress passed the country's first draft act, a model of inequalities and ineffectiveness, the worst of which was that any draftee could avoid service by paying a substitute three hundred dollars to enlist for him for three years. Some men made a career of deserting, and then reenlisting, as many as thirty times. It was a lucrative profession if you stayed out of battle—which many of the substitutes did.

The immigrant Irish-Americans, who had not cared for the war to begin with, became more and more sullen under the draft's inequalities. They felt they had known far worse treatment than the Negroes of the South, and now, to cap it all, they—the poor—would be the ones drafted. There were men only too willing to use this dissatisfaction for their own ends, notably Samuel Tilden and his pro-Southern Copperhead party, Boss Tweed, and Benjamin Wood who owned the *Daily News*. The *News* repeatedly printed reminders that the immigrants had not survived the horrible conditions of the ships that brought them to America in order to be killed.

The actual drafting was delayed in New York until July 11, and then the rioting broke out. There were two hundred thousand Irish in New York, and at one time they formed a mob of fifty thousand along Third Avenue. For four days, the rioters stormed through the streets, looting shops and burning the homes of the rich.

The small police force, which included many Irish, did its best to restore order, but the men were overwhelmed by the sheer number of rioters. Well-to-do and middle-class households ran to cover, up the Hudson and out to Westchester and Long Island. All transportation out of the city was at a premium.

Charles Tiffany neither fled the city nor did he hide behind barricaded doors at home. At the height of the rioting, word came that a mob was forming to march up Broadway to Tiffany's and other "rich shops." Charles Tiffany's reaction was to shutter the windows, bar the doors and pass out rifles to the staff. The men filled hand grenades with powder and posted themselves at strategic spots around the store. Charles surveyed his little army and felt assured it was more than equal to any rabble. The test of actual battle did not come, for just before the mob reached Tiffany's, the police managed to turn it aside. With the danger past, the employees laid down their guns and faced the delicate task of disarming the grenades. Charles stopped them. "No," he said, "You don't know how. I'll do it myself." And that is what he did.

NATIONAL LINE.
AMERICAN TELEGRAPH COMPANY.

Communicating with Philadelphia, Pittsburgh, Cincinnati, Louisville, St. Louis, Memphis, New-Orleans, and all Stations West and South.

Principal Office—Telegraph Building, 145 Broadway, N. Y.

BRANCH OFFICES.—*Astor House; Metropolitan Hotel; New York Hotel; Everett House; Bentley's Dispatch, [cor. Broadway and 22d St.;] 5th Avenue Hotel; Harlem Railroad Depot, cor. 4th Avenue and 26th St.; New Haven Railroad Depot, cor. 27th St. and 4th Avenue; Murray Hill House, cor. 6th Avenue and 40th St.; also at 91 South 7th St., Williamsburg, and 269 Washington Street, Brooklyn.*

Terms and conditions on which Messages are received by this Company for Transmission.

The public are notified that, in order to guard against mistakes in the transmission of messages, every message of importance ought to be repeated by being sent back from the station at which it is to be received to the station from which it is originally sent.— Half the usual price for transmission will be charged for repeating the message, and while this company will as heretofore use every precaution to ensure correctness, it will not be responsible for mistakes or delays in the transmission or delivery of repeated messages beyond an amount exceeding five hundred times the amount paid for sending the message, nor will it be responsible for mistakes or delays in the transmission of unrepeated messages from whatever cause they may arise, nor for delays arising from interruptions in the working of its telegraphs, nor for any mistake or omission of any other company over whose lines a message is to be sent to reach the place of destination. All messages will hereafter be received by this company for transmission subject to the above conditions.

J. KENDALL, Gen'l Sup't,
145 BROADWAY, N. Y.

E. S. SANFORD, Pres't,
145 BROADWAY, N. Y.

Dated *St Louis* 1861.

Received *Sept 7*

To *Tiffany & Co*

Continue sending Swords same as sixteen forwarded today. Send rapidly as possible & advise by telegraph of Each shipment

J. C. Fremont
maj Genl Com'g

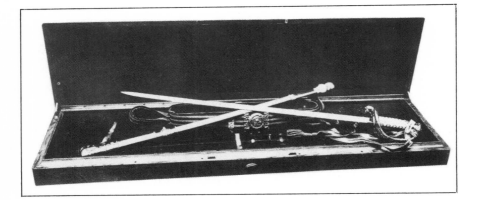

(Left) Civil War order for swords which poured in to Tiffany's were promptly filled ''for all loyal states.''

(Above) Gen. George B. McClellan, Commander of the Union armies.

When the victory of the North was assured, there was a great demand for commemorative swords for the returning heroes. It was a small and poor town that did not present its favorite officer with a sword. Tiffany's turned out hundreds of them. The most noted were the two which were to be given to the most popular officer in the Army and Navy. This scheme was not only a popularity contest but a means through which the ladies of the New York Sanitary Commission hoped to raise money for their work with the wounded Union soldiers. The drawing was part of a large fair, at which the "wealth and beauty of the city gathered to act as saleswomen," to sell donated merchandise and to collect one dollar for each vote cast for the most popular officers. Either the ladies were unusually good saleswomen or the contest was genuinely popular: the fair netted over a million dollars.

The swords offered for the contest, although more elaborate, were representative of the type Tiffany's was sending all over the country. They were described in loving detail in *Leslie's Weekly:*

The General's Sword: the grip of oxydized silver: on the obverse side, in low relief, a head of Mars, surrounded by a trophy composed of military insignia and weapons of the past and present times; on the reverse side, a figure of Victory with a laurel wreath in her uplifted hands, the joyous sounding cornets at her feet, and·over her head a diadem of stars. The guard, slender at each end, swells into a rich medallion, upon which is sculptured the wrathful Medusa; at the back of the grip is the head of a ram, identical with that familiar ornament of the sacrificial altar of the Greeks. The shell of the guard . . . is filled with a fine relief representing the combat between Hercules and the Nemean lion. The whole is surmounted by a spirited piece of solid sculpture . . . the helmeted head of America. Set in the helmet are rubies, diamonds and sapphires, representing the national colors. The scabbard is sterling silver, the tips in richly carved relief, laurel leaves etched in gold. The inscription: "Upon Your Sword Sits Laurelled Victory."

The Navy sword was far less ornate, apparently on the assumption that gunboats had played a lesser part in the war. As might be expected, the Army sword was won by General Grant and the Navy sword by Admiral ("Damn the torpedoes, full steam ahead") Farragut. The swords cost Tiffany's two thousand dollars to make and created for them good will and publicity worth much more. The admiral was awarded a special sword by the Union League Club, possibly to make up for his less splendid prize. This so pleased him that he had Tiffany's make a brooch for his wife, similar to the cypher in diamonds in the hilt.

The ending of the war brought a flood of unprecedented spending, this time by the rascals who had sold the government defective guns and powder, the scandal of Lincoln's administration. The new rich did not care if they were accepted by the society of old rich, which laughed at the newcomers' love for excessive adornment and vulgar tastes.

The Old Guard capitalists called them the Sybarites of the Shoddy, while their wives glanced with mingled disdain and envy at the new parade of diamond stomachers, diamond tiaras, diamond necklaces and diamond brooches which lit up the boxes at the opera and the theaters. Nothing like it had ever been seen on this side of the Atlantic. Hair was powdered—with real gold and silver dust. Not to be outdone, the men began the fashion of using diamonds of the finest water for waistcoat buttons.

While Tiffany's had no part in the fraud of defective weapons, it did not hesitate to accept the eagerly proffered money of those who had. In the winter following the end of the war, six hundred balls were given in New York, and the aforementioned stomachers, tiaras and other jewelry might individually cost from a hundred thousand to more than a million dollars.

The new rich did not live through their hectic days on such innocent refreshments as the tea and barley water so fondly recorded by naïve lady novelists. Far stronger stimulants and sedatives were required for the "fashionable and over-wrought hostesses preparing themselves for even greater dissipations," as one diarist wrote. One such palliative found on many a lady's dressing table between the gold dust and the diamonds was a bottle of Tilden's Extract, which could be purchased at any apothecary's shop for six cents the half ounce. The Extract was "hasheesh" (as it was then spelled) in liquid form.

With the booming market for diamonds—which lasted throughout the Gilded Age—Tiffany's main problem was not to sell jewels but to find enough to satisfy the demand. Under these easy circumstances, it was logical for Charles Tiffany to look around for another challenge —and he found it in his silverwork. Tiffany's had already established its dominance over the American silver market, but as yet was little known in Europe, where the traditions and skills of the great masters in silver went back unbroken to the Middle Ages. Tiffany decided to challenge the Europeans in Paris, at the Exposition of 1867. Winning the medal for silverware would be the highest accolade.

Charles Tiffany would compete on his own terms. While he had been turning out elaborate tankards and other commemorative pieces, he knew that this was the special province of the Old World masters, a field where it might be difficult to surpass them. So Tiffany wisely decided to show plainer articles, the kind that could be used in any substantially wealthy household. Under the supervision of Edward C. Moore, John's son, Tiffany's made water pitchers, coffee services and tea sets, done so beautifully and yet so simply that there could be no mistakes in workmanship; errors could not be glossed over or covered up, as was possible in more ornate pieces.

The results at the exposition were beyond the expectations even of Tiffany. The grace of the designs, their stark simplicity so unusual in those days, and the skill of the craftsmen so impressed the judges that Tiffany was awarded the grand first prize for domestic silver plate— a terrible shock to the older craftsmen, notably the English.

The London *Spectator* commented: "We confess that we were surprised and ashamed to find that at the Paris Exposition a New York firm, Tiffany & Company had beaten the old country and the world in domestic silver plate." The London *Art Journal,* with a touch of condescension toward the colonies, noted that "The establishment of Tiffany & Company is the largest in the New World. It is of great importance, therefore, that they minister to pure taste in America; they are doing so, if we may judge, by their contribution."

The New York *Herald* could not let these patronizing tones go by. The paper pointed out that Elkington's of Birmingham, the largest manufacturer of silver plate in the world, paid Tiffany the highest compliment by buying half a dozen pieces directly from the showcases after their offer to buy the entire lot was refused. The Tiffany pieces were copied exactly by Elkington's, the paper said, no doubt in order, "to minister to a pure taste in England. The pieces bought were all ordinary household articles . . . A massive tankard of artistic merit and great value or an elaborate christening cup to be produced only on state occasions, Birmingham could comprehend. But a water pitcher for everyday use and at the same time a work of art—that was a revelation to them."

Behind the triumph in Europe were years of work and training, plus the development of new methods of producing silverware which revolutionized the industry. Ever since the days of Cellini, the fabrication of gold and silver pieces had been virtually all hand work, done with hammer, forge and file, a slow and costly process. But after Tiffany entered the silver business, new methods had to be found to do things faster, simply to keep up with the demand.

The master craftsmen at Tiffany's invented mechanical means to speed manufacture, without compromising the results. Moreover, in the preceding decade, Moore's shop, which produced exclusively for Tiffany's, had grown until it covered an entire block and employed five hundred men. Speed as well as quality paid off. When a city official wanted a dinner set, valued at over thirteen thousand dollars, Tiffany's turned it out in thirty days; competitors would have needed months to complete the order.

New production methods were not the only reason for the rise of Tiffany's. Edward Moore, the director of the factory, once named the other reasons: "First, the nationality that we put into our productions; second, the novelty of our manufactures and design; and third, because there are few new designs from England—they are only reproductions of their old styles."

Asked, if all this was true, why the European artists claimed such superiority over America, Moore's reply was blunt: "I think it is their insufferable conceit—nothing else."

It is interesting to note that just as the 1970's mourn the dying off of good craftsmen and their irreplaceability, so did the 1860's and 1870's. Good silversmiths were so scarce that the factory trained its own apprentices, as many as a hundred and twenty-five at a time, most of them from the Cooper Institute. The works usually took teenage boys, but none younger than fifteen, and paid them from the start—an innovation. The wages depended on the work produced and skills displayed; when the apprentices reached twenty-one they were supposedly skilled craftsmen. Tiffany had a complaint about the public schools which sounds familiar: "We have adopted this method of training our own employees because of the absence of education in art, or industrial or technical skills in the schools in this country."

In these years, Charles Tiffany made one of his few wrong guesses. He decided to make his own watches. The store had always sold a great number of timepieces, so many that it employed five mechanics whose sole chores were to go about the city, winding and checking customers' clocks.

Watchmaking seemed to have been one of Tiffany's best ideas—on paper. As a first step, the firm opened a branch in Geneva. It then erected a watchmaking factory, the largest ever built in Switzerland, to join the mass production of the New World to the superb handcrafts of the Old. Unfortunately, the superb handcrafters of the Old World did not take kindly to the new-fangled methods. They refused to adapt. After what seemed a fair trial, Tiffany, not one to back a loser, closed the plant. He went back to buying his watches and clocks from the Swiss, probably what those Old World mountain types had in mind all along.

Tiffany did not let this setback color his enthusiasm for what the Swiss could produce. At the same time that he was confronting the obstinate workers, a marvel was created that was "superior to any yet offered for racing, gunnery and scientific purposes . . . noting time to the nicety of ⅕ of a second, in such a manner as to prevent the possibility of error." America knew the product as the "Tiffany Timer." We call it a stop watch.

Sportsmen and, possibly, scientists bought them by the gross and lent their names to the Tiffany Timers ads. One finds the names of many of Tiffany's friends and associates: Leonard Jerome, grandfather of Winston Churchill (who founded Jerome Park and the Jockey Club, and who liked to clock his fast horses), August Belmont, O. N. Cutler, J. V. Sprague, J. C. Griswold and many others.

The rapidly growing "uptown" business had become too big for the old quarters, so again a move to a new store was planned. The business also had become too big for one man or partnership to run; besides, there were certain legal advantages in reorganizing into a corporation, Tiffany & Co. The meeting to do so took place on May 1, 1868.

Two thousand four hundred shares were issued, with a par value of a thousand dollars a share. Charles L. Tiffany received 1,124 shares and was elected president and treasurer of the company; G. F. T. Reed, still head of the Paris office, received an equal number and was elected vice president; Charles T. Cook, who had started as a delivery boy twenty years before and who was so highly regarded that he succeeded Tiffany as president, got 91 shares and became assistant treasurer; Edward C. Moore, head of the silver firm, received 61 shares, and at the same time sold his business to Tiffany & Co. for fifty-five thousand dollars. George McClure, Tiffany's gemologist and diamond expert, was issued 200 shares and made secretary. While Cook received only a small amount of stock, it played a significant part in the history of Tiffany's ninety years later; the woman who inherited some of Cook's shares was to precipitate the struggle for control of the firm which eventually was to bring Walter Hoving into the company.

A new store would be a tremendous step forward for Tiffany's. It would erect its own building at a time when merchants only leased quarters. As the *Times* reported happily: "It is fast becoming the test of commercial standing to own your own store." A. T. Stewart had been the first to build his store, on Broadway between Ninth and Tenth Streets in 1862. Tiffany's was three years abuilding, delayed by constant changes in the plans because business was expanding so rapidly; space it had intended to rent out had to be converted to the company's own use. With all the delays, Tiffany's managed to open its store exactly three weeks ahead of that of Messrs. Samuel Lord and George Washington Taylor.

Charles Tiffany gambled on the expansion of the city and moved

(Above) Pink topaz and 1,722 diamond tiara, pendant and necklace set.

*Tiffany's draped
in flags for
Columbian Exposition.*

far uptown, where he might settle down and wait for the business
section to catch up to him. He liked Union Square, an oasis in the
ugly, jumbled thoroughfare which once beautiful Broadway had become. At that time, Union Square, slightly larger than it is now, was
a great oval with tall trees and acres of green grass, surrounded by a
high ornamental fence and a wide drive, with three huge fountains
in the center. As yet, there was not a single business establishment on
the Square, which was ringed with large houses, set in their own
grounds, many of them occupied by Tiffany customers.

In the midst of this pastoral setting, on the west side of the square
where it met Fifteenth Street, stood the Church of the Puritans, a
small, ivy-covered wooden building. During the Civil War the church
had been famous for the fiery Abolitionist sermons preached by the
pastor, a certain Dr. Cheever. Now the building was empty and for
sale, and Charles Tiffany snapped it up for the site of his new store.

Tiffany's, Stewart's and Lord & Taylor were not only pioneers in
owning their own stores; they were pioneers in construction. All three
stores had outer walls of iron, that odd type of architecture indigenous to New York. The stores were hailed as the city's first fireproof buildings—as indeed they were. Stewart painted his iron to
resemble marble and, before long, everyone forgot that it was not.
(When Stewart's, later bought by Wanamaker's, burned in the 1950's,
the press was amazed that the ''marble'' shell did not crack.) Lord
& Taylor chose to copy London's Crystal Palace, a ''lace work in iron

and glass.'' Tiffany delighted the taste of the solid burghers by paint-ing his store a no-nonsense ''drab,'' that misnamed Victorian shade which combines the pleasing glow of greens and browns. The press also praised the merchants' ''thrift.'' Not only were the buildings handsome but they ''cost from ⅕ to ⅒ which would have been re-quired for marble.'' Although the new store had 78 feet fronting the Square and 115 on Fifteenth Street, Tiffany's cost a comparatively modest $750,000, exclusive of the real estate. Parts of the iron had been precast; 1870 was more modern in its methods of licking the costs of construction than the 1970's are permitted to be.

The store's opening in 1870 was preceded by the national disasters which almost seemed necessary to Tiffany's pattern of growth. The business community still suffered a hangover from Black Friday of 1869, when Jim Fisk, Gould and their fellow speculators had almost cornered the gold market and were thwarted only by the prompt ac-tion of the federal government, which sold its own gold and collapsed the soaring price. Curiously, or not so curiously considering Tiffany's history, the shenanigans in the gold market benefited the store.

The New Jersey *Journal* reminded its readers:

Bargains may be obtained at Tiffany's because of the low price of gold. The proprietors of the said establishment are now (as they always have been) disposing of their goods on a strictly gold basis.

It follows that while Messrs. Tiffany and Company (as was to be expected of them) conscientiously adhere to the highly honorable rule

Tiffany's draped in black for McKinley's death.

they have so long adopted, that purchases made at this house, as com-
pared to purchases made elsewhere, are made at a saving of some
twenty or twenty five per cent . . . We take it for granted, there-
fore, that such of our readers who persist in patronizing the Metro-
politan establishments in search of Holiday gifts (notwithstanding the
claims of our Home dealers) will as a matter of course call upon
Messrs. Tiffany & Company.

One wonders whether the *Journal's* advertisers persisted in remaining with the paper.

Payment in gold is but a memory, but headlines in the newspapers,
which would have baffled readers of 1837, would seem current news
to New Yorkers of 1971. Here is a sampling from *The New York
Times* of 1870:

𝔓rinter's 𝔖trike 𝔈nded

THE CUBAN SITUATION

SUITS FILED AGAINST MAYOR AND CITY SNOW STILL LIES ON CITY'S STREETS

1870: ERA OF MURDER

RIOTERS MARCH AGAIN

From the editorials:

The Police need not act
as grand inquisitors;
they believe themselves to be
judge, jury and counsel,
all rolled into one.

From Letters to the Editor:

Why does the city
keep empty land in Central
Park while the middle
classes are being driven out
of the City by excessive rents?

The physical appearance of New York would have been quite as baffling to a ghost from 1837. There were now a million inhabitants. Telegraph wires so crisscrossed Fifth and Broadway that some claimed one could not tell whether the sky was cloudy until the raindrops fell. The city remained filthy. The streets were paved "abominably, with irregular blocks of stone, so that a drive uptown was a wear and tear on the nervous system." One fashionable physician, Dr. Fordyce Barker, forbade his convalescent patients to take the air because of the jolting necessary to get out of the residential quarter. Because few of the vehicles had rubber tires, the noise "made open windows a purgatorial trial . . . not to mention the flies and the smells."

Of New York's million, one-half lived in 40,000 dwellings of from five to fifty rooms; the other half in 20,000 dwellings, mostly of one room; 8,500 cellar cubicles housed over 24,000 immigrants. The rich were very rich and the poor were very poor. A good address on Fifth Avenue rented for six thousand dollars a year; a house on Forty-second Street, four thousand dollars.* Women worked six days a week, fourteen hours a day, as clerks—when they could find work at all—and were paid five dollars a week. Since every mistake was taken out of a girl's pay check, she often owed her boss at the end of the week. Tiffany's would hire no women clerks. The men, very correct, dressed in dark suits with frock coats and stiff collars.

There were 450 churches and 5,711 saloons; there were seventy thousand arrests for drunkenness and disorderly conduct in 1870. Charitable societies, however, congratulated themselves on one small victory. While the hordes of homeless boys—the street Arabs of the Alger books—seemed numberless and hopeless, only 944 girls under sixteen were arrested—which was genuine progress, because the number in 1860 was 5,880.

Union Square was twenty-three blocks from Charles Tiffany's home on Madison Avenue, still exclusively a street of private houses. He walked to work, rain or shine, snow or sleet, and then walked back home again. It was a form of exercise much in vogue, and the press noted that "most important men followed this routine so that they did not need diet fads nor health foods." The ladies, of course, did no more walking than necessary. It was difficult in the styles of 1870, the last year for the vast crinolines, which were being superseded by the "upholstery look," still constructed, however, on whalebone foundations called jupons. All dresses were made with a porte-jupe (shortened inaccurately to "jupe" in the States), a mechanical device that

---

* Many economists multiply by four to translate sums into 1971 values.

enabled the wearer to lift the whole skirt high enough so that she could cross streets without dirtying the hems.

Such was the city and such was the look of the people when the new store opened its doors for the first tour—by invitation only—on November 10, 1870. The press took one look and became ecstatic. The *Times* ran a continuing story for three days, taking the lofty view that everyone read every word of the *Times* every day, and beginning one of the later installments with the comment: "It is not necessary to describe the exterior as this has been printed the day before."

The *Times* hailed the store as "A Jewel Palace . . . the largest of its kind in the world." One day's story was devoted to the setting: the great crystal chandeliers, the gas bulbs without shades; the stark simplicity of the white ceiling, the iron beams left exposed, so that "the rich gleam of diamonds and the colored jewels, the gold and the chased silver afforded their own decoration." The *Times* man also was much taken by the bronzes on the third floor: "the most magnificent to be found in any city in America or Europe . . . everything will be found, from the "Return from the Chase," by the famous Jean Pierre Mene to "Last Moments of Napoleon" by Vela ($675)." "Andromeda" ($950) was still New York's favorite.

The *Times* also noted, with Victorian circumlocution (after all, a lady did not even admit to having legs), that "There is another feature too greatly disregarded by city stores, namely a retiring room for ladies and children. Very many ladies residing in towns adjacent to New York invariably bring their children [shopping] and such toilet rooms are an absolute necessity." There was another innovation which most of the papers missed. The *Times* man saw it, but for once was a trifle uncertain. He gave it a good try: "A dummy engine located in the basement also hoists goods and people from one floor to another on a sliding platform." Another reporter called the contraption "a railroad going up." (The first elevator in New York had been installed in the 1850's, but few people knew about it since it was in a very elegant hotel.)

The New York *World* headlined its story: "A New Palace of Trade: A Mine of Wealth and a New Palace of Beauty." In those days, before wire services, stories like these were picked up and printed verbatim in papers across the land. The *World* had never seen anything as impressive as the first floor with jewels valued at over two million dollars and "property valued at $1,500,000 . . . case after case of solid silverware in an apparently interminable line . . ." The reporter was bowled over by a "miniature watch of a very unique design, a tiny cupid's quiver suspended from a small chain. On pressing down the feather of the center arrow, the front of the quiver flies open, showing a still tinier watch dial, scarcely a third of an inch in diameter. This tiny watch keeps good time and costs $500.''

On opening day, fifty clerks were kept busy by the crowds who jammed the store, taking the advice of the press literally: ''Worth a visit by all, even if you cannot afford to buy.'' Charles Tiffany helped out, darting from counter to counter, waiting on old customers and friends and enjoying the whole show. He is described at this time as being as brisk and quick as he had been thirty-three years before, and as he remained until a few months before his death at ninety. A medium-tall man, somewhat slight of build, he held himself so straight he was often judged to be taller. One acquaintance said that he gave the impression of leaning backward when he was standing still. His most notable features were ''his bright blue eyes above a Roman nose, his florid complexion and his direct gaze.'' The short ''under-the-chin'' whiskers, which he had sported as a youth in the days when mustaches and full beards were frowned upon, had been allowed to luxuriate. He never needed to wear glasses.

In the city he was never seen dressed in any clothes but the formal clawhammer coat, gate's-ajar stiff collar and high silk hat, which also made him seem taller. On chilly days he favored a double-breasted chesterfield, with velvet collar. He not only walked to work, arriving at his desk at 10 A.M., but never, throughout his long life, missed a day through illness. He even walked to work every day during the blizzard of 1888. (Six hundred of his employees, knowing the boss, also made it.) He was amused that sales during that famous catastrophe were even smaller than they were on his first day of business; on one day of the storm, Tiffany's took in exactly ninety cents for two boxes of plate powder.

In contrast with the callous manner in which most firms dealt with their clerks and workmen, Tiffany's developed the kind of personnel policy that created an esprit de corps which continues to this day. It is not unusual in the 1970's to find employees who have worked for the firm for fifty or sixty years. (The record now is held by William J. Tanz, a sixty-six year veteran of the diamond department who made his first buying trip abroad in 1967, at the age of seventy-six.) Tiffany's personnel policies were unusual enough in the 1870's to be noticed in the press.

Just treatment, liberal pay and a quick recognition of talent has drawn into his [Tiffany's] employ a magnificent body of men. There is not a man or boy in his employ whose name he does not know and

Busts, groups in bronze and elaborate clocks at
Tiffany's were in the best of taste in the Nineties.

for whom he has not a word, given in that manner which makes it a personal compliment.

Mr. Tiffany carries in his high forehead and keen eye the sagacity which enables him to pick out his men, and in his mouth and chin the firmness and benevolence that enables him to hold them. Preference is always given the native American and numbers of his artisans can trace back their American descent for generations. [This was at a time when other firms boasted about their European artisans.]

Some years later, the New York *World* carried a front-page story under the headline "How Some Big Men Write." Interspersed through the page were facsimiles of the great men's signatures. Of Tiffany, the graphologist wrote, "Mr. Tiffany writes as prettily as a young lady [in those days a compliment, since good penmanship was much admired] but the design is good and bold. The writing shows a leaning toward the arts, but again, the lines are all clear and bold. The language is that of the Street [Wall] but the highlights [artistic] are there all the same." The analysis was made when Mr. Tiffany was seventy-four. The signature is indeed unusual—firm, and youthful without a single quaver or sign of age.

Charles L. Tiffany, eighty-seven, and Charles T. Cook in the Union Square store.

Charles Tiffany was one of the very few business leaders who could write in the handsome copperplate script, similar to the handwriting which Tiffany & Co., together with other top firms, required for their correspondence, employing a small army of young scribes with only this talent. It was well into the twentieth century, and long after other firms had been using the typewriter, that script as the correct method for formal communication was finally supplanted at Tiffany's.

Stories of how Tiffany's, then and now, stood behind every purchase are legion. Pliny Fisk, who was associated with the firm of Harvey Fisk and Company in the last century, related an experience he had with Charles Tiffany:

Mr. Tiffany was a customer of ours, a very quiet, very dignified gentleman. Tiffany always stood behind everything he sold. When I married my second wife, I wanted to give her something nice. I went to see Mr. Jacques at Tiffany's and decided on a small string of pearls at $10,000. Tiffany's told me that in ten years they would be worth $30,000. I had some personal difficulties and ten years later my wife and I were living apart. My wife wrote me and said she needed some money. I took the pearls in to Tiffany's and they gave me $32,000.

However, one widely printed story showed Charles Tiffany as being far from sagacious. He was a central figure in the greatest diamond fraud ever perpetrated and its success hinged on the fame of Charles Tiffany as a gem expert. The "great diamond swindle," which "duped some of our soundest and shrewdest financial men," as the *Times* noted, as well as the Rothschilds in Europe, grew out of the unbounded credulity, irrational speculation and rascality of the times. Gold, silver, fresh-water pearls, rubies and emeralds had already been found in America when the news came, in the late 1860's, of the discovery of diamonds in South Africa. It was enough to touch off a diamond fever in this country, setting the stage for the hoax.

It was the scheme of an ex-gold miner from Kentucky, Philip Arnold. With a fellow Kentuckian, John Slack, he had made a small strike during the California gold rush. But by 1869 the days of the bonanza were over, and Arnold took a job as assistant bookkeeper with the Diamond Drill Company, in San Francisco. The Drill Company handled only poor, rough diamonds; nevertheless, assisted by a co-worker, J. B. Cooper, Arnold learned all about diamonds, as well as the simple tests to distinguish them from quartz and other rocks. By 1871, Arnold knew as much about diamonds as anyone in America who had not actually visited the mines in India or Africa.

During those years, Arnold continued prospecting. On one trip to Arizona he saw the wife of an Indian chief wearing a necklace of sparkling stones, which he took to be rubies, and bought the baubles on the spot. Early in 1871 he and Cooper returned to Arizona and discovered enough rubies (which later proved to be garnets) to decide that they had the makings of a fortune. Arnold got in touch with an old San Francisco associate named Asbury Harpending, who was dispatched to London to sell stock in the "ruby mines" to British financiers.

Meanwhile, Arnold decided that diamonds, after all, were the better bet and left California. (Cooper got cold feet and dropped out of the scheme.) Arnold next showed up in San Francisco in February of 1872 with his old partner Slack. They brought with them a couple of buckets of garnets, an assortment of flawed emeralds and rubies, one "diamond" (white topaz) weighing 108 carats, and a bag of diamond pebbles not unlike those used by the Drill Company. It is possible that Harpending contributed to the assortment from London. They also brought with them a fearsome story of a cache deep in dangerous Apache territory, where they had murdered their Indian guide and left his grave to mark the spot of the diamond claim.

Approaching another mining man, George D. Roberts, they asked permission to store the bag in his safe for the night. Naturally, Roberts squeezed the story out of them, and after swearing him to secrecy, Arnold and Slack departed. Roberts immediately took the find to a San Francisco banker, William C. Ralston. By morning, the town's leading jeweler had made the simple tests he knew and pronounced the diamonds genuine.

Ralston, the cautious banker, wanted one more proof of the value of the find; an expert, chosen by himself, must be allowed to survey the site. Arnold agreed, gambling on the probability that no expert in diamond fields would be available. Ralston chose General David D. Colton, whose probity and knowledge of gold mining could not be questioned, but who knew nothing about diamonds.

The con game began in earnest. Colton, Arnold and Slack set out by rail and horseback to what is now Moffat County, Colorado. Colton was taken aback, as he had assumed he was going to Arizona. This was to throw claim jumpers off the scent, Arnold told him. (As a matter of fact, the episode would go down in history as "the great Arizona diamond swindle.") Alighting from the train, Colton was blindfolded and ridden on a horse for three days and then permitted to dismount at the "claim." Immediately he saw a large ant hill sparkling in the sun; the sparkle was diamond dust. Colton dug in and around the hill as Arnold directed, discovering a number of stones. Taken back to San Francisco, Colton's gems, too, were found to be diamonds.

Ralston became frantic. Here was the opportunity of a lifetime, but the deal would take more money than he could raise by himself. West Coast investors raised part of the money; William M. Lent, who later became president of the company, was one.

For the assault on the Eastern financiers, General Samuel L. M. Barlow, a respected member of the New York bar, was retained as counsel. Harpending returned from Europe, and the group turned to Wall Street for help. Barlow brought in another general, Benjamin F. Butler, and General George B. McClellan, one-time commander of the Union armies. Among the financial men were August Belmont and Henry Seligman—to give an idea of the quality of the money involved.

Belmont, Seligman and their associates made but one stipulation: before they invested they wanted the opinion of Charles Tiffany. This was agreed to and a document drawn up which specified that if Tiffany and yet another mining expert certified the diamonds to be real the syndicate would pay Arnold and Slack six hundred thousand dollars to release all rights to the claim.

Tiffany agreed to see the gems, and the viewing took place at General Barlow's opulent residence, down Madison from the Tiffany mansion. Arnold, who could have cut the heart out of a riverboat gambler without his knowing it, was betting six hundred thousand dollars that Charles Tiffany knew no more about diamonds in the rough than any other man in America. He was right; Tiffany's experts bought from the European cutters who delivered the stones shining and beautiful. Tiffany did know the tests for a genuine stone and he made them. Arnold's psychology could not have been better. The financiers trusted Tiffany and his reputation for honesty, and Tiffany was swayed by his belief in the honesty and expertise of Colton. Tiffany gave his judgment: "I cannot fix the exact value until my lapidary has a chance to inspect each stone, but I can assure you they are worth at least $150,000."

By morning, details of the "secret" meeting were known up and down Wall Street. Fortunately for the Rothschilds—or so it seemed at the time—their representative on the West Coast had already snapped up a number of shares for the great banking house. (Tiffany invested eighty thousand dollars in the new company.)

While final negotiations took place, Arnold and Slack announced that they could not bear to stay in the effete East. They would go

back to God's country and await mining operations, leaving their bag
of gems as security. However, they did not go West. Arnold sailed
for London, where he found two agreeable American sailors. By
paying them five hundred dollars each, he engaged them to help him
secretly buy thirty-seven thousand dollars' worth of what were probably the poorest diamonds ever shipped out of Kimberley, and then returned to America. It was not too much of a chore for Slack and
Arnold to sprinkle the diamonds over the mesa; when approached
from Denver to the east, it was only fifteen easy miles from the nearest railroad.

Meanwhile, on Tiffany's advice the syndicate hired Henry Janin,
the leading mining engineer in the country, to make the final inspection of the claim. He knew no more than his predecessor about diamond
fields. Janin went out to the site with Lent, Harpending (the company had been named the Harpending Mining Company), Arnold and
Slack. They repeated the farce of the blindfolded trip to the site,
where the Janin group turned up 250 carats of large diamonds, over
500 carats of small ones and four pounds of "rubies" (garnets).
Janin gave his opinion that the claim would yield about five million
dollars to the acre. Since the mesa covered some three thousand acres,
it would seem to have been the most valuable property ever discovered.

Slack, who had sold his share to the new company for a hundred
thousand dollars, was left to guard the claim and was never heard of
again. Whether he decided to decamp or whether that hostile Apache
really was lurking, no one will ever know. Arnold, who knew when
to get out of a good thing, announced that he had not realized that the
claim was so rich and had been hoodwinked by the Eastern establishment. Reminded of the contract and the legality of the written word,
the new company forced five hundred thousand dollars on him and
suggested he go back to Kentucky, where country boys belonged.

There was much grumbling among the general public that it had
been cheated of its chance for riches by the great moguls. Curiously,
at the height of the fever, *The New York Times* printed a story on
the front page of its issue for August 30, 1872, headlined "An English
Opinion of the Arizona Diamonds." The gist of the cable to the editor
of the *Times* was that Rittar, Levinson & Co., diamond brokers of
London, had become suspicious in April when "an American bought
a large number of diamonds in the rough, paying no attention whatever to the weight or quality of the stones." The *Times* continued that
"they intimate these were used by the alleged discoverers of the diamond mines in Arizona. The *Times* expresses astonishment that
Messrs. Latham, Barlow and Gen. McClellan should have been induced

to allow their names to be connected with the enterprise."

The public paid no more attention to the *Times* than did the promoters of the new company. Baron Rothschild, in Paris, cabled his fellow investors: "America is a rich land. It has given us many surprises. It reserves many more."

The surprise was soon provided by a young government geologist, Clarence King, who had recently completed a survey of the area where the diamonds were found, and had discovered no trace of precious stones. He felt his professional reputation was at stake.

He sought out Janin and questioned him in great detail. When Janin told the story about the blindfolding and the long ride, King asked if it had not been uncomfortable riding in such terrible weather. Janin assured him it had been a pleasant ride—"We had the sun in our faces for the entire three days; it was quite warm."

King made some calculations and decided Janin was either not telling the truth or had been taken in. For one thing, the territory where Janin had located the claim had been buffeted by heavy storms and rain during the period.

Using maps and a system of deduction worthy of Edgar Allan Poe, King deduced that the claim had to be on the edge of the Uinta Ridge, east of Salt Lake City. On Table Rock, a plateau of some six thousand feet at the head of Ruby Gulch, King and his party discovered diamonds which Janin had missed. They went him one better. A workman ran up chuckling to King with a stone and said, "Look, Mr. King. This mine not only has diamonds, it cuts them, too." Arnold had been careless. In his assortment was one partly polished stone. There was also evidence of stones ground into the earth by heavy heels, and one diamond was found on top of a tree stump.

King wired San Francisco: "An unparalleled fraud." The company begged him not to make his finding public until officers could visit the site themselves. For some reason, King agreed. He had made his find in the middle of October. On November 11, Colton and Janin (who had made the first two surveys) were taken to the site by King. In freezing weather—it was twenty below zero—they reached the site and the same conclusions as King, who pointed out in his later testimony that this was the work "of no common swindler."

The story did not break until November 23, pushing from the front page of the *Times* the story of the arrest of Jay Gould, on a charge of defrauding Erie Railroad stockholders out of nine million dollars. (Gould was released on bail of one million dollars.)

The public did not give up its dream so easily. Janin announced that he still believed there was an unlimited wealth of diamonds in the hills. A dispatch from Salt Lake City pledged faith in the Janin report and continued that "leading capitalists of the city are putting up money for an expedition to the spot." In fact, one miner turned up with diamonds and a story of a new discovery near Table Rock. But the *Times*, in a two-column story on page one, noted: "It has been from the first the most adroit and skillfully managed affair in the annals of fraud."

Nevertheless, even the *Times* reporter apparently could not quite believe what he had written, for a few paragraphs later in the same story he raised the possibility that there was a fabulously rich diamond mine: "The theory and belief is gaining ground here that the men who placed the diamonds *have* [italicized by the *Times*] some source of supply—some veritable and actual diggings from which they obtain them . . . Only time will tell. We shall know some day how it was."

"How it was" for banker Ralston and the master swindler Arnold was tragic. Ralston's bank was declared bankrupt and his body was found floating in San Francisco Bay. Arnold did not fare any better. Back home in Kentucky, he set himself up as a banker. In an argument, he invoked the code of the hills by shooting a competing banker in the arm; the man's partner retaliated by killing Arnold.

As for Charles Tiffany, he said nothing in his own defense. Asked by reporters for an explanation for his incredible goof, he made the only statement possible: "We deal only in cut gems at Tiffany's and that's what fooled me. I had never seen a rough diamond before."

Eventually the country stopped laughing at the smart Wall Streeters who had been clipped, and let the story die. Tiffany did not forget. He knew that he and his company could not afford to remain as ignorant about diamonds as they had been proved to be. Somehow a way had to be found to prevent the company from being made to appear as foolish as it had in the great diamond swindle.

Once more, fortune favored Charles Tiffany. In the years before the great hoax a young man was growing up in New Jersey, almost on Tiffany's doorstep, and studying at night school in Manhattan. Still in his teens, he was already on his way to becoming the world's foremost gemologist and—what was more important, in the light of the diamond hoax—mineralogist. His name was George Frederick Kunz.

Charles Tiffany and George Frederick Kunz came into each other's lives, appropriately enough, over the matter of a stone. The year was 1876, four years after the hoax, and Kunz was a precocious twenty, already a skilled if amateur mineralogist and a fierce champion of American semiprecious stones, which were so beautiful and so unap-

(Above) Illustration for story on Tiffany Exhibit at Chicago World's Fair.

George F. Kunz at thirty-two.

preciated. Spring came, and with it a surge of courage. Kunz "buckled in youth," as he recalled many years later, wrapped a choice tourmaline in a piece of gem paper and hopped on a horse car bound for Union Square. Charles Tiffany was as accessible as always; Kunz remembered that he walked as fast as he could past the clerks, along the elegant crimson-and-black carpet and up to Tiffany's desk, where he spilled out his "drop of green light" before the great expert. The sixty-four-year-old jeweler-merchant prince was as fascinated as the boy. He admired the stone and discussed its fine points courteously. What is more important, he bought it on the spot.

Kunz "felt the check crinkling in his pocket and star-gazing, tripped over curbs and walked all the way home." After this, Kunz sold the firm many stones before he joined the staff the following year; he became the store's gem expert and a vice president at the age of twenty-three.

An archaeologist as well as a mineralogist, he was also honorary curator at the American Museum of Natural History, in New York, and it sometimes seemed, Lord High Everything Else.

Kunz was born in New York City on September 29, 1856. His father was something of a botanist, who spent his Sundays walking through the woods above Forty-second Street, sometimes venturing into the wilds above Fifty-second Street—a "turbulent wilderness." Little George tagged along.

When George was eleven, the family moved to Hoboken. Here were treasures indeed. The so-called Elysian Fields were on the outskirts of the town; the railroads were cutting through for tracks, the Bergen Tunnel was being excavated, all spilling out specimens of a richness the boy could scarcely believe. He spent all his free time clambering over the holes, and came home with his pockets bursting from the weight of rock. They seemed so precious to the boy that he hid his loot each night under his mattress and loose floor boards. Soon he could call his treasures by name—green quartz, pectolite, zeolitic minerals— with the ease with which his contemporaries called off the names of their marbles.

Young Kunz's first sight of a real collection was at Barnum's old Museum at Broadway and Ann Street, a few weeks before it burned down in July of 1865. "I hung suffocated with pleasure . . . over the exhibit. Since then I suppose I have looked on more wealth of gems than any other person, but nothing has been as thrillingly beautiful as those first, not even precious, stones."

Too poor and too shy to get in touch with dealers, he continued his lonely, stubborn way, collecting over the Jersey countryside. His family did not appreciate his passion, but as often happens, young George did meet a sensitive adult when he most needed help. Benjamin Chamberlain, already known as a collector, gave companionship and encouragement to the brilliant boy. (Chamberlain's collection, along with Kunz's, is now in the Museum of Natural History.)

At fourteen, George felt he had enough specimens to begin exchanges with others, he recalled, beginning the stream of correspondence which inundated "the vaults of several museums and my home." He also realized that he would get ahead faster if he had more formal education. He worked days and studied nights at Cooper Union.

Before he was nineteen he had completed his first collection. What-

Barnum's Museum on Broadway (left) circa 1859.

ever it lacked in quality it more than made up for in weight—it must have been the heaviest collection in the world; the four thousand specimens weighed two tons. Kunz was determined to sell his collection, both for the money and the recognition he would gain as a serious collector. When the University of Minnesota paid four hundred dollars for it he was "smothered in pride."

Kunz came into his own when he went to work for Tiffany's. He was encouraged to go to the ends of the earth to track down lovely stones, many unknown to most jewelers and which interested few of them. For many years scientists and the artistic world were more aware of Kunz's early findings than the affluent circles of society.

Kunz once showed Oscar Wilde a handful of his prize semiprecious stones. Wilde himself was an enthusiastic collector. "My dear Kunz," he exclaimed, "these are exquisite. I believe I admire them more than precious stones, for those are of only four obvious colors. But there is not a color on land or sea which is not imprisoned in these heavenly rocks . . . The barbarians, the Egyptians, the Romans and the Persians realized this and used all of them, but we moderns have never conceived such beauty. I see a whole renaissance in art." (Another Tiffany connection, Louis Comfort, son of Charles, would be closely associated with Wilde as they spread this appreciation in the cult of Art Nouveau.)

In the course of his quest for jewels for Tiffany's, Kunz learned to speak and write in all modern languages, to read ancient Greek, Sanskrit and Arabic as he pursued the history of gems and bought them, a million dollars' worth at a time. He would never forget his first enthusiasm, the semiprecious stones of America. Kunz was personally gratified when he could say in the 1890's, "No lady with a quarter yard of diamond and emerald bracelets up her arms or three yards of Oriental pearls around her neck now scorns a star sapphire or beryl bracelet for less formal moments."

Traveling in America, Kunz visited every one of the States in his search for diamonds, rubies, emeralds and sapphires. He found semiprecious stones in every state. He considered that Maine supplied the finest tourmalines. The second largest emerald in the world was found in North Carolina, and a laborer, digging a sewer at the corner of Thirty-fifth Street and Broadway in Manhattan, picked up the finest large garnet to be found in the United States. Kunz found that Montana had the finest sapphires; Utah, the best topazes and garnets. A lilac-colored variety of spodumene was discovered in California in these years and named kunzite.

The discoveries inspired Kunz's great roundup of American gem

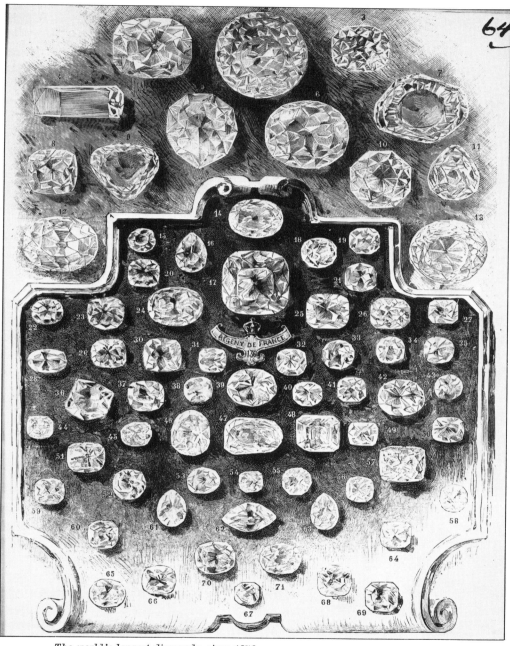

The world's largest diamonds, circa 1878.

1. The English Lottery.
2. The Great Mogul.
3. The Hope Blue.
4. The Shah of Russia.
5. The Florentine.

6. The Koh-i-Noor after cutting.
7. The Koh-i-Noor before cutting.
8. The Pole-Star.
9. The Nassak.
10. The Pasha of Egypt.

11. The Sancy.
12. Star of the South.
13. The Orloff.
14. The Regent and Mazarins,
    and lesser stones.

stones for the Tiffany exhibit at the Paris Exposition of 1889. The collection included rough crystals as well as beautifully cut stones; the fresh-water pearls were outstanding. Three-fourths of all precious stones found on earth were represented, and came from eleven states and territories: Tennessee, Ohio, Maine, Connecticut, Arizona, California, North Carolina, Virginia, New York, Massachusetts and Iowa. Because this was to be an all-American display, even the cases were fashioned of native materials. Boxes were made of California redwood, Alaska cypress and native cherry and maple. Linings were of elk, moose calf, black raccoon, reindeer and alligator skins.

This was not only the first comprehensive presentation of American gems but the first international tribute to the culture and craftsmanship of the American Indian. All the pieces in the exhibit—brooches, rings, vinaigrettes, sleeve buttons, pendants, even match boxes—were inspired by designs of the American Indian. A brooch, fashioned of brown pearls from Tennessee, was copied from the carved masks worn by the medicine men of the Chilkat. Pink pearls from the Miami River in Ohio traced the pattern of basketwork of the Hupa Indians; tourmalines from Maine decorated a brooch designed from the Sitka peoples of Alaska; the horsehide war shields of the Sioux inspired

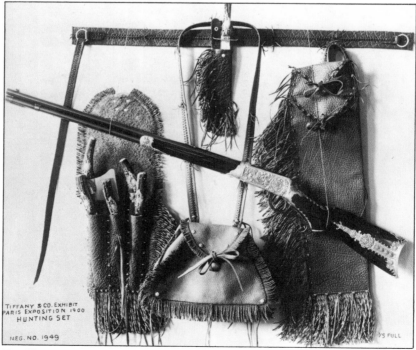

Far West motif in exhibits at Paris Exposition.

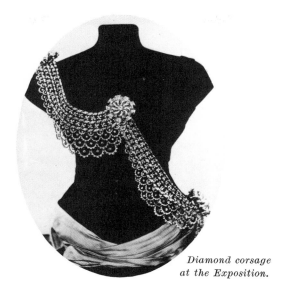

*Diamond corsage
at the Exposition.*

another pin. The art of the Navajo, Zuñi, Cherokee and Inuit was also shown, all to the amazement of "civilized" Europe.

Tiffany's also used an Indian and Western motif for a tea set, valued at ten thousand dollars; among the most admired objects was a massive silver lamp, in a design matching the tea set, and a giant solid silver urn with feet and handles in the form of buffalo heads.

In addition, Kunz sent for the exhibit the two bushels of pearls found in an abandoned mound in the Little Miami valley in Ohio, arranged before an altar. There were objects from another mound in Florida, an exquisite arrowhead made of smoky quartz from North Carolina and an array of topazes, beryls, and zircons worked in silver representing the various tribes. There were two hundred Indian pieces in all, valued at five hundred thousand dollars.

Of course, as jeweler not only to America but to most of the crowned heads of Europe, the Tiffany display contained other gems, the finest acquired by Kunz. These jewels alone were worth two million dollars and the silver and gold tankards, pitchers and tea sets were valued at equally impressive prices. In this portion of the exhibit, the *pièce de résistance* was a plaster bust, decorated with a "corsage" made of two thousand diamonds that extended from the right shoulder across the breast to the left hip, with a diamond rose at either end. Around the neck of the bust were four strings of Oriental pearls, fastened together with a clasp of magnificent emeralds. Displayed on velvet in front of the bust was a diamond necklace with a center stone of over twenty-five carats—one of the French crown jewels—valued at forty-five thousand dollars, the whole necklace priced at $175,000.

Many of these pieces were sold to collectors and jewelers at the fair, and to agents of the royal houses of England, Russia and Austria. What remained was the irreplaceable sampling of the gems of America, for which Europe was not yet quite ready. Size and show, not to mention origin, in the treasure of a shah or an emperor still counted.

Tiffany's brought its native display home intact and pondered what was to become of it. Kunz, naturally, clung to the hope that this remarkable exhibit might be kept intact; there was nothing like it in the world. The American Museum of Natural History was the obvious repository. Late in 1889 the museum, through its president, Morris K. Jessup, did indeed approach Tiffany's. The museum and its trustees were looking for a donor, and in the meantime were inclined to dicker. Negotiations dragged on from November until March of 1890, the museum calling in various experts to determine whether the price of fifteen thousand dollars, which Tiffany's had put on the collection, was reasonable. Three separate experts submitted their opinions, together with their bills. All agreed that the collection was ''impossible to be duplicated,'' besides being ''worth a deal more than $20,000,'' and ''no time should be lost in acquiring these irreplaceable gems.''

By March, Tiffany's was growing impatient and threatening to break up the collection among a number of collectors. At this point the name of J. Pierpont Morgan enters the saga. Morgan had made his first acquisition only two years before—a manuscript purchased from a friend of his son's. He did not begin to collect seriously until the summer of 1891; his well-known descents upon the treasures of Europe were in the future. Morgan was now intimating that he might help the museum. By March 12, Charles Tiffany had made up his mind to settle the whole question. He sent off a polite but stiff note to Jessup saying that before April 30 ''We must ask you to give us a check for $15,000 from the Museum or formal instructions to charge this to the account of J. P. Morgan.''

Morgan agreed to pay, and on March 19 the legal agreement was written by Tiffany's and signed by Jessup: ''We [Tiffany's] agree to sell and deliver to the American Museum of Natural History for the sum of $20,000, $5,000 donated by ourselves, the gems and gem stones called for in the typewritten catalogue.''

There is an amendment: ''Tiffany also agrees that it will make identification on the stones, hidden so as not to mar them but which will mark them permanently.''

This agreement, filed away in the old oak archives under the roof of the museum, untouched for eighty years, holds a curious relevance for collectors and the contemporary public.

In 1964, Murf the Surf, in a much-publicized caper, engineered the incredible theft of stones from the museum which belonged both to this collection and the one which was put together by Kunz ten years later in 1900. The great Star of India from the 1900 collection and many of the diamonds from the 1889 exhibit were included in the haul. The Star of India and the star ruby were recovered with much fanfare; the diamonds were not. It is the opinion of the museum's gem curator that these stones are possibly in the safes of private collectors. If and when they should come on the market—and most stones do, eventually—the ineradicable secret markings made by Tiffany's will still identify the stones. Someday, when the name of Murf the Surf will elicit only a puzzled frown of incomprehension, the diamonds can be identified and returned to their proper place in the museum.

Kunz remained the loyal champion of American gems, but early in life he gave his heart to the pearl. He traced its lore through history and traveled around the world to places where he might catch a glimpse of famous specimens. As a scientist, he experimented with pearls. After one such experiment, Kunz wrote that the pearl was indeed the queen of jewels. Apparently soft, she is in reality tough, as a reigning sovereign must be. Kunz tested what he called the pearl's "feminine durability." He placed three pearls on boards of increasing hardness: soft pine, oak and mahogany. Then he proceeded to grind the pearls with his heel into the wood. None was even scratched, he reported, as "the pearls sank clean through the boards."

Of course, Kunz took an avuncular delight in the discovery of the American fresh-water pearl. He never tired of telling the story about a man who was cleaning mussels out of his pig pen in Morley, Ill., and found a pearl worth five thousand dollars—Kunz's punch line: "It was literally a case of pearls before swine."

The largest fresh-water pearl in America was found in Arkansas; a perfect rose-white it weighed 103 grains and was sold for twenty-five thousand dollars. (Kunz's favorite, the Tiffany Pearl, was also perfect rose-white, and weighed 100 grains, as the reader may recall.) A pearl weighing 68 grains, found in Wisconsin, fetched fifteen thousand dollars. In 1896 pearl fever struck on the White River, in Arkansas; thousands of families left their homes and their jobs to converge upon the banks. Pearls worth half a million dollars were found in three years. Kunz divided the number of diggers by the man-hours spent and estimated the profits per person were just over one dollar a day. By 1928, a total of fifteen million dollars in pearls was discovered in American waters.

The American pearl was treasured as highly as the Oriental. Tiffany alone assembled two necklaces that sold for over a million dollars each, and at least a hundred in the range of a hundred thousand dollars and over. Opera star Lillian Nordica owned one of the more publicized ropes, which Tiffany had collected for her. Once, meeting Kunz, she threw her arms around him and announced: "Dr. Kunz, I do believe that if I were on a sinking ship and could save only one thing it would be these pearls."

No one could have had as much fun out of his profession as Kunz. He collected for Tiffany's—and Morgan and the Metropolitan and the Museum of Natural History—with the enthusiasm of that boy of eleven. His excursions into international sleuthing were as gay as those of a child let loose in his grandmother's attic. He learned to suspect the value of famous old jewels; they were too big and there were too many of them. In Moscow he found that jewels were judged by size only. "Certainly," he reported back to Tiffany's, "there is an emerald four inches long, but the entire crystal has been polished with all its fissures and imperfections. What we call a gem emerald uses only a thousandth of the original crystal. The Stephenson emerald, found in North Carolina and now in the Bement collection, has only one rival in the world, that belonging to the Duke of Devonshire, which is $\frac{1}{4}$ ounce heavier."

Like most gem collectors, Kunz had heard rumors about a many-colored diamond necklace, the property of the Romanoffs, supposedly the most fabulous in the world. He saw it when it had been left for cleaning with the crown jeweler.

"I decided," he said, "that it was just too good." When the jeweler was not looking, Kunz scratched on the back of a stone with a fingernail. The scratch confirmed his suspicions; the necklace was made up of second-rate diamonds, skillfully enameled on the backs to give the rainbow effect.

This was quite all right in India and in medieval Europe, Kunz noted. In fact, the craftsman who could give precisely the right shade to the backing of a diamond was considered a great artist. The technique of cutting a diamond to bring out its true brilliance was a skill not yet discovered. (Those who attended the exhibition *The Year 1200* at the Metropolitan Museum in 1970 could see how, over the centuries, the backings had cracked or flaked off on many of the gems.)

Kunz used his educated fingernail freely. He *always* scraped turquoises, since these stones, once so highly prized, are possibly the easiest to imitate. Marie Antoinette and her jewelers were among those

Lillian Nordica as Wagnerian heroine.

taken in. Kunz managed to get close to her famous set of turquoises set in diamonds when they were on display in Paris. Kunz's scratches indicated that the "turquoises" were only fossil bones stained with copper salts.

Not a fingernail but a small magnifying gadget, which he had invented, satisfied the doctor that the famous emerald of Cologne was not an emerald at all but a peridot. Always the champion of the semi-precious, Kunz quickly added that this was not bad, just incorrect. The peridot was another of his favorites. Kunz loved to recount that except for the pearl, the peridot is one of the few jewels formed within the life span of a man—in fact, created in a few days, though it does take a volcanic eruption to accomplish the feat.

Volcanoes are also responsible for a stone which Kunz felt had never been properly appreciated, the opal. Kunz wrote a poetic description: "Millions of years ago, as the earth dried up and the mountains poured forth lava, little squid died in the long drought. Then the hot waters of the volcanoes, containing soluble silicia, ate into the bones of the squid, mingling with the lime. Finally, the water ate away the bone, leaving the deposits we call opals. Shake an opal; you can hear the waters of prehistoric days awash."

All his life Kunz was concerned about the belief that opals are unlucky. The only scientific explanation he could think of for the superstition was that they are fragile; jewelers find them hard to work with, and if cracked, the water which colors the stone rushes out and the opal "dies."

The opal probably received its unlucky reputation from a too literal reading of Sir Walter Scott's *Anne of Geierstein*. The mysterious heroine wore an opal in her hair, and the stone was supposedly bound up with her life. It sparkled when she was gay, shot out red gleams when she was angry; holy water sprinkled on it quenched its radiance. The lady came to a tragic end; the opal and the lady mingled in a heap of ashes.

Kunz noted that Scott was irked that the foolish women who read his novel took all this nonsense seriously. However, another author, Rudyard Kipling, whom nobody could possibly call foolish, wrote to Kunz: "I am relieved to have your authority for it that the opal is not unlucky, as that was a belief early instilled into me: and I have always liked the opal beyond all other stones. . . ."

There is also a story that J. Pierpont Morgan refused to collect opals. This simply is not true. Morgan commissioned the trip which Kunz took to the Mexican opal mines, and combined the stones which Kunz brought back with the Bement Collection, later given to the

Museum of Natural History.

Just as Kunz had brought his tourmaline to Tiffany, other hopefuls began sending their finds to Dr. Kunz. As he said, "It is hard to imagine discovering a gem lode sitting at a desk in New York," but this did happen, twice.

On one occasion, he received an envelope from a miner at Yogo Gulch, in Montana, asking about a sample of gold ore enclosed in the letter; the anxious miner wanted to know if the blue crystals dotted through it cheapened the price of the gold. The blue crystals were sapphires, and Yogo Gulch became the most valuable sapphire mine in America, providing the best-quality gems found on the continent. (Kunz added: "They never did find much gold.")

Many years later, in 1902, another package was sent to Kunz's office. The sender thought he had found an unusual tourmaline and asked to have it tested. The ore came from an abandoned mine at Pala Mountain, in California, where an old prospector had once reported finding traces of spodumene, a noted ancient gemstone which no one had been able to find for years. Kunz, given as he was to enthusiasm, reached heights that day. Before him was a specimen of the "extinct spodumene," of a "gloriously lilac or orchid color, very hard . . ." A fellow gemologist, Dr. Charles Baskerville, named the find "kunzite." It can be seen in a variety of dazzling cuts at the Museum of Natural History: there is a pear-shaped jewel of 191 carats; a pillow shape of 224 carats and a brilliant of 542 carats from mines in Brazil which were discovered later.

Kunzite gives off enough light to take its own picture. Also, when exposed to strong light, it will glow in the dark for half an hour. These qualities are shared by a milk-white diamond from Brazil which Kunz named tiffanyite; later, Kunz found in Madagascar another pink gem, which he named morganite, so that the three men are joined together in *Webster's Unabridged* for all time as common, or lower-case, nouns.

The ability to glow is true of most diamonds. Kunz made this discovery in a homely fashion, in the connubial bedroom. He was already in bed, when his wife, who had stepped into her wardrobe room, uttered a little cry. She came out staring at her hand. Even across the room, Kunz could see the light of her ring; it shone like a firefly. Naturally, Kunz had his wife recount exactly what had happened. She had hung up her dress without turning on the closet light. As she did so, she brushed her ring against another dress; the glow resulted. It is an experiment anyone can make.

Everyone who has talked or written about Kunz has remarked on his charm and his bewildering number of interests. He seems to have been rebuffed only once in his life. At his club he started a discussion on his favorite subject, gems, with Teddy Roosevelt. After a few moments, Roosevelt looked puzzled. "You're talking to the wrong man, Kunz," roared T. R. "Ivory is my life, Doctor, ivory."

Another amusing episode occurred in 1896 during the visit to the United States of the celebrated Li Hung-chang, Viceroy of China. It was of this visitor that Ulysses S. Grant had declared: "There are three great men in the world, Gladstone, Bismarck and Chang, but the greatest of these is Chang." Chang's first pronouncement on his arrival in New York was that the one thing he wanted to see was the Tiffany diamond. In the words of W. S. Gilbert, this presented a nice dilemma. The imperial viceroy, possessed of more power than the Empress of China herself, sat in his suite at the Waldorf, awaiting the diamond. The diamond had been out of the store only once, when it was shown at the Chicago Exhibition of 1893, and there was an absolute rule that it was never to be taken out again. For some reason, Kunz was the only one of the firm's officers available to deal with the problem. Under the circumstances, Kunz shrugged off policy, and took the diamond over himself.

Kunz found in Chang "that air of frankness and naivete I have found in all great men."

"Surely it is not one single diamond," said Chang.

Assured that it was, he examined it once more with childish delight. Once more his face clouded. "You are sure?" he asked again. "It is not three or four pieces stuck together?"

Kunz bowed, took the diamond, revolved it slowly and tugged at all the corners, gesturing that Chang should do the same. The viceroy did so. When he was finally convinced that this was indeed one single stone, "his delight knew no bounds."

There is probably not a single child who has visited the Museum of Natural History who has not lingered long in the Hall of Minerals. After trailing from case to case, there is probably not a child—or his parent—who has not rested gratefully for a minute on the granite base that supports a huge chunk of black ore. Not many of them realize that they are sitting in front of the biggest specimen of jade[*] (nephrite) ever found *in situ* and the largest ever polished. The ore is not black, when seen in a good light, but a very dark green. The slab is seven feet long by two and a half feet wide and weighs 4,718 pounds. The polishing was a considerable achievement; it was done

---

[*] In his book *The Curious Lore of Precious Stones* Kunz relates that it was Sir Walter Raleigh who gave the word "jade" to the English-speaking world. The Indians used the Spanish word for colic, *hijada*, to identify the mineral, since they believed that jade was the specific for the ailment; Raleigh, a true Englishman, ignored the Spanish pronunciation.

by Tiffany's, since the stone was discovered by Kunz.

Kunz on his way to Russia, on another of his endless collecting tours, had heard that large jade masses might be found near the small town of Jordansmuhl, south of Breslau in Silesia. He had only a single day available for the side trip. As he tells the story: "I called on the owner of the quarry, Herr von Kriegsheim at around six in the morning, and asked his permission to look for jade. Von Kriegsheim was so astonished that any one asked permission—he had been robbed so many times, it turned out, that he was resigned to vandalism—thât to show appreciation for my courtesy he asked me in and gave me a magnificent breakfast. He then sent me off, with peasants to show the way, and a cart. When I discovered the great mass, I, of course, came back and reported the event to the owner. However, von Kriegsheim insisted that it belonged to me because I had found it."

Since German law forbade dynamiting, the great rock was loosened by a dozen men operating a heavy crowbar imbedded in a log twelve feet long. Later, Kunz had the satisfaction of writing that prehistoric jade objects found in Europe did not necessarily come from Asia, as had been the belief until that time.

At this time, 1899, Kunz was completing his second collection of gems and *objets d'art* for the Paris Exhibition of 1900. After the acclaim accorded the American collection of 1889, Kunz had approached Morgan and Tiffany with the idea for an even more inclusive collection, with the whole world for his field. Well pleased with the first, they told him to go ahead.

When Kunz was finished, the collection was not only more extensive, he had greatly exceeded his budget, having spent close to a million dollars. Morgan was ill and bedridden. The deadline was fast approaching for the last possible moment when the collection could be shipped to Paris. Still no final approval from 219 Madison Avenue. Kunz began to fret that the deal might fall through. He admitted to himself that "to make a collection even under tacit orders and then to sell it are two different things. No one, not even a jeweler such as Tiffany, can keep a collection such as this indefinitely."

At the last possible moment, Morgan felt well enough to come to see what Kunz had wrought. This time there was no haggling; Morgan the banker had become Morgan the collector. The great man spent exactly one hour looking over the collection and approved payment on the spot.

Kunz, looking back, was certain that he had never let his uneasiness show. He reported back to his friends that when the press interviewed him and asked how he had dared invest Tiffany's money to such an extent, he had replied carelessly, ''Oh, I knew there'd be Mr. Morgan to pay for it.'' Privately he confided to his diaries: ''I was rather pleased with my own aplomb.''

Morgan was also pleased with his purchase when it was awarded the Grand Prize at Paris. Included in the collection was the new pink stone from Madagascar which Kunz had named morganite; there was also the great star sapphire, the most perfect found to that date. One gains some concept of the size and extent of the 1889 and 1900 collections by examining the catalog which the museum published when the two were combined and displayed as the Morgan Collection. The catalog listed 2,176 specimens of gem stones and *objets d'art* made of precious and semiprecious stones, and 2,442 pearls.

Among the gems listed are the great hyacinth(garnet) portrait of Christ, which a cardinal commissioned during the Renaissance, and the four-thousand-year-old Babylonian axhead of banded agate, which Cardinal Borgia, later Pope Alexander VI) had ''liberated'' from Constantinople when he was head of the Propaganda Commission of the Vatican. (Kunz found it in Poland, where it had come into the possession of a certain Count Tyskiewiecz.)

Kunz remained the all-American collector at heart. If the collection held a 57 carat yellow beryl from Ceylon, there was one of 14½ carats from Litchfield, Conn. There were 600 and 300 carat topazes from Ceylon, and one of 193 carats from Cheyenne Mountain; a mass of aquamarine, weighing fourteen pounds, the heart of a great crystal

NEG. NO. 2414

Pink tourmaline butterfly, at Pan-American Exhibit, 1901.

found at Maramboya, Brazil, and a diamond weighing $15^{12}\!/_{32}$ carats from the Kettle Moraine in Wisconsin.

To conclude the history of the association of Morgan, Kunz and Tiffany with the museum, there is a touching story which contradicts the legend that Morgan showed himself capable of tenderness only once, when he made the romantic gesture of marrying his first wife, knowing that she would die within the year.

In December of 1907, Kunz, through Tiffany's, had found an exquisite branch of crystallized gold in California. Morgan thought it would make a splendid addition to the museum, since Kunz and other experts had given their opinion that it was "the finest specimen yet discovered." But Morgan, ever punctilious, felt that Mr. Jessup of the museum should see it first. Jessup was ill—as a matter of fact, he was on his deathbed (Tiffany's sent out the announcements of his death shortly afterward) and could not come to Morgan's home. So Morgan bundled up his treasure and took it to Jessup's bedside.

The gesture is especially moving if one recalls that this was during the 1907 Panic, which was ended single-handedly by Morgan, now a sick old man of seventy himself. He had spent weeks without sleep, suffering from colds and painful migraines, and had, in fact, been so completely comatose only a short time before that his doctors and his family feared that he might die.

In his search for gems, Kunz had roamed deserts, and slept in the muck of swamps, in Arab tents, South African kraals and Siberian outposts. As he neared the end of his life, he was asked what had been his most colorful experience. Kunz did not have to think twice. It was in 1892; he was again in Russia, again collecting for Morgan. His goal was Troitsk, near Orenburg in the Urals, where he had heard that rare amethysts were to be found. To reach it, he had to climb a 5,000-foot mountain before he could catch a train for Orenburg. After this hike through virgin forest, which lasted from 7 P.M. until 2 A.M., he caught his train and, after that, still had to ride 200 versts (roughly 125 miles) in a droshky.

Then, in Orenburg, as Kunz told later, he was confronted by an emergency. The Czarevitch, later Nicholas II, was on his way to St. Petersburg from Siberia. There was to be a huge official reception, and Kunz was the only foreigner invited. In that stiffly formal world, protocol demanded that guests assemble in full evening dress at ten in the morning. Kunz had left New York without white tie and tails. He felt he must attend the reception; yet he felt quite as strongly that because the Western world would be represented in his person he must be properly attired. Fortunately he never traveled anywhere without his Prince Albert. He also had scissors. Kunz spread the full-skirted morning coat out on the floor, and went to work. He drew a pattern on it, and proceeded to cut the semblance of an evening tail coat.

He had scarcely finished his tailoring and was admiring the results in the mirror (''Not bad at all,'' he complimented himself) when there was a knock on the door and his host entered. Knowing Kunz's impatience with protocol, his host had managed to wriggle out of the invitation so that Kunz could mingle with the crowd and observe first-hand the barbaric hordes pouring in to goggle at their ruler. (Notices had been sent about by horsemen ordering the populace to appear and *cheer* on pain of death.)

Kunz forgot his ruined morning coat. He changed, dashed out, and managed to get in the front line of the mob; he was standing beside the triumphal arch when the Czarevitch stopped, preparatory to acknowledging the tribute of his faithful subjects. Unfortunately, at that moment a photographer clicked his lens. The future Czar, with memories of anarchists burned into his consciousness, thought the sound was the click of an assassin's gun and fainted. The Czarevitch took to his bed and made no further appearance.

The episode was a stroke of luck for Kunz. He had been worried when he learned that the heir to the throne was coming to the spot where he was on a jewel-buying trip, since it was the custom, much encouraged by royalty, to shower princes with the choicest gems of the province. The Czarevitch's scare gave Kunz a head start. While the young prince rested, Kunz slipped out of town, three hours before the royal cortège was scheduled to leave. (The wretched notables, among whom Kunz had just missed being included, stood in the broiling sun for that entire time, and went home without their audience.)

It was not a restful trip to Troitsk. There was always the possibility of being hauled up by the Cossacks; the road itself was a deathtrap, scarcely passable; furthermore, only a few months before, three travelers had been killed by robbers. Kunz traveled with a loaded revolver on his lap.

When he reached his destination, he saw that his difficult trip had been more than worthwhile. Kunz had never seen such amethysts, either in size, color or perfection. The owner was an old peasant woman, known to her neighbors as the Czarina Ujakra, because of her gems. She owned twelve amethysts, worth well over a hundred thousand dollars. Kunz concealed his excitement, but this time it did him no good at all; the expert had met his match in the peasant. He reported: ''The American left with the amethysts he wanted, but he paid every penny that they were worth.''

The Czarevitch, later Nicholas II, who was killed with his family by Bolsheviks.

Kunz continued on his active, inquisitive way, gathering, during his life, knowledge and honors, but little money. One newspaper noted that American business had made and saved hundreds of millions of dollars through the discoveries of the doctor. Besides the honors heaped upon him by his own country he was made an Officer of the French Legion of Honor; a Knight of the Order of St. Olaf, of Norway; and an Officer of the Rising Sun, of Japan.

His interests extended to the study of meteors, on which he became an authority. While attempting to saw through a meteor, in his living room, he came upon the first diamond discovered in a meteor.

Kunz was the author of *Gems of North America* (1890); *The Book of the Pearl* (1908); *The Curious Lore of Precious Stones;* (1913); *The Magic of Jewels* (1915) and *Rings* (1917).

When Kunz died on July 29, 1932, *The New York Times* pointed out that most people thought of him only as director of the United States Bureau of Standards—which he was. But the fact was that he was also an officer or founder of a dozen other organizations.

At his funeral the Cathedral of St. John the Divine was filled, and the bishop and three priests officiated; Tiffany's was closed. There were delegates from all of his clubs and organizations, both learned and honorary, and the faculty of Columbia University marched in the procession, headed by its president.

The whole world paid tribute to the boy who had come from the Elysian Fields of New Jersey to show his small treasure to Charles Tiffany. The contributions made by the joint association of Kunz, Morgan and Tiffany resulted in one of the most outstanding gem collections in the world.

It cannot be forgotten, however, that the field trips, the honors at the world exhibits, the cases at the museum, all had their beginning because Charles Tiffany, on that long-ago day in the 1870's, took time to examine a piece of tourmaline placed on his desk in the store on Union Square.

F rom the time of its establishment on Union Square, Tiffany & Co. had become something more than a princely mercantile establishment; it was looked upon as a museum that happened to sell its exhibits. The store was a "must" visit for the inner circle of old wealth. Mrs. Harold Peabody, of Boston, recalled in her diary, *To Be Young Was Very Heaven*, her first trip to New York. Mrs. Peabody, then Marion Lawrence, came with her parents, the Reverend and Mrs. William Lawrence (her father was soon to become Bishop of Massachusetts). The Lawrences, Brahmins of Brahmins, who visited Europe once a year, barely nodded to the Cabots and did their American traveling in Pierpont Morgan's private railroad car when they did not hire one themselves, had their

(Above) Queen Victoria: the ultimate accolade.

itinerary carefully arranged: "We went to see the Statue of Liberty, but did not venture out upon the water. We then saw the Brooklyn Bridge, Grace Church, and then Tiffany's." The Metropolitan Museum was left until the next day.

As the country amassed wealth, it developed an awareness of something beyond the "mere articles of luxury"; there was a mysterious new ingredient called taste. The New York *Post* informed readers that Tiffany's was "a school for taste . . . a teacher of art progress." The New York *Mail,* too, discovered that "the Country is now developing a taste for the beautiful in art ornaments and things of actual use. It is quite as easy to display good taste in the selection of articles which are necessary to our daily comfort as it is in those which are mere matters of luxury. . . . Tiffany & Co.'s immense establishment is a palace of bewilderment and seems to embrace every article that the most aesthetic can demand."

Among the articles "most worthy of examination that give the house a distinctive character for the improvement of popular taste" were the bronzes, now more popular than ever, and also larger and more expensive. The *Post*'s self-appointed critic was already beginning to separate the highbrows from the lowbrows.

To a gentleman from the rural districts the finest work of the French artists is a goodly image and no more; while to a man of cultivation and travel it has an historic meaning in representing the progress of art and skills and recalls the Museo Bourbonico, the Hotel Cluny and the South Kensington Museum. On entering the building, one cannot fail to notice the heroic "Nubian Slaves" of Toussaint, which were recognized the other day by the Grand Duke Alexis as the counterparts of the statues which guard one of the grand staircases of the Winter Palace in St. Petersburg. These figures, in smaller and more convenient sizes, are exhibited above in company with. . . . Sappho gazing over the cliff from which she is about to plunge . . . Cleopatra in her immortal beauty, Isis seated upon the mysterious Sphynx and the "Dying Gladiator" butchered to make a Roman holiday.

There was a new department devoted to glassware and cloisonné; a "revival of the sixteenth century is shown in the clocks and candelabra of the *goutte d'eau* pattern, the crystal pendants falling like the spray of a fountain, a style so rococo . . . that it would be quite unsuitable in an apartment unless taste and knowledge had not harmonized the furnishings."

By 1880, Tiffany's was showing "a very magnificent statue, 'The

First Dream of Love,' and a very beautiful and pleasing statue called 'After Supper': a duplicate of this piece has been ordered by the Emperor of Austria.'' (At an art sale in the same period an oil of a milkmaid called ''Why Don't It Come'' went for eight hundred dollars; a Turner was sold for seventy-five dollars.)

Charles Tiffany was a good enough businessman to know that no matter how many newspapers praised his store, a position of tastemaker could be given only by the judges, the arbiters of taste, at the great fairs and expositions. He put his mind and the skill of his workmen to the task of being recognized by this particular world.

The results were gratifying. At the Centennial Exposition at Philadelphia in 1876, Tiffany's so outdistanced competitors that it received the Gold Medal, as well as special recognition for its superb exhibits of jewelry, watches, silver inlaid with niello and wedding stationery. This was the trial run for the Paris Exposition two years later, which Charles planned to attend to receive the expected honors. His hopes were justified: he won the grand prize for silverware, a gold medal for jewelry; and the skill of his workers was honored with six gold medals. Charles was awarded the Cross of Chevalier of the Legion of Honor; a more exceptional tribute came from the Czar of Russia—the gold medal of honor, Pramia Digna. The quality of the new customers was even more gratifying. Among them were the Prince of Wales and his brothers, the Duke of Edinburgh and Prince Leopold; the Grand Duke Alexis of Russia, an Austrian grand duke, four German princes, nine Rothschilds and a long list of lesser notables, four museums, and a Japanese gentleman, Minoda Chojiro, who was as enamored of Tiffany's products as Charles Tiffany had been of those of his country since the time he opened his store.

As a result, Tiffany's was able to announce that it was now Imperial Jeweler, Royal Jeweler, and both gold and silver smith to many glittering houses. In 1883 the firm was appointed jeweler to her Most Gracious Majesty, Queen Victoria herself. Within a year, her example was followed by the Czar and Czarina of all the Russias; the Emperor of Austria; the kings of Belgium, Italy, Denmark, Greece, Spain, Portugal and Roumania, as well as the Emperor of Brazil, the Khedive of Egypt, the Shah of Persia and the Infanta Dona Eulalia of Spain.

Charles Tiffany was fully aware of how this roll of royal clients would affect the customers in his own country—now beginning to engage in the heavy traffic in titles which occupied American society for another twenty-five years. Tiffany got his point across by a capital use of reverse snobbery. He made no show of his awards in his win-

*The six-prong
Tiffany setting.*

dows, nor by running the ''by appointment to'' ads and labels which
appear on English products. He had no need to, since the public, as
usual, was kept informed by the press. A typical story ran: ''In a
private office in the rear of the store hang the letters patent from the
crowned heads of Europe, enough to placard the show windows. A
single one of these would make the fortune of a silversmith or jeweler
in England. There, if a butcher enjoys the sublime distinction of
serving H.R.H. with a single chop he hastens to put over his shop
door the everlasting ostrich tips and the motto ''Ich Dieu'' [*sic*],
which wouldn't be a bad one for his butchership either. There is nothing that shows Mr. Tiffany to be more strongly American than the
non display of these bits of royal parchment. He pays his countrymen
the compliment of thinking that they ask for no foreign endorsement
of their taste.'' The private office was Mr. Tiffany's own, and important sales, then as now, were discussed privately. The effect of
those walls must have been overpowering to the select rich who were
invited there, especially if they were not quite sure whether the article
was worth the Tiffany price tag.

Charles still helped the press along occasionally. An article in *The
International Review* by an author named Edwin C. Taylor extolled
American artisans as the leaders in the art of silverware and detailed
exactly how Tiffany's had achieved world leadership. The article was
widely reprinted by newspapers, which neglected to state, if they
knew, that Edwin C. Taylor was an employee of Tiffany's.

About this time, the Tiffany ring setting was first shown, and soon
was in great demand. Although much has been written about the setting, the store does not know exactly when—or by whom—this superior way was devised to show off the large, perfect brilliants which
the firm now carried. In the new open setting the gem was held by
only six small prongs, so that any fault would be seen. The old (or
closed) setting had covered all but the face of the stone—a necessity

The Tiffany Diamond, actual size.

with the off-color or flawed gems marketed in the earlier days.

A small-town jeweler vented his irritation at the giant, and the way he himself was forced to give it publicity. He wrote:

I wonder if Tiffany & Co., realize how much trouble they have created for jewelers everywhere when they originated the styles of wedding rings and diamond mountings which bear the name "Tiffany." Every time a jeweler shows a customer the rings or mountings he has to mention the hated name a dozen times and advertise his big New York competitor. I get around the difficulty to a certain extent by never mentioning the name but always saying "You wish the narrow English shape wedding ring, I presume?" . . . But for the life of me I cannot think of a name for the mountings. Maybe some of Tiffany's neighbor jewelers on Fifth Avenue can help me out, for it is inconceivable that they would advertise a competitor every time they sell a diamond mounting.

Curiously, an acquisition which has become synonymous with the name of Tiffany, and which has attracted more visitors to the store than any other single item, was purchased, cut and held for several years without a line of publicity. This is the great Tiffany diamond itself; the stone whose fame spread even to China in later years, and which, from its glass case set into the wall behind the diamond counter, dominates the first floor of Tiffany's today; it is valued at $2,000,000.

Found in the Kimberley mines in South Africa in 1877, the diamond was purchased at once for $18,000. It was taken to Paris, where experts studied the stone for a year before it was cut from the original 287.42 carats to 128.51 carats—not an unusually great loss in proper cutting. The stone is just over an inch wide and seven-eights of an inch from top to bottom. The cut is unusual in that the brilliant has ninety facets instead of the conventional fifty-eight, causing it to gleam like a small sun. Curiously, the extra facets were cut not to give more sparkle but to make the gem smolder as if lit by an inner flame.

The only explanation for Tiffany's early reticence about the diamond would seem to be that, as in the case of the Tiffany fresh-water pearl, diamonds with a yellow cast were being found in great numbers in South Africa; Charles might have been afraid that the Tiffany diamond would be only one of many. This has not proven so. Almost a hundred years later, the Tiffany diamond is still the largest flawless and perfectly colored canary diamond ever mined.

The wealth and honors that Charles Tiffany had accumulated over these years made no difference in his personality or distaste for personal promotion, but they were bound to affect his manner of living.

Charles Tiffany, like Morgan and the Rockefellers who followed, was never interested in social climbing. In the eyes of New York's pre-Revolutionary aristocracy—the Livingstons, the Beekmans, the De Peysters and the rest—the Astors, Vanderbilts, Tiffanys and Morgans were all lumped together as new rich. Morgan's biographer, trying to place him, suggests that the Morgans, and such other staid families as the Tiffanys and Rockefellers, would be termed high bourgeoisie in Europe—solid, assured, serene in their position to do as they pleased in the settings they preferred. The joys of Newport (and Newport's notorious flies, poor climate and weedy beaches) never tempted them. If they compared themselves with a European model, they must have mused that a designation that was good enough for

Kimberley mine, where the Tiffany diamond was found.

king-maker Jacques Coeur, the great fifteenth-century banker, was good enough for them.

Charles Tiffany was comfortable in his handsome, dignified house on Madison Avenue and saw no reason to trade it for a bogus French chateau on Fifth. In the 1860's he acquired a country estate at Irvington-on-Hudson, in the fifteen-mile stretch along the river that was later known as "Millionaires' Row." Along the row lived Pierpont Morgan, the Rockefellers, the Vanderbilts, the Wendels, Henry Villard and George Jay Gould.

Three houses already stood on the sixty-five-acre tract. The oldest was a pre-Revolutionary structure built by the original landowner, a farmer named Dutcher, who came to the United States in the 1600's. Two large square stone houses, almost identical, were built by later owners at the foot of the gentle hill crowned by the main house. The two remain, handsomely preserved by loving owners, architecturally severe and pleasing. Each has ten or eleven large, high-ceilinged rooms, eight original fireplaces, and is surrounded outside by loggias and terraces hung with ancient wisteria vines.

The original house, renamed Tiffany Hall, is gone, torn down in the early years of this century. A visitor can still stand beneath one of the giant trees which dot the property and have a magnificent view of the Hudson and the shoreline to the west. Tiffany's children and friends had urged him many times to tear down the big wooden house with its huge Dutch fireplaces and doors, and build something more in keeping with his position in the world. Charles would have none of it—though he did refurbish the twin houses below for his children.

The informal manner of living at Tiffany Hall seems to have protected the family from the kind of fears that plagued the Goulds, who "needed guards twenty-four hours a day to watch the walls and the shrubbery." One of the hazards of the times was the bomb-throwing anarchists. A commentator on the Gilded Age noted that "No rich man could turn down his gas light at night without wondering if he would be attacked before dawn."

In or out of the city, Charles Tiffany was not a recluse. In his conservative fashion he "belonged" to society. He became a member of the Union Club in 1868—a sign then, as now, that a man was accepted as a member of the city's most select social group. (A. T. Stewart never made it.) His favorite sport was fishing, often on the banks of the then fresh and glorious Hudson; he also joined the South Side Sportsmen's Club of Long Island and was one of the founders of the Restigouche Salmon Club at Matapedia, Canada. He helped found the

The young Mrs. August Belmont ready for a drive at her Newport home, about 1885.

Union League, and joined the New York Club, the Jockey Club and the West Island Club of Rhode Island. He was a founder of the New York Society of Fine Arts, a trustee of the Museum of Natural History as well as the Metropolitan Museum of Art. With these and other activities, social, financial and philanthropic, Tiffany was one of the "select group of prominent citizens" who were asked to contribute a thousand dollars each to the Metropolitan in 1871, when the founders who met the year before found their infant endeavor in need of money. Among the contributors, besides Tiffany, were Theodore Roosevelt (father of Teddy), Pierpont Morgan, James Gordon Bennett and Levi Morton.

It was natural that Tiffany, the backer of Kunz and his collections, would have more in common with the Metropolitan Museum than other trustees. In fact, the association was closer than was generally apparent. There are Tiffany-made fakes in the Metropolitan which even some of the staff were not aware of until a year ago.

General Louis Palma di Cesnola, the first director of the Metropolitan, was trained neither as an artist nor an archaeologist. He seems to have been a dashing soldier of fortune, with an eye on the main chance. He had fought in the Italian revolution, the Crimean War and the Civil War. For the last service he was appointed United States consul to Cyprus. Impressed with the amazing news of the wealth uncovered at Troy and Mycenae, Di Cesnola mused on the possibilities of Cyprus, another spot well used by ancient civilizations. He dug indiscriminately during his six-year tenure as consul, bringing out over ten thousand artifacts of Egyptian, Assyrian, Phoenician, and early Greek cultures; what he must have destroyed dismays the imagination.

When Di Cesnola returned to the United States in 1876, he offered his hoard to the struggling Metropolitan. New York loved dress and jewels and show, but was little interested in art. John Taylor Johnston, president of the museum (William Cullen Bryant was vice president), bought the lot on his own initiative and bond for sixty thousand dollars. He also appointed Di Cesnola director of the museum. (Ground for the present structure had been broken in 1874, but the collections were still in quarters in the old Douglas Mansion, at 128 West Fourteenth Street.)

Mixed in with the iridescent glass, Bronze Age vases and broken shards—and, some said, illegally reconstructed statues, which led to a blazing international scandal a few years later—were two gold armlets, authenticated as having been sent by Eteandos, King of Paphos, to Curium about 300 B.C. The armlets were of virgin gold, so soft they could be bent with the fingers. Each weighed about a pound, and bore the signature of the King on the inner side. The treasure, along with the other collections, was transferred to the new building, at the present site, when it opened in 1880. (The red-brick edifice, now hidden by additions, was promptly judged "hideous.")

Then, on September 15, 1887, guards discovered that the cabinets holding the Cypriote gold had been broken into and the armlets stolen. A few days after the robbery a small package was delivered to the office of the director. Inside were the bracelets—or rather, what looked like the bracelets.

Back in 1877, Di Cesnola had replicas made of several pieces of the treasure for museums in Europe. Tiffany's was given the commission. Di Cesnola wrote in a letter to Charles Tiffany: "If it were not for your name stamped upon the ones you have made, I believe it would be almost impossible to decide which are the originals. They are so faithfully reproduced, they must prove most useful."

And they did, ten years later. As soon as the robbery occurred, Di Cesnola got in touch with Tiffany's in the forlorn hope that the firm still had facsimiles of the armlets. Tiffany's did have them, and they were given to the museum with Tiffany's compliments. For some weeks the press made much of all this, at the same time quoting the museum that it would be but a matter of weeks until the originals would be back in their cases. Since the museum was overly optimistic, the story gradually vanished from the papers.

In the spring of 1970 a curious visitor asked about the armlets. Were the ones in the museum the originals or the Tiffany copies? A young curator replied indignantly that the Metropolitan never retained copies; however, having a professional's natural curiosity and love of truth, he checked the armlets. He found that they do bear the stamp of Tiffany's put there nearly a hundred years ago so they could never be fobbed off as the real ones.

Shortly after making the Di Cesnola duplicates in gold, Tiffany's made one of its most spectacular silver sets, the famous Mackay family silver service. John Mackay, who was born in Ireland, struck it rich at Virginia City, Nevada, with the Comstock Lode. In all, the "Prince of Miners" took more than two hundred million dollars from the lode before he went East. There he and his wife were so royally snubbed that they went to London, where they entertained real royalty in splendor. Mrs. Mackay was described in the European press as "a great lady in the tight circle of international society . . . mastering several languages and all the social graces of the newly acquired fortune."

For his silver service, John Mackay had 14,719 ounces sent from his mine to Tiffany's, with instructions to make the most ornate service possible. Tiffany's did—charging Mackay $125,000 for the job—working out such elaborate designs around the motifs of the shamrock of Ireland and the thistle of Scotland for Mrs. Mackay's ancestors that there was no visible spot of the service which was not ornamented. Each piece also carried the family crest and the Mackay monogram. The Mackay crest inspired some humorous remarks in the press, but one newspaper liked the idea: when Prince Colonna, who married one of the Mackay daughters, came to the United States, the crest would be proof that his bride was "raised in this Country, not just dragged up."

A Mackay candelabra.

A prime example of the ornateness and weight of the service was a celery vase, which, though only sixteen inches high, contained 150 ounces of silver. A pair of candelabra, thirty-six inches high, held fifty-eight candles and weighed more than 500 ounces. In all, there were 1,350 pieces in the service which was sent to the London house, where it "became a tradition to use it at stately receptions for members of the Victorian court and the families of the great houses of Europe."

The service went to John's son, Clarence, and on to his son, John II, intact. Since then it has been broken up. Some fifty-eight pieces, including the candelabra, were presented to the University of Nevada. Parts of the service belong to other members of the family, including the younger John's sister, Mrs. Irving Berlin. Unless the dies turn up in some moldering cellar or carriage house, the younger generation cannot fill out their services: when the order was completed, old John Mackay bought the dies so that his service could never be duplicated.

Another collector of silver, on a scale even greater than Mackay's, was Mrs. Charles Morgan, the wealthy widow of a shipowner, who spent so much time at Tiffany's that she regarded it as her second home. When she died at Saratoga in the summer of 1885 ''all her treasures [including a million dollars' worth of Tiffany jewels] were at Tiffany's, as usual.'' Mrs. Morgan, with a genuine knowledge of art, put together the first important American collection of paintings. However, her first love was silver; she designed many small figures which Tiffany's executed for her, as well as a pair of candelabra which cost thirty thousand dollars. But the most impressive was Mrs. Morgan's design of a group of Indians lassoing a buffalo. Tiffany's made this up in solid silver at a price, the press reported reverently, ''beyond cost.''

About this time, the Tiffany Blue Book devoted an entire page to something new—along with diamonds and pearls ''beyond cost''— which was bound to fascinate a dedicated walker like Charles Tiffany: the American pedometer, invented by Benjamin Church, ''the well-known engineer of the Croton Aqueduct.'' The catalog pointed out that ''Tiffany's, the sole agent, supplies a table (for computations) with each pedometer. Price $5.''

This gadget supplied its share of Tiffany stories in the press. One of the more often quoted concerned a young wife who suspected that her husband was ''larking about.'' She bought a pedometer one day and concealed it in the back pocket of his trousers. That night, the husband made the usual remarks about a hard day at the office. The wife yanked out the pedometer and showed him he had walked exactly eleven miles while seated at his desk. ''Whom were you walking with?'' she demanded.

''Why,'' said the husband, a quick thinker, ''I met Mrs. Swope, the clergyman's wife, and we did walk a bit.''

''Oh, no, you didn't,'' cried the wife. ''She was walking with me! Oh, Edward . . .'' A burst of tears, and the wife went home to Mama in the accepted fashion.

For gentlemen the catalog of 1885 suggested toothpicks at five dollars; whistles to call cabs and dogs at twenty-five dollars, or pocket pin-cushions, engraved with a monogram or coat of arms. Men's jeweled sleeve buttons were $439 a pair and up, while ''bronze busts of eminent men, suitable as gifts for professional men'' were sixteen dollars. Tiffany's did not as yet frown on diamond rings for men, let alone refuse to sell them, as it was later to do. In the early 1880's the store featured a ''gypsy ring'' for men, the diamond ''buried in gold.''

Popular items for women were shopping bracelets, with pencil attached, in gold, richly jeweled, a hundred and eighty-five dollars; fan holders, twenty-four dollars and up; vinaigrettes, five dollars to three hundred dollars; shopping bags, nine dollars to one hundred dollars; laces for parasols, fifty dollars to three hundred dollars; and "magic pencils," three hundred dollars.

It was during this period that Tiffany's produced its most unusual inkstand; in fact, for once, it is correct to say that the creation was unique. The customer was a writer of Western stories, named Howard Seely; one of his better-known books was entitled *A Nymph of the West*. Whether the inkstand was connected with the Nymph, Seely did not choose to tell. What he did was send Tiffany's a small human skull, which he explained was that of a famed Mexican beauty; he wanted it turned into an inkstand for his desk. Tiffany's, never one for questioning a customer, set to work. The eye sockets were fitted with inkwells, covered with silver lids, connected to springs attached to the jaw. When this was pressed down, the eyelids opened.

The inkstand provided only a one-day story for the press. But the mystery of the Mummy's Eyes, which came a short time later, was a sensation for weeks. The European papers, the French in particular, shuddered deliciously, speculating as to what those barbaric Americans would be up to next. Matters began simply enough—at least in a store which had just shipped off a human skull. A Mr. W. E. Curtis dropped by with a bag of stonelike objects which he wanted made into a necklace for his lady love; the "stones," he added casually, were mummies' eyes. No trouble at all, said Tiffany's. And then the trouble started.

A youth of sixteen was set to polishing the eyes. Almost at once he became ill; he had headaches, was bilious, began vomiting, and had to be sent home. He was out only a couple of days but, not unexpectedly, refused to work with the eyes. His place was taken by a "strong, hearty Frenchman, about 45 years old weighing 200 pounds"; he showed the precise symptoms of the first workman, adding that he noticed "a strong metallic taste in his mouth." A third workman, "a middle-aged German," volunteered to take over; to the previous indispositions he added another; he broke out in a rash. By this time, the papers were hot on the story of the "Mummy's Curse."

An expert was found who stated that the stones were petrified human eyes from Peru, and the arsenic used in preserving them was making the workmen sick. Tiffany's expert, George Kunz, admitted that he was stumped. However, he did turn up his own expert, a Professor Baird, who said he knew all about Peruvian mummies, eyes and all. The mummies themselves came from the rainless region around Arica, where the bodies were dried in a sitting position in the sandy soil of the nitrate beds. Furthermore, Professor Baird told Kunz, the eyes were not human at all but were those of a species of cuttlefish; he had first seen specimens thirty years before. These particular eyes dried into a hard ball; they were sawn in two and polished (the golden-brown color closely resembling that of the human eye), and placed in the mummies' empty eye sockets. He added that certain alkaloids generated in the drying process might prove poisonous. There the matter was dropped (the press did not record whether Curtis received his necklace). But the problem was pursued by Kunz for his own edification. He felt forced to amend the findings of his own researches with the note that "on the other hand, Professor Raimondi, the most eminent ethnologist in Peru, believes them [the eyes] to be human, and Dr. Tschudi of Vienna is said to support him."

On a homelier plane, Tiffany's introduced aluminum flatware to the New World. The *Tribune* was impressed with the display: "The spoons are about one fourth the cost of gold, and are expected to be widely used." The *Tribune* was no more wrong than Louis Napoleon; he had been so enchanted with the new metal that he put away his gold and silver services and served guests on a service of aluminum which cost him as much as silver. Pierre Lorillard, founder of the tobacco company, was far more prescient in the use for aluminum. Impressed with the lightness of the metal, he asked Tiffany's to make horseshoes for his racing stable.

But Tiffany's did not reach its eminence by polishing the eyes of mummies or casting aluminum horseshoes. Charles Tiffany concentrated on catering to the expensive desires of the very rich. Mackay had his silver service; the Goulds, Astors, Vanderbilts, Bradley Martins, Havemeyers and Whitneys served guests at their more intimate parties of a hundred or so on solid gold. Tiffany's made J. Pierpont Morgan handsome services in both gold and silver. These scarcely seemed enough to his fellow directors of the New York Central, whose shaky fortunes he had so deftly saved for them on a leisurely afternoon cruise in 1884 on the *Corsair;* on the following Christmas, they

Eyes of cuttlefish or humans?

presented him with a $50,000 gold dessert service.

Tiffany's still meant diamonds, as it had since Charles made his coup in 1848. Neither he nor the press which crowned him king could have imagined how popular the gems would be thirty-five years later, when experts estimated that individual Americans owned over a billion dollars' worth of diamonds, more than all the crowned heads of Europe together, excepting Queen Victoria. Tiffany's for years sold more than six million dollars' worth of diamonds a year—and as much or more in pearls, emeralds, rubies and sapphires. The amount when translated into modern money values is staggering. A nine-carat diamond classed as "pure white and perfect" could be bought for two thousand dollars in the 1880's. Such a gem today, if truly white and perfect, would cost close to seventy thousand dollars.

All this meant an unprecedented demand for diamonds. The discovery of the mines in South Africa helped the supply. But a more romantic and constant source remained the same as it had been in 1848: the treasures of the royal houses of Europe, whose members found themselves in need of money. "Fat, frivolous" Queen Isabella II, a hearty and apparently not quite bright nymphomaniac, who was deposed from the Spanish throne in 1868, sold Tiffany's over $1,600,-000's worth of gems, which the Spanish Bourbons had been hoarding for a hundred and fifty years. Most of Isabella's jewels became the property of Mrs. Leland Stanford, but one diamond had its own more poignant history. Tiffany's sold H. A. W. Tabor, the Colorado miner, a 6.62 brilliant, which he gave to Baby Doe on their wedding day; when the Tabor fortune vanished, Baby Doe sold it back to Tiffany's.

At other times, Tiffany's picked up the Brunswick yellow, 30 carats and the Duke's favorite stone, at an auction in Geneva (the Duke had earlier turned down an offer of $60,000 and presumably Tiffany's bid was higher); the famous collection of Hungarian Prince Esterhazy (for a hundred thousand dollars); and a large ruby which had once adorned the chubby neck of Catherine the Great. Sultan Abdul Hamid of Turkey offered a diamond-and-emerald necklace, which Tiffany's bought for $1,250,000. Wherever jewels were available, at auctions or through private and discreet hands, Tiffany's was there.

But it is the French crown jewels with which the house of Tiffany is inextricably entwined. To do full justice to the story, it is necessary to go back, long before Tiffany's first purchase in 1848, to the days when the jewels were accumulated, and when they were subsequently lost and dispersed.

Until the Revolution, France possessed the finest and largest collection of gems in Europe, housed in the royal Garde Meuble. Upon the outbreak of the Terror in 1792, criminals released from the prisons first emptied the wine shops and then plundered the Garde Meuble. They marched drunkenly through the streets with their loot, leaving a splendid trail to a tree near the walls where they carelessly buried much of the jewelry. Although this cache was quickly recovered, still missing was an estimated 90 percent of the treasure. This accounts for the fact that pieces of the collection kept floating into view, and out again, during the next hundred years. (The Regent, the most valuable diamond in the lot, was found ten years later, hidden in an old loft. France has held on to the Regent, valued at two million dollars in 1792).

Cardinal Mazarin is credited with laying the foundation for the

Cartoon of senators' wives who planned to bid for French jewels.

Jewelers inspecting French crown jewels before sale.

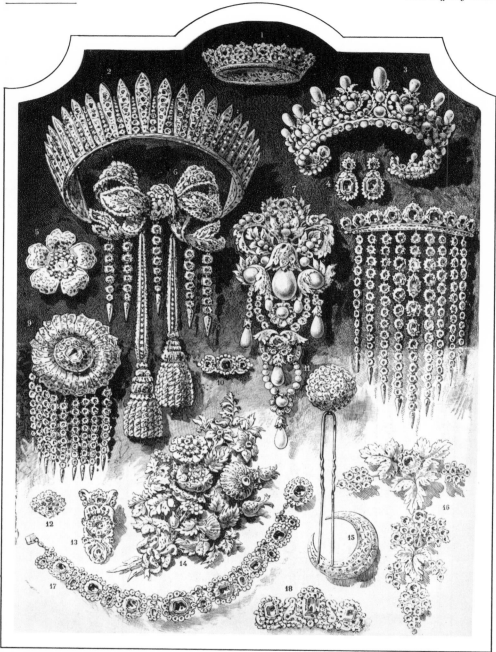

The French crown jewels.

1, 12, 13. *Diamond and*
   ruby ornaments.
2. *Russian diadem.*
3. *Pearl diadem.*
4, 10, 17, 18. *Sapphire*
   and diamond ornaments.

5. *Wild rose.*
6. *Diamond knot with*
   tassels.
7. *Pearl and diamond*
   brooch.
8. *Comb, with diamond*
   pendants.

9. *Buckle fir girdle.*
11. *Hairpin with*
   jeweled ball.
14. *Bouquet for*
   the breast.
15. *Crescent.*
16. *Sevigne brooch.*

collection in the 1600's. Mazarin amassed enormous wealth, and when he died, he left his eighteen best diamonds to Louis XIV (probably to deter the grateful monarch from confiscating his entire fortune) with the proviso that they be known as The Mazarins. Later Bourbons added to the collection, and after the collapse of the republic, Napoleon Bonaparte repatriated many of the crown jewels as he conquered Europe; Empress Eugénie collected jewels in a fashion that outdid American millionaires. By 1870, the French crown jewels were once again a great treasure. Eugénie was always tinkering with her gems; her jeweler, Bapst, reset them for her every year. (This fact is pertinent because it influenced Tiffany's when the French government's sale of 1887 took place.)

Eugénie, as opposed to Louis Philippe in 1848, had time to plan ahead before she escaped, like him, in a hackney cab. The Empire fell in September 1870, but the nervous Eugénie had removed many of her jewels from the Tuileries the month before. A confidant, Comte de Montglas, took all he could manage to England, where he deposited them with the very reluctant Bank of England.

The story behind the 1887 sale lies in the phrase "all he could manage." Somehow a number of cases were left aboard a small ship, the *Borda*, in the harbor of Brest. There they bobbed around for two years, the populace frightened off by the label "explosives" on the rough boxes. Finally the French government brought them back to Paris in 1872; among the jewels were the Regent and five Mazarins.

Eugénie herself sold a hundred and twenty-three lots of jewels in 1872 at a sale at Christie's. From 1872 until 1883 the French fussed about what to sell and what to keep. One commission stated flatly that the combs and brooches and necklaces had no historical significance for France because of Eugénie's passion for resetting. There was one preliminary sale in 1883, and it was extraordinarily discreet. Only one tiny notice in a French newspaper stated that certain pieces had been sold "to eight crown jewelers and Tiffany and Company."

The Paris sale of 1887 was another matter; it was publicized around the world. The sale opened in the Hall of State on May 12, and continued for several days. There was much buzzing and speculation when the great house of Tiffany made no move to bid as lot after lot, one through nine, was sold. Then lot number ten was announced. This was the so-called great necklace of Eugénie, consisting of 222 large diamonds of the first water, set in four rows, and acknowledged to be the single finest piece to go on sale. Tiffany's bid it in for 183,000 francs. When interviewed, the firm's representative said that the first nine lots had gone at too high prices because of their supposed historical associations, and the house was not interested in that aspect of the jewels. (Tiffany's was well aware of the opinion of the French commission that they had no historic significance.)

Seven Mazarin diamonds were listed in the catalog; Tiffany's got four of them by paying 128,000, 81,000, 155,000 and 71,000 francs for them respectively. The purchases were on consignment ''for lady millionairesses on the other side of the Atlantic,'' the French press reported. Eugénie's most spendid comb was another piece she did not get out of the country. This was set with 208 large diamonds, including two certified Mazarins, ''the eighth on the left side of the comb proper.'' From the band fell nine flexible streamers of solid diamonds, which reached to the shoulders and, in happier days at the Tuileries, had swayed when the Empress moved—''a perfect waterfall of diamonds.''

The comb was broken into eighteen lots. Tiffany's took the six finest —including the eighth Mazarin—for 218,000 francs. Another purchase was a ''huge briolette of diamonds'' (a species of dog collar), which the firm sold to Colonel James D. Safford, the second husband of the daughter of President Andrew Jackson. Tiffany's also acquired a sapphire-and-diamond comb, the Savigné brooch and two diamond and ruby bracelets. Only once were they outbid. A certain Mme. Gale got a belt and buckle, described as having 295 diamonds, including two brilliants of 25 carats, of a rare aqua shade. Tiffany's man was able to buy the belt and buckle from the sagacious Frenchwoman the following day.

The night after the sale ended, Mrs. Joseph Pulitzer, wife of the owner of the New York *World,* was noted at a fashionable Parisian ball, the great Eugénie necklace ''clasped around her handsome neck.''

In all, Tiffany's bought twenty-four of the sixty-nine lots, nine times the purchases of the next biggest buyers, the Orléans princes. Tiffany's spent approximately five hundred thousand dollars and felt it had done very well. The French government thought so, too, since it had expected to raise a third more than it did. Most of the jewels were brought back to New York and shown at Tiffany's with much fanfare on the part of the press, which called them, inaccurately, Marie Antoinette's jewels.

No less an expert than Dr. Kunz felt that 1887 marked a milestone in the history of Tiffany acquisitions: the French crown jewels; four of the largest diamonds to come out of Africa that year; and finally from London his own contribution: ''I acquired a number of gems when the great collection made by Henry Philip Hope in 1850 was sold all over the world by his heir.'' An assessment printed at the end of 1887 estimated that the Tiffany vaults held forty million dollars in precious stones.

Not all of the French jewels were sold on consignment. Tiffany's great gem exhibit for the Paris Exposition of 1889 was arranged around a diamond necklace, the center stone being valued at forty-five thousand dollars and identified as a part of the French treasure. Mrs. Bradley-Martin * always claimed that all the stones in her ruby necklace from Tiffany's were from the French crown jewels.

The eighties and the nineties were a period when a newly dubbed multimillionaire could prove his financial status to his associates by sending his wife to balls and the opera loaded down with enough jewels to cause her knees to buckle. But the women of the time were made of stern stuff; they not only bore the heavy burden uncomplainingly, they themselves demanded more, the better to outshine their friends. A lady of fashion under full sail would wear a tiara on her head. Clasped about her throat would be the omnipresent dog collar, below which would be diamond necklaces and ropes of pearls. A brooch or two would glisten on her bosom, and clasping her waist would be a stomacher, shining with the full brilliance of diamonds. It is easy to understand why the first tier of the new Metropolitan Opera House was immediately named the Diamond Horseshoe when it opened in 1883. Diamonds by the thousands outshown the house lights.

If America as a whole owned more diamonds than all the courts of Europe, three women—Mrs. John Jacob Astor, Mrs. Clarence Mackay and Mrs. Leland Stanford—were *each* said to own more jewels than any of the crowned heads, with the exception of Victoria and the Czarina of Russia (and Kunz, as we have noted, took a dim view of the Russian gems).

Mrs. Astor received the most publicity. Ten mounted policemen were employed to escort her and her eight hundred thousand dollars' worth of diamonds to and from Mrs. William K. Vanderbilt's fancy-dress ball in 1883. Among the jewels she wore was a pair of solitaire earrings, each diamond ''as large as the end of a man's thumb.''

But the acknowledged Queen of Diamonds was Mrs. Leland Stanford. Tiffany's purchased most of her collection for her, including a million dollars' worth from the cache of the unfortunate Isabella of Spain. This included four matching sets of diamond pieces, each one composed of a necklace, corsage, earrings, tiara, bracelets and brooches. One set ''emitted violet rays by day''; a second was com-

---

* The Bradley-Martins felt they had blocked a recession with their spectacularly lavish fancy-dress ball. The poor felt differently—and so strongly that the Bradley-Martins were forced to leave the country.

posed of yellow diamonds; the third, of pink diamonds; and the fourth, of pure-white stones. Tiffany's also sold Mrs. Stanford a large pear-shaped black diamond and a necklace of varicolored diamonds, judged to be the finest necklace in the country and valued at a hundred and thirty thousand dollars. She owned sixty pairs of diamond earrings, which she kept in order on a string of black tape.

Incredible as it may seem, Mrs. Stanford was reported to have once worn all her jewels at a private dinner given by William E. Dodge. Her dress was of black tulle, embroidered in silver, with voluminous folds, which she needed as a background on which to pin her assortment of jewels; she also wore many necklaces, rings and "other ornaments."

The New York *Sun* once (in 1889) tried to give its readers a rundown of the wealth of jewels in the country; it filled a column of the small, eye-straining type of the time, and admitted the job was not complete (the list would run to several columns in the larger type used today). The headline was, *They Have Jewels Galore.*

The article noted that Hetty Green, "who does not give a rap for a diamond except for the cash it represents," kept hers locked up in safe-deposit vaults. She always paid cash, appearing in Tiffany's with a paper bag full of bills. Mrs. Hicks-Lord, continued the *Sun*, wore a "superb necklace said to have cost over $100,000 but from the standpoint of the experts not the equal of Mrs. Stanford's, because of the rarity of the latter's stones." Mrs. J. B. Hagan, "wife of the California millionaire," had a ruby valued at ten thousand dollars, which had once been given to Lola Montez by Louis of Bavaria. Conspicuous among the costly collections of jewels in New York, the *Sun* went on, "are those of Mrs. Christopher Myer, widow of the aged rubber manufacturer. Mrs. Myer . . . is a young and handsome woman, and at many of the elegant receptions is resplendent in her jewels . . . diamonds, sapphires, pearls and turquoises." Miss Isabella Singer, "daughter of the sewing machine man," who married the Duc de Decazes, was showered with diamonds and pearls from Tiffany's. "Making allowances for the enthusiasm of her press agent," the *Sun* said that Minnie Palmer, of Chicago, "probably has $250,000 in diamonds, including the Cleveland stone of 42½ carats, which cost $10,-000." Mrs. A. J. Drexel, Mrs. Thomas A. Scott and Mrs. Clarence L. Harper, of Philadelphia, each had "a fortune in diamonds." A "unique and costly" necklace in the possession of Mrs. Robert Johnson of San Francisco was formed of many costly stones "in the exact counterpart of a snake. The solitaires are set in gold folds, the plates,

VOLUME XIII.

NEW YORK, MARCH 28, 1889.

Entered at the New York Post Office as Second-Class Mail Matter.
Copyright, 1889, by MITCHELL & MILLER.

NUMBER 326.

A BARE POSSIBILITY

MISS F: I think I shall go as Cleopatra, but I don't know where to go for the costume.

MISS A: You will find all you need at Tiffany's.

overlapping each other are perfectly flexible . . . the resemblance to a snake is very striking.''

Mrs. August Belmont owned ''the finest collection of sapphires in the Country.'' Mrs. Pierre Lorillard collected ''brilliant and costly jewels,'' and Mrs. Robert Hoe, wife of the press manufacturer, had ''a fortune in diamonds,'' the same phrase designating the collection of Mrs. Henry Clews, wife of the author of *Twenty Years in Wall Street*. The finest sapphire belonged to Mrs. John Astor's sister-in-law, the formidable Mrs. William Astor, who, black-gowned and black-wigged, received the Four Hundred wearing the costliest necklace of emeralds and diamonds in America. Although one single Gould rope of pearls was valued at a million, the *Sun* assured its readers that the finest collection of pearls was owned by Mrs. Marshall O. Roberts, founder of the Y.W.C.A. of the City of New York.

Not all the comments were so full of awe. The jewelry-laden *grandes dames* and belles of the eighties were a source of considerable merriment for humor magazines, such as *Puck* and *Life*.

On one cover, *Life* ran a drawing of two elegant ladies on a couch. The title, ''A Bare Possibility,'' was quite daring for those days.

Puck was even more to the point. It ran a full-page drawing of a ball scene, the women in their low-cut, wasp-waisted dresses, each wearing a numbered badge. The tag line: ''If the ladies will go to these affairs and wish to show off their diamonds without danger from thieves, we respectfully submit the above as one way of doing the thing properly.'' In an upper corner of the drawing is a glass case containing numbered boxes of diamonds; above the case is a sign reading: ''These are genuine diamonds and guaranteed to belong to the persons as marked. [Signed] Tiffany & Company.''

Another woman with a famous collection of jewels was Mrs. Frank Leslie, whose husband owned *Leslie's Weekly*, one of the leading magazines. She both collected and designed, and even her small black-and-tan dog had a collection of diamond-studded collars. (The most expensive dog collar [for a dog] was made for a Gould, at a cost of fifteen thousand dollars.) After her husband died, his widow found the publishing company close to bankruptcy; she needed a large source of credit. As reported in *Jewelers Weekly*, she solved her problem, with the unwitting help of Tiffany's, by making the grand purchase.

No larger or finer sets of stones are to be found in the Country [again!] than a large pair of solitaire earrings owned and earned by this same lady [Mrs. Leslie].

They have an almost unequalled depth and brilliancy and were bought at Tiffany's for $10,000. At the time she bought them, Mrs. Leslie was struggling as mortal seldom does to restore the standing of her business. . . . Finding it difficut to secure credit, she came to the wise conclusion that, as she was reputed to be a remarkably prudent woman, it would at once raise her credit if it were known that she had spent a large sum of money for jewelry. Instead, then, of paying a few thousand dollars on account to her creditors she boldly bought the stones, knowing that the papers would spread the news. They did, and in consequence of the seemingly rash purchase, raised her credit to $100,000 and saved her from ruin. Today she has a splendid business and is worth over a million.

Society names and an occasional title titillated the masses, but they were equally interested in the careers and the wealth amassed thereby of the professional beauties and the queens of the stage. "Mrs. Langtry (the Jersey Lily) came over one day from Philadelphia," the *World* chronicled, "to see the Tiffany jewels and to invest a few spare thousand in their black pearls. She says she does not want any more diamonds, having already about $40,000 worth, most of which is represented in a necklace in which every stone is over five carats in weight." An admirer of Mrs. Langtry also gave her a mirror, ten feet high and elaborately carved, with little cupids tossing garlands to each other. The Divine Sarah Bernhardt came to Tiffany's and bought herself a $3,000 silver toilet set, with a washbowl described as big enough to bathe in.

Diamond Jim Brady was probably Tiffany's most flamboyant customer. He owned hundreds of cuff links and waistcoat buttons, not to mention rings. He also was a very generous man, dropping by regularly to buy "little nothings" for his girl friend of the moment—such as a diamond bracelet or a single pearl for five thousand dollars. Jeweled garters were another acceptable gift. The item dubbed Ne Plus Ultra (two jeweled hearts set side by side) went for two thousand dollars. Actresses and socialites who could afford the garters all wore them. In December of 1880, Tiffany's sold five hundred pairs, at prices ranging from a modest two hundred dollars to five thousand dollars. Lillian Russell wore a pair in the shape of large spiders, the bodies made of huge emeralds, the legs encrusted with diamonds and rubies.

This was also the time when Diamond Jim displayed his imagination with a gift for Lillian that may never have been matched for vulgarity. He asked Tiffany's to make (and they made it) a solid-gold chamber pot; in the center of the bottom, peering up, was an eye.

The age of diamonds continued into the twentieth century. Now it was steel and oil fortunes which descended on Tiffany's. Charles M. Schwab of U.S. Steel was typical of the tycoon customer: one afternoon he walked in and walked out again in less than an hour—he had a 60-carat diamond for his wife; and Tiffany's, his check for ninety-one thousand dollars.

Whether the clerk knew Mr. Schwab by face would have made little difference; his check or his ability to pay would not have been questioned. Long before credit cards were thought of, Tiffany's had its own system, which enabled the firm to advertise that "suitable items would be dispatched for out of town selection."

A reporter of the St. Louis *Post Dispatch* recorded that he "happened to drop into Tiffany's to make a small purchase. While there, a gentleman from St. Louis entered, and after examining a large amount of expensive jewelry, directed that several costly articles be put aside for him, saying he would send a certified check as soon as he reached home, on receipt of which they were to be forwarded.

" 'There is no necessity for that,' the salesman replied, 'you can take them with you and send us the money when you get home.'

" 'But you don't know me,' was the astonished answer. 'I never was here before in my life, and I am not acquainted with anyone connected with the establishment.'

" 'That's all right,' was the rejoinder, 'take the jewelry with you. We have no anxiety concerning payment.'

"The St. Louis gentleman was a man of large wealth, but not especially prominent. After he left I asked the salesman how he could carry on business in such a manner. He laughed and introduced me to the credit clerk."

The reporter was told that Tiffany's was acquainted with the financial standing of the citizens in every large city, partly through Dun's Financial Service, "but a great many of [their] best customers, particularly foreigners and ladies, do not appear on the lists of that company." Seven employees of Tiffany's were kept busy getting the information from other sources. To make identification certain, Tiffany's also possessed photographs of everyone listed.

" 'That gentleman who just came in, we never heard of before, but as soon as he mentioned his name,' the credit manager explained, 'and place of residence, our errand boy brought it to me. I turned to my book, found that we had a photograph and within five minutes knew we could trust him with any amount. . . . We are able to extend our trade all over the country. When we give credit to anyone who had supposed himself unknown to us we are sure to retain him forever.' ''

And so the decade of the 1890's drew to a close. It had been the Gay Nineties for some; never had so few had so much. But it was not so gay for the dollar-a-day laborers, the strikers at the Homestead Steel Plant, the starving marchers in Coxey's Army, the little merchants caught in the Panic of '93. It was a decade of change. No one would cut up and sell telegraph cables again—Marconi had invented the wireless, and Thomas Edison had given the first viewing of pictures that moved, in his kinetoscope. The world moved on with the century.

Charles Tiffany did not seem to have changed at all. Still straight and erect, he kept businessmen's hours and tended the store. He was a widower now; his household was run by his unmarried daughter, Louise. The last big family party had been given at the great house Charles had built for his son, Louis, on Madison Avenue at Seventy-second Street. In it was celebrated the fiftieth wedding anniversary of the Charles Tiffanys. All the children were there, and a great gathering of friends. The next day, December 1, 1891, the newspapers reported that it was one of the most elaborate receptions ever given in New York, period. The story was brief because Mrs. Tiffany did not like to see her name in print—nor details of the Tiffany private lives.

In 1900 Charles was prepared to ''whoop it up,'' in the words of the *Tribune,* for McKinley and Roosevelt. Interviewed, Tiffany told the *Tribune*'s man that he felt the election of William Jennings Bryan would have a serious effect on business: ''and my business would be seriously disturbed. At present it is doing very well and I want it to stay so.''

For Lillian Russell, a solid silver bicycle from admirers.

SHAKER SISTER MISTOOK MILLIONAIRE FOR A TRAMP.

Aunt Aurelia Gave Charles L. Tiffany, Head of the Big Jewelry House, One of the Most Enjoyable Meals of His Life.

And He Surprised the Whole Community by Showing the "Tramp's" Appreciation in a Present of a Handsome Silver Service.

It might be called a romance of two cities but that one of them is a little Shaker village up in New England.

Charles L. Tiffany, head of the great jewelry house, was at Poland Spring House enjoying the Maine mountains and climate, and one afternoon went for a long walk. He didn't find the cow pastures and the blackberry lots as smooth walking as it is in Central Park, but it was beautiful. He went on and on.

At last he stopped to take his bearings. He was lost. Nothing but stretches of sweet fern, dotted here and there by giant bull thistles, covered the vast hillsides around him.

AUNT AURELIA.

AUNT AURELIA'S ROOM IN THE SHAKER VILLAGE.

Mr. Tiffany did what any sensible man would have done. He steered by the sun, and after an hour and a half of struggling through blackberry brambles and over beds of ferns and ground hemlock he came out on a rocky road. At the top of the next hill was a tiny village with snow-white houses against

was "Trustees' office. Visitors are Always Welcome." Seeing a cool-looking well with an old-fashioned sweep, he went up to the door with the intention of asking for a drink.

Aunt Aurelia, one of the sweet-faced, tender-hearted elderesses of the village, answered the bell. The sight of the weary, travel-stained stranger told its own story. No knight of the road was ever turned away from that hospitable

good woman, but if there is anything I can do to help the community"—

"Nay, nay! Thou art tired, and the men have finished the haying. Thou shalt rest a little, and then go thy way again."

Mr. Tiffany began to enjoy the experience. A glance at the little mirror in the room explained why she took him for a wanderer. A little after, in spite of his protests, he was sitting in the dining-room downstairs, with the Shaker sister bustling around the room.

Mr. Tiffany has enjoyed many good meals in the course of his active life. He knows, for instance, what a dinner can be at the Holland House or the Waldorf-Astoria. But in all his life he has never enjoyed a lunch as much as he did that one.

Perhaps the romance of it added to the flavor of the meal. The fact that everything served came from the farm of the Shakers was another thing. The light bread, he was told, was made of flour ground out in their own mill. The honey was from the row of hives down among the clover in the orchard; the preserves from the dark cellars; the berries from the sunny gardens, where the little Shaker lassies in their demure sunbonnets worked all day pulling weeds and killing time.

But it was the ordinary meal of the Shakers. The reporter for the Evening World has dined in that little room with Sister Aurelia, and knows whereof he speaks.

At last the guest could eat no more, and rose with a sigh of regret. From the back window of the room could be seen the woodshed and a pile of wood.

"Who splits all that wood?" asked Mr. Tiffany.

"Oh, the boys do it. There was a poor fellow along here a month ago who split nearly a cord in one day. We gave him a suit of clothes for it."

Mr. Tiffany glanced at his soft hands and hesitated. "I am not much on split-

---

Newspapers told the story of the lost tramp.

When a reporter commented that the general opinion was that Bryan would have little power as President because both Houses would not have a Democratic majority, Tiffany shot back: "But we want a man with power."

He still was a great walker, and on one of his walks had such a quaint experience that the whole country was amused—and touched. In the summer of 1900, while staying at the Poland Spring House in Maine, Mr. Tiffany, aged eighty-eight, set out on one of his hearty strolls. According to a contemporary story, "he did not find the cow pastures and blackberry plots as smooth as Central Park or Tiffany Acres," but the countryside was beautiful and he went on and on. At last he stopped to take his bearings; he was lost. "Steering by the sun" he struggled through brambles, thistles and scrub pine until he finally saw "on the top of a hill, a tiny village with snow-white houses against the blue sky." Weary and worn, his clothes torn and ragged, his face hot and scratched, he walked up to the nearest house. He soon realized, from the dress of the woman who came to the door, and the long hair of the men, that he was in Shaker Village, a few miles from the Poland Spring House. Noticing the cool-looking well, he asked for a glass of water.

A newspaper of the times tells the story well.

Sister Aurelia, one of the sweet-faced elderesses of the village, answered the bell. The sight of the weary, travel-stained stranger told its own story; no knight of the road was ever turned from that hospitable door. Several times the knight tried to explain who he was but the explanations were silenced as the good woman brushed off his clothes, made him lemonade and then invited him to sit down at the noon meal they were having.

"It is a dreadful thing to be out of work, sir, but thee should thank God thee has thy strength and health," said Sister Aurelia.

"I am not exactly out of work," Tiffany replied, "but if there is anything I can do to help . . ."

"Nay, nay, thou art tired. Thou shalt rest a bit and then go on thy way again. I hope thee will find work soon."

When the time came to leave, Charles was handed a pasteboard box, which he later found contained three ham sandwiches, four doughnuts, two pieces of apple pie and a glass of grape jelly. That night, while the splendid dining room of the hotel was filled with elegantly dressed people, "Mr. Tiffany and another rich New Yorker slipped away, walked to the shore of the lake, spread Sister Aurelia's lunch on a flat rock and ate every crumb of it."

Not many days later a coach drove up and a footman delivered a package to Sister Aurelia at Shaker Village. In it was a $300 set of silver spoons, knives and forks, each piece marked "Aurelia." Enclosed was a card: "In return for the kindness you showed me after my encounter with the blackberry brambles last week. [Signed] Charles Tiffany."

This is one story Tiffany never told. But Sister Aurelia did, laughing over the mistake that she had made.

In the meantime, Tiffany began to have thoughts along familiar lines; business was outgrowing the Union Square store, and the tide was moving ever northward; it was time to move farther uptown. As the plans for a new store fell in shape, Charles went up to Irvington-on-Hudson, to spend the autumn days at Tiffany Hall. One October dusk a chill came with the dying of the sun. Charles, never one to baby himself, went to put a log on the fire in the library where he was sitting "instead of summoning a servant" (as the *Times* commented). He fell and injured his hip. It was slow to heal. In February he was still confined to his bed in his house on Madison Avenue. A large celebration had been planned for his ninetieth birthday on February 15. His illness forced a cancellation; instead a delegation came to the house, leaving a ceremonial greeting on parchment signed by 1,192 associates, and a massive gold loving cup. The Chamber of Commerce sent up a request to copy an oil portrait of him (which now hangs in the Tiffany board room). The Sunday *Times* published a long tribute on its editorial page.

Two days later, Charles Lewis Tiffany died of pneumonia; at his bedside were his daughters and sons, Louis Comfort and Burnett Y. Tiffany. He was buried from the Madison Avenue Presbyterian Church. In its lengthy obituary the *Times* dwelt on Tiffany's "great wealth and the large amounts he gave to charity. . . . His philanthropies were as great as they were unostentatious."

The young man from Connecticut, who had started out with a borrowed five hundred dollars, left an estate of thirty-five million dollars.*

---

* This may not seem like a large fortune today, but Cecil Rhodes, the diamond king of Africa, died the same year, leaving twenty million dollars.

C harles Lewis Tiffany
was the first and the last Tiffany to run Tiffany & Co. He was succeeded by Vice President Charles T. Cook,* an associate for years, in
whom he had often expressed his full confidence. Long before he died,
Charles Tiffany knew that neither of his two sons would follow in his
footsteps. His older son, Louis Comfort Tiffany, was born out of his
time; he would have been more at home with the rebellious youth of
today than he was with the earnest, business-minded young men of
his generation. As Louis Comfort Tiffany's authorized biographer
wrote: "He was born with a silver spoon in his mouth but the spoon
was immediately tucked away and he was seldom permitted to remember its existence. His parents did not believe in spoiling children

(Above) Louis Comfort Tiffany, the young painter.

by allowing them to live on a scale their fortune warranted.'' As an adult, Louis Comfort made up for this by living on a scale considerably grander than his fortune warranted.

At the time of his father's death, Louis Comfort Tiffany was already world famous for his stained-glass windows, his iridescent Favrile glass objects and his interior decorating; he was a leader in the Art Nouveau movement that swept Europe and America at the turn of the century and had a far greater influence on taste than even his father's ''school for taste.''

It was a stroke of luck for Tiffany & Co. that neither Louis Comfort nor his younger brother, Burnett Y. Tiffany, ever had control of the firm. Louis Comfort—or LCT as the world knew him from the signature attached to many of his works—won fame, but lost a fortune doing so. He was a poor businessman, who paid no attention to the costs of his products as long as he achieved the desired artistic effect.

Burnett apparently never did much of anything and did not do even that very well. He was once briefly mentioned in the newspapers in connection with his divorce; after what was termed a ''clandestine marriage'' a detective hired to get divorce evidence did so, but had to sue to collect half of his $1,000 fee. Later, Burnett, never connected with the store, spent most of his life in California. As one member of the family remarked, ''We never talked much about Uncle Burney.''

Nevertheless, unlike other tycoons of the times—who struck ne'er-do-wells from the family rolls and wills according to the Victorian code—Charles always had a welcome for Burney. He came East for the celebration of his parents' fiftieth wedding anniversary, and was left one-eighth of his father's estate, some $4,375,000 (LCT received three-eighths, or $13,125,000 *).

If Charles Tiffany and his wife did not believe in spoiling their children with money, neither did they spoil them in other ways. The youngsters were brought up along severe Presbyterian lines: morning prayers, sensible food and clothing, church together every Sunday and not much else for the rest of the day.

While still in his teens, LCT let his father know that he did not plan to join his firm, but wanted to be an artist. He was sent to the Flushing Boarding School in the hope that that strict institution could shape his nature more to his father's liking. But the school had no effect. His real education—as an artist—began shortly after in the studio of George Inness, already a famous landscape painter, who

---

* Louis's sister Annie also received three-eighths of the estate; the remaining eighth was left in trust for the unmarried sister, Louise.

*Medallion on testimonial book
from employees on golden
wedding anniversary—
Mr. and Mrs. Tiffany.*

took LCT as a pupil, the only one Inness ever had. The studio was a meeting place for young men interested in the arts, and Louis blossomed in the friendly environment.

In 1867, the year Tiffany's won its first international fame at the Paris Exposition, LCT took the first step in his artistic career; at nineteen, he exhibited a painting at the National Academy of Design. After that, nothing would do but Paris. He spent the next two years with Paris as his headquarters, studying and working hard. There he met another American artist, Samuel Colman, with whom he was associated for years. Together they toured Spain and North Africa, painting as they traveled. On this trip, LCT acquired the taste for Oriental and Moorish art which would influence him all his life. On his return to New York he moved out of the Tiffany mansion to live with several other young artists, at the Y.M.C.A., just across from the National Academy of Design.

While he worked at his painting—he always worked hard at whatever interested him—he did not neglect his social life. Tall and handsome, with bold eyes and a reddish-brown beard and mustache, he was a dashing and popular young man about town. In 1870 he became the youngest member ever elected to the Century Club, where achievement was more important than blue blood. ("Do you know, there's a club down on Forty-third Street that chooses its members for intellectual eminence? Isn't that a hell of a way to run a club?" a member of the Athletic Club once remarked in honest puzzlement.)

In 1872 Louis Tiffany married Mary Woodbridge Goddard of New Haven, a pretty girl, but who was in poor health. After the birth of a daughter, Mary, on April 3, 1873, she became more sickly. The next year, hoping that a change of climate would help, LCT took the family to southern France, where a son, Charles, was born in Menton—he died two weeks later. The family returned to New York, where another son, again named Charles, was born in 1878; and a year later, a daughter, Hilda. By this time, LCT was achieving a reputation as a painter, with such pictures as ''Duane Street,'' a study of tumbledown houses in drab browns and gray. As one critic commented: he was a ''very clever painter of naturally unromantic, not to say, hideous localities,'' indicating that LCT was a forerunner of the Ashcan School of Luks, Sloan and Henri which was to distress the artistic sensibilities of the critics thirty years later. LCT's paintings, as well as exhibits from his father's firm, were represented at the Philadelphia Centennial Exposition in 1876 and the Paris Exposition of 1878. However, the medals and honors went to his father.

Just how good an artist LCT would have become if he had concentrated on painting is a question. He himself had doubts about his talent. Moreover, the movement in England to eliminate the arbitrary distinction between the arts and the crafts was spreading under the aegis of William Morris. Painting alone was too narrow a scope for an artist, or so the credo went. Why shouldn't an artist, as Morris did, design furniture, stained glass, utensils and wall decorations, bringing beauty into the articles used in everyday living?

Louis Tiffany had been conditioned to this reasoning all his life. The homes of Americans were filled with Tiffany bronzes, enameled works, *objets d'art* and especially silver. Edward C. Moore, who still supervised the silver factory, had helped make the reputation of the firm by turning out articles for everyday use of exceptional beauty, precisely as Morris was advocating. It was a logical step for the son of the firm's president to turn toward decorating the whole interior of a house.

Soon after the Philadelphia exposition, an artistic woman named Candace Wheeler founded the New York Society of the Decorative Arts ''to encourage profitable industries among women in embroidery and tile and china painting.'' LCT's old traveling companion, Samuel Colman, was involved, and he persuaded Tiffany to teach a class in unglazed pottery making. This kind of artsy-craftsy dilletantism bored LCT and he soon suggested that he, Miss Wheeler and Colman form a more businesslike partnership and use their considerable talents in a more professional and profitable fashion. The company, called Louis C. Tiffany and Associated Artists, was formed in 1878, and flourished for three or four years. It was given impetus and direction when LCT met Samuel Bing in Paris that spring. Bing, who had much admired Moore's silverware in the Tiffany exhibit at the Paris Exposition, was certain that Moore had created a ''new style,'' although strongly inspired by the Oriental art which had always been featured in the Tiffany store.

The new company started out well. Its first major commission was for the drop curtain for the Madison Square Theatre; it was praised by Oscar Wilde on his visit to the States in 1882. This was followed by an even more comprehensive order: to decorate the Veteran's Room of the Seventh Regiment Armory in New York, at Park Avenue and Sixty-fifth Street, which, like the theater, was then under construction. The Seventh had always been New York's elite regiment; its members would carry ideas to wealthy homes if the officers liked the results. Critics variously praised and condemned LCT's decorations, but the Seventh liked the room—it struck a new note that caught the military imagination. (The room is still in use, exactly as conceived.) At the opening, the thousands of visitors who trooped through were as overwhelmed by the Pentagon prose of the memorial booklet as by the room itself: "What most impresses and what is most worthy to impress . . . is the practical and yet poetic adaptation of decorative material to the purpose in hand . . . by the very accordant chime of all side decorations, the clamp and clang of iron, the metallic lustres, the ponderous beams (with axe cuts showing on them) and all clearly and undeniably assimilable and matchable with the huge hard, clanging ponderosities of war and tramping regiments and armories." (This was written by a general, at the least.) The room has worn well; possibly the "clanging ponderosities" have faded and softened, but the whole effect is of space and no-nonsense masculinity.

Suddenly the rich of New York wanted their homes done in the latest mode. The Union League Club commissioned LCT's company to

Veteran's Room, Seventh Regiment Armory, New York.

do over its rooms. Other commissions followed: the home of Mark Twain, in Hartford; the new mansion of Cornelius Vanderbilt II up Fifth Avenue; the home of the Metropolitan Museum president, J. Taylor Johnston—which gave a professional cachet); Ogden Goelet's house; and the yacht of James Gordon Bennett. All were exotic, whether Oriental, Byzantine or plain imaginative design; all were luxurious, costly, and lighted in the "soft, diffused glow" which was to be associated with Tiffany glass and Tiffany lamps.

LCT's most prestigious commission was the partial redecoration of the White House—East Room, Red Room, Blue Room and State dining room—for a fee of thirty thousand dollars. Tiffany considered his chief contribution the replacement of the ground-glass screen which divided the downstairs living space from the corridor. LCT designed a ceiling-to-floor curtain of opalescent glass, which afforded privacy to the family. It was handsome as well, with a pattern of national emblems in brilliant colors. (When Teddy Roosevelt became President in 1904 and took his turn redecorating, he ordered *his* decorator, LCT's erstwhile associate and friend Charles F. McKim, to "break up in small pieces that Tiffany screen." Why he took such a dislike to it he did not say. Possibly, as he had once hinted to Dr. Kunz in another context, because it was not made of ivory.)

LCT's preoccupation with glass, which would one day be synonymous with his name, had already been going on for a matter of years. He used it in his own home in the Bella Apartments at 48 East Twenty-sixth Street. The description in *The Art of Louis Tiffany* * also shows the strong Oriental yet modern touch.

[The lobby was] lighted by stained glass windows, which reached up into the peaks of the gables where the beams themselves showed the light in a rich, dull color scheme, lighted here and there with plates and studs of bronze. . . . The roof slopes were set with thick glass tiles . . . and the windows were made up of rounds of glass of uneven thickness. What with the staining and carving and inlays of metal and glass, the dark brown beamed ceiling was a foil to the warm India red of the walls and trim.

A novel effect is the treatment of the window sashes and was to be seen in the gable. The stained glass sash was heavy, and to raise it there was need for a strong pulley. [Here, Tiffany anticipated the modern concept of incorporating such functional devices into the

---

* A privately printed publication of 502 copies, of which ten were printed on parchment and 492 on Japan paper. The author was Charles de Kay, a friend of LCT's. The foreword states that the book was written "at the request of the children of Louis Tiffany, so that they will understand their father's ideas on art." Actually the idea was Tiffany's own, and he certainly edited, if he did not write, much of the book.

decorative scheme.] Mr. Tiffany used a large wooden wheel and chain and exposed them to view, turning them into decorative objects by simply providing a handsome wheel and chain. . . . The whole apartment shone with the articles and colors Tiffany liked: Oriental Ceramics and textiles, brass and bronze, silver and dull gold.

LCT continued his experimentation with glass. His goal was to produce all the colors in a window, even one with figures, without any painting, drawing or etching of the glass itself, as was the debased custom of the period. LCT himself wrote: "By chemistry . . . and years of experiments, I have found means . . . to produce figures in glass in which not even the flesh tones are superficially treated—built up of what I call 'genuine' glass." One of the first windows fashioned in this manner was that of St. Mark for the Episcopal church at Islip, Long Island.

The Tiffany windows became enormously popular and were widely imitated, appearing everywhere in New York, from the stations of the "El," the elevated rapid transit system, to apartment-house lobbies and modest homes.

While his fame spread rapidly, Louis Comfort's private life was saddened by the death of his wife in 1884. Two years later he married Louise Wakeman Knox, the daughter of a Presbyterian minister, by whom he had three children.

By this time there is no doubt that Charles Tiffany was proud of

Stained-glass window showing LCT's use of glass as free-flowing medium.

(Top) Dragonfly hatpin.
(Bottom) Heavy jeweled pendant.

his son's achievements, so much so that LCT was put on the staff of the store, with the title of Director of Design. However, Louis concerned himself chiefly with his own designs, which now included jewelry, and a separate floor was designated for all of his creations. In his jewelry, which again reflected his favorite Oriental or East Indian motif, the emphasis was on workmanship; LCT mixed metals and enamels, precious and semiprecious stones the way Kunz had advocated and which anticipated the work of Jean Schlumberger.

As described in his biography, LCT's jewelry was exotic: "A dragonfly hatpin is enamelled and set with opals in a platinum base. A marine motif, half crab, half octopus, with the writhing feet split in two, is arranged as a brooch, and set with opals, sapphires and rubies. A girdle of silver, ornamented with enamels, has berries formed of opals . . . a decoration for the head is a branch of black-berries, the berries clusters of dark garnets. Another design is the dandelion full-blown with seeds." More elaborate was the peacock necklace . . . "the main piece of which is a mosaic of opals, amethysts and sapphires. The back of the big centerpiece has a decoration of flamingoes and the lowest point of the pendant below is a single large ruby, selected, not for its cost, but for the shade of its red."

Such subtleties were not appreciated by a society which valued jewelry only by how it would impress others, and notably by the cost and size of the gems rather than beauty of design and workmanship. LCT's jewelry was expensive and perhaps it was not beautiful (so little remains that it is hard to judge). In any case, his jewelry did not sell, even though Tiffany's salesmen were given the added incentive of a special 10 percent commission on it.

Another venture proved an artistic success but a personal financial loss for LCT. With his old friend, James Steele MacKaye, a playwright whom he had first met in Inness' studio, LCT contracted to decorate the new Lyceum Theatre for fifty thousand dollars. A small house, on Fourth Avenue near Twenty-third Street, it was fondly termed "the drawing room of drama." One commentator remarked that the elite went there to learn how to dress and how to decorate their homes. The Lyceum was noteworthy for another reason: LCT worked with Thomas Edison and it was the first theater to be lit by electricity. Unfortunately, after the novelty wore off, the Lyceum proved to be too far from the theater district, and closed after a year; a protracted lawsuit failed to win LCT his fee.

Charles Tiffany now asked his son to design a new house for him, on the lot he had purchased at Madison Avenue and Seventy-second Street. LCT obliged with a charming wash drawing, but the actual architectural work was done by McKim, Mead and White, who had done most of the mansions on Fifth Avenue.

In a city grown accustomed to European castles duplicated along Fifth Avenue, the house on Seventy-second Street was acclaimed the grandest—and it was the largest—of all. The style was referred to as being "akin to the Domestic Renaissance of the Low Countries." The new house rose five stories (the building was 115 feet tall and occupied a hundred square feet), built around a central courtyard lined with glazed bricks. The top story was a studio for LCT, although he also retained his old one on Twenty-sixth Street. As described by de Kay, the at-home studio was done with "colored tiles and the cinnabar red so beloved by the Japanese; iridescent glass shelves full of ceramics in subdued tones meet the eye in every direction." The house had fifty rooms and resembled a fort from the street, since there was only one outside window (a bay) on the first two stories, the rooms receiving their light from the courtyard. The lower walls were of blue stone, while those above were covered in dull-yellow bricks, mottled in black. There were two projecting wings, a number of gables and dormer windows, one tower, and a "great archway, or porte-cochere" which led into the courtyard.

The Charles Tiffany house at 72nd and Madison where LCT lived.

Children of LCT and sister with wife's sister. (Left to right) Hilda Tiffany,
Alfreda Mitchell, Charles Tiffany, Mary Tiffany, Mrs. J. G. Piatt and Charley Mitchell.

Mary Tiffany, who married Dr. Graham Lusk, and her sister,
Hilda, in 72nd Street house.

There is a small mystery about the house. All the newspapers called it the Charles Tiffany House. Charles commissioned it, and paid for it, but, as it neared completion, he decided he would not live there. He had apparently thought of a patriarchal compound with his children and grandchildren gathered around him, for the house was designed with accommodations for distinct family groups. While one writer stated that Charles "obstinately refused" to live in the house, it is more probable that as the magnificence multiplied, he simply changed his mind. He was happy at 255 Madison; he could walk to work from there. Uptown, he would have been at the mercy of a coachman, the weather or the elevated train. Like Morgan, he preferred to stay where his habits had made him comfortable and happy. LCT moved into the fifty lofty rooms and the cavernous studio with his second wife and their three girls, together with his son, Charles, and the two girls by his first wife.

LCT was now so well established that he could afford to be a decorator "to the trade only" and only on projects which interested him. As designer also for Tiffany's, he attended the Paris Exposition of 1889, where he had not thought to exhibit any of his creations. At the exposition, he was startled to see a stained-glass window, which he considered much inferior to his, being highly acclaimed by the crowds. This was a blow to his esteem until he realized that he had been too busy at home to export his windows, and his fame. That could be easily remedied. He renewed his acquaintance with Bing, who was the center of the new art movement that was sweeping the continent, and arranged for him to display windows which LCT would make and, ergo, LCT would be as famous in Europe as he was at home. In justification of LCT's egotism, that is exactly the way everything worked out.

Bing—whose shop, several years later would be called the Art Nouveau and give its name to the movement—was urging his artist friends toward a new approach to their canvases, a breakdown of colors into components. Art must leap from canvases to walls, know no boundaries. That, in fact, had been Tiffany's idea all along.

Having made his point with the windows, LCT concentrated on one of his early loves, his Favrile (from old French *fabrile,* meaning handmade) glass. This iridescent type of glass had been produced on and off for years by glass blowers trying to imitate the rainbow-colored shards turned up by archaeologists at Troy and Mycenae and by Di Cesnola on Cyprus. The aim was to reproduce instantly the many-colored tints wrought by nature in glass buried for centuries.

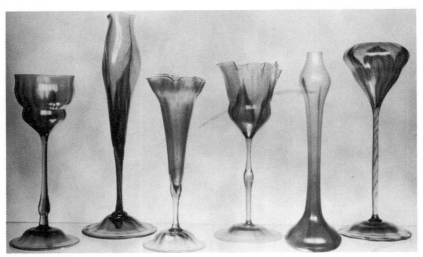

Shapes in Favrile glass.

To make his glass, LCT set up a factory at Corona, Long Island, and in 1896 publicly showed the results of his years of experimentation. His Favrile was so superior to earlier iridescent glass that it was an immediate success and became a symbol for Art Nouveau.

"We shall never have good taste in our homes until people learn to distinguish the beautiful from the ugly," said LCT. And the beautiful in this case was his Favrile glass, which could be blown into a variety of articles for everyday use. As their creator said, "these [shapes] could be remarkable with brilliant or deeply toned colors, usually iridescent, like the wings of certain butterflies, the necks of pigeons and peacocks, the wing covers of various beetles." Favrile was generally used for flower vases and table decorations, but it could also be used in mosaics, tiles, table services, toilet boxes, trays, snuff and cigarette boxes, lampshades and many other things that could be made from china or metal.

The rapid manner in which the Corona glassworks turned out products—all sold by Tiffany & Co.—caused some of LCT's fellow artists to criticize him for "commercialism." Which bothered him not at all; the more Favrile articles appeared in more homes, the more the taste of the country was improved. The factory also produced table lamps and floor lamps, with glass shades and sculptured bronze bases. Since Tiffany had first worked with Edison at the Lyceum Theatre, many of the lamps were designed for the new electricity— a welcome relief from the harsh glare of the first hanging bulbs. There was scarcely a town where the lamps did not have their glass shades, by LCT or his clumsy imitators.

The most famous Tiffany design was the lily-cluster lamp, the bronze base formed of lily pads, the slender column of the lamp rising to the branching blossoms. The design was also used for matching wall brackets. One of the loveliest installations is still in the large reception room of Morgan Hall, a residence of the Y.W.C.A. in New York—a gift from LCT. The free form of the side lights is particularly graceful. (This design won Tiffany the grand prize at the Turin Exhibit of 1902. His wisteria pattern dates from 1904.)

All the products of the plant were enormously popular, and LCT personally supervised the work from design to completion. After the death of his father, Louis was made a vice president of the store, but his chief interest always remained with his own endeavors. If he had inherited the business sense of his father, as well as his taste, he would have become wealthy in his own right while spreading his ideas of beauty. But he allowed no one to watch costs; it is ironical that while being charged with commercialism, the business was suffering losses— presumably made up by his father—because it was not commercial enough.

While the price of lamps ran as high as five hundred dollars, some of the Favrile glasswork—such as the small ''paperweight'' vases,

Lily cluster lamp.

which are considered the most complicated and whose manufacture baffles modern glass blowers—sold for under fifty dollars. The glass was blown in all manner of designs: flowers, leaves, trees, rough or smooth "lava" swirls, dimpled or "accidentals" (not accidental at all but carefully planned); pure colors blown in such a way that they gave the effect of abstract paintings, the same effect LCT achieved in his windows.

Tiffany's discovery in his youth of the Byzantine chapels on Italy's east coast was a continuing inspiration. His design for a Byzantine chapel for the Columbia Exposition of 1893 combined all his products: stained glass, tiles, metalwork and mosaics. It was considered the most modern exhibit and was a hit of the fair, along with the jewels and silver of his father's store.

Just before this, LCT's firm decorated the H. O. Havemeyer home (which then stood on Fifth Avenue at Sixty-sixth Street), with the chapels of Ravenna setting the pattern. The Havemeyer fortune was such that Louis was given carte blanche. Mrs. Havemeyer was delighted with the result, and so was Bing when he saw the house on a visit to New York to spread the word of Art Nouveau. Bing breathed an enraptured sigh and announced that "nothing and no one [else] could have achieved such a unified concept in an interior."

As in the Italian chapels, the walls were mosaics, but white, supported by ten white pillars at the entrance to the art gallery, which contained the great collection of paintings, now in the Metropolitan Museum. Aline B. Saarinen has this description in her book *The Proud Possessors:*

The walls of the music room were covered with Chinese embroideries. On the blue and gold Chinese rugs stood special, richly carved furniture, rubbed with gold leaf and varnish to look like the ivory inre that inspired it. The furniture and the woodwork in the library were based on Viking designs and Celtic motifs. . . . The two-story upstairs gallery was noted for the golden or 'flying' staircase . . . suspended like a necklace from one side of the balcony to the other. A curved piece of cast iron formed the spine to which, without intermediate supports, the stair treads were attached. The sides of this astonishing construction, as well as the balcony railing, were a spider web of gold filigree dotted with small crystal balls.

The death of his father in 1902 provided Louis Tiffany, for the first time, with many millions of his own at his disposal. He could afford to build himself a country house, a house that would not only be a museum for his treasures and creations but would put into effect all his ideas of architectural beauty. He had already left Irvington, and settled his family for the summers at Cold Spring Harbor, on the north shore of Long Island, in The Briars, a home large and comfortable, but not more elaborate than his father's Hudson River estate. Now LCT purchased 580 acres overlooking Cold Spring Harbor and set about building a country home that, as Robert Koch, author of *Rebel in Glass,* wrote, "was unlike anything ever done before or since." LCT named this stately pleasure dome "Laurelton Hall."

The house sprawled for 275 feet across the top of a hill, and three stories down the side. The main entrance was on the top floor, level with the land which slopes to the Sound. There were over eighty rooms (which included twenty-six bathrooms) and a staff of sixty-five. There was a bowling alley, a gymnasium and a squash court. Fifteen greenhouses supplied floral decorations with a different motif for the house each week; a "genuine Babylonian hanging garden with rare and exotic imported plants" (from a rhapsodic story in the Brooklyn *Eagle*) was a botanical paradise. There were stables, a separate art gallery (with a front wall from an Indian temple) to house LCT's paintings, and a separate chapel. The chapel's altar had been designed for the Cathedral of St. John the Divine in New York, but when the cathedral's style was changed from Romanesque to Gothic, the altar did not conform. So LCT installed it at Laurelton.

How much he spent on the estate is not known. Estimates have been as low as two million dollars and as high as the seventeen million dollars given in *The Saturday Evening Post* in 1953. Whatever the cost, it was not a factor that disturbed LCT. As the New York *World* reported:

Louis Comfort Tiffany and his architect were on the horns of a dilemma. Laurelton Hall needed a heating plant and the waterfront was the logical place for it. Plans called for a sixty foot smokestack. With that rearing its ugly head you might as well face a glue factory. Tiffany and Terwilliger [his architect] pondered. . . . The next morning, Tiffany sought out the architect, a wash drawing of a minaretted tower in hand. It looked like something from the Arabian Nights.

"Can you do this?" Tiffany asked.

Terwilliger looked at the drawing. "How big will it be?"

"Sixty feet," said Tiffany and Terwilliger whistled.

"We can do it," he answered, "but have you any idea of what it will cost?"

Mr. Tiffany smiled gently. "I don't want to know," he said.

Two-story entrance court of Laurelton Hall.
Water flowed into pool from left and out trough
in floor at right. Water also filled vase in center,
changing it to ''exquisite, ethereal color,'' but
also causing vase to explode occasionally.

Stained-glass window.

Wisteria lamp which dripped blue or purple blossoms was one of most popular designs.

Elaborate pendant necklace with uncut semiprecious stones.

In the living room, a glass window of "The Bathers."

(Top) Dining alcove in Laurelton Hall showing LCT's use of glass walls, which could be folded back, making the room part of the gardens. (Bottom) dining room, with decorations from Middle East.

(Top) Laurelton Hall, seen from Long Island Sound side, and one of Hall's many pools with palms, dragon. (Bottom) the Chinese room, with intricately carved bronze walls and LCT's Chinese art collection.

This same incredible attention to detail and cost-be-damned attitude characterized the whole enterprise. There was the matter of the living-room fireplace. LCT had conceived it as taking up most of one wall and being surmounted by a cement canopy supported by pillars. The fireplace was built and torn down nine times before LCT was satisfied. There were any number of recherché touches. A bronze replica of the hand of Queen Elena of Italy, which LCT considered the most beauti-ful hand in the world, rested on a table in the living room; incoming mail was placed on the bronze palm. There was a Chinese room, done with carved walls, a Japanese room, and a smoking room, where armor hung on the walls, one side taken up with a picture entitled "The Opium Fiend's Dream." "It is oriental," said the *Eagle*, with a shudder, "and shows a stupified victim lying on the floor, surrounded by a dozen or more of oriental women who are lavishing their at-tentions on him."

The house was written about for over a decade, with a number of the manuscripts supplied by a Tiffany employee and de Kay. The house itself was a mélange of styles, mainly Moorish, although Tiffany once told reporters that he had gotten his inspiration from the Grand Canyon, meaning that he wanted the house to glow with color.

The three-story entrance court, encircled by two-story pillars crowned with a dome of Tiffany glass, had a remarkable fountain and pool in the center. The water came into the court in a small open stream that flowed into the pool and out the other side of the court in a covered trough that ran under the outer wall. From there the water cascaded in a succession of pools to the shores of Long Island Sound, a hundred yards away. The most spectacular aspect of the pool was the pale-blue, crystal-clear glass vase, tall as a man, which stood in the center, slowly filling with water from the bottom and then overflowing down the sides. This changed the color of the water until it became, according to de Kay, "so ethereal, so exquisite, that one seeks in vain for a simile." Unfortunately the action of the water had another effect; every so often the vase cracked and exploded.

A different account of the vase and the pool remains a curious memory for a neighbor who, as a little girl, was taken by her mother to see the wonders of the Tiffany house. She did not like the house.

_____

It was frightening, everything gloomy and overhung, all those hang-ings and bright ugly tiles. It was terrifying, like something out of a bad story.

As for the vase, I thought it the silliest thing I had ever seen. Why would grown-ups put a big vase in the middle of a room and then be

*so careless as to let it fill up with water and spill out again? I re-
member all I was interested in was what happened to the water. I let
go of my mother's hand and dashed over to the window where I could
see the water falling into the Sound. I was quite relieved.*

She remembers many an afternoon spent on the grounds, playing with
the Tiffany children. She was not allowed by her mother to go inside,
possibly for fear she might wander into the smoking room and en-
counter the opium fiend. Or even, for that matter in those days, the
lovely, quite sexless, glass window in the living room, the nude
"Bathers."

At any rate, "the gardens were the most beautiful anyone, child or
grown-up, could imagine. The minaret [smoke tower], the trees and
plants, the many fountains—this was fairyland, as every child dreamed
it to be."

The most notable room, by modern architectural standards, was
the dining room. The whole length of the room facing the Sound was
made of ceiling-to-floor glass panels, which could be slid open to make
the outside gardens a part of the room. It was the first use of the glass
wall, now so popular in American architecture. Another novelty was
a one-mile-long tunnel from the entrance of the estate to the service
door so that delivery men would never mar the artistic effect of
Laurelton. LCT, too, bowed to such plutocratic conventions. And his
great-grandchildren remember that he always wore white, from head
to toe; he insisted on always being immaculate, even if he had to
change two or three times a day.

LCT had taken on yet another architectural chore, this one in New
York. He purchased the house on Seventy-second Street from the
estate for $665,000—the press took the view that this was more than it
was worth. To the five stories he added another three, still keeping
the top floor for a studio. Like a patriarch, he insisted that his children
and their families give up their homes and move in with him, with
some unhappy results for one son-in-law who was forced to move out
again at a considerable loss of money.

As he grew older, LCT developed a taste for magnificent parties,
thereby mixing pleasure with business. The socially elect and other
friends at these parties were often his customers. He combined all his
artistic talents, not to mention considerable money, in February of
1913, when he staged an extravaganza which *The New York Times*
called "the most lavish costume fete ever seen in New York." Since
the *Times* had covered both the Vanderbilt and Bradley-Martin ex-
travaganzas, that was citation indeed.

LCT was as meticulous in staging his parties as he was in everything else. For this gala, the first notice was a formal Tiffany invitation to four hundred guests (that favored number in Manhattan) requesting that they keep Shrove Tuesday, February 4 open, as a further invitation would be forthcoming for a fete on that date. In due time, the second notice was sent around, written in hieroglyphics on a roll of papyrus, sealed with twine and wax. Thoughtfully enclosed was a full translation of the text:

> *Hail to thee, Great Ones—Happy Friends (both)*
> *Men and Women, saith the Lord (Mistress)*
> *of the Throne of the World.*
> *Come to Me and Make Glad Thyself*
> *at the Sight of My Beauty.*
> *Queen*

Invitation in hieroglyphics to Shrove Tuesday ball.

The invitation "expected that all will come to this fete in the costume of the period, either as Egyptians, Nomad Tribes, Greeks, Persians, Ethiopians, Romans, Syrians, East Indians or Arabs."

A committee was appointed to approve costumes, and arrangements were made, adding a rather cheap note, for guests to rent them "if necessary, at from ten dollars upwards." The committee took its duties seriously, and newspapers gravely noted that "eight yards of cloth have been draped to make one beautiful costume" and "Egyptian vases are being scanned . . . to be correct in costume."

The affair did not take place at Laurelton Hall, as some modern writers have quite logically supposed. The Hall was a summer place and, among other things, almost impossible to heat. The locale was the

Louis Comfort Tiffany dressed
for his ball as potentate of Middle East
with jewels and four ropes of pearls.

*Ruth St. Denis "in brown thin gauze" dancing in LCT's extravaganza
which the* New York Times *called "the most lavish costume fete ever seen in New York."*

(Top left) *An Egyptian Queen.*
(Bottom left) *LCT's daughters,*
Mary, Julia and Dorothy.

(Top right) *Roman soldier.*
(Bottom right) *John W. Alexander*
as a mummy.

(*Top*) *Guests playfully struck Egyptian poses.*
(*Bottom*) *In group are Dr. Andrew Piatt, Miss Cecelia Beaux,*
Henry Sleeper, Mrs. Henry P. Davison and Dorothea and Rosamond Gilder.

Tiffany Studios, at 345 Madison, near Forty-second Street. The enormous room had been transformed into a replica of the ancient city of Alexandria (or so Louis Tiffany said). A terrace had been erected at one end, supposedly overlooking the sea, and the tops of palm trees and masts of ships were visible. Guests were seated on piles of Oriental rugs, and musicians (hidden) of the Philharmonic played as the pageant got under way. It would have done Cecil B. De Mille proud. In the limited space Tiffany managed to move a crowd of extras that included water sprinklers, porters, merchants (with real gold wares), suitably attired women wandering through the scene, and slave girls who danced and sang for the "benefit of the prospective purchasers."

The big moment came when Cleopatra was carried in in her palanquin, borne by practically naked "Ethiopians." "Beautiful children scattered thousands of lotus petals in her path . . . when Antony joined her on a crimson divan they were again entertained by the dancers." There was even a gladiatorial combat; Cleopatra (who appears in her pictures to be somewhat stouter than the soldiers and fighters) stepped forward, made a gesture with a thumb down, and the victim was carried off stage.

As in George Bernard Shaw's play, a body was carried in rolled in a rug, and unwrapped. This turned out to be Ruth St. Denis, "her body lightly covered . . . with thin brown gauze," who did an Egyptian dance. Paul Swan, in an "abbreviated leopard skin" was her partner. After more of this, Delmonico's served supper.

Louis Tiffany himself was labeled an Egyptian Potentate (a little out of period); he wore an intricately wound turban, studded with jeweled pins, the largest over his forehead, rich and full draperies with a species of embroidered cape in the back, more jewels scattered about the folds and four ropes of enormous pearls strung round his neck. Later, he said he was a Persian.

Mrs. John D. Rockefeller, Jr., came as Minerva in white draperies with an "Athenian helmet and breastplate of beaten gold;" her husband was a Persian prince in "elaborate raiment." Elihu Root, Jr., came as a Roman soldier, and Mrs. Root was a "richly attired" Moorish woman. Walter Damrosch was also a Roman soldier, but Mrs. Damrosch went Egyptian in purple, green and gold. Mrs. Cass Gilbert wore a mass of veils in yellow and all her jewels, except the ones her husband wore as a Persian prince in blue and dull crimson silk with a headdress banded in jewels. Persia was well thought of : half the guests seem to have been inspired by it.

Mrs. Edward S. Harkness showed much imagination, coming as Zuleika, Potiphar's wife, almost covered with jewels. Her husband was an anonymous Egyptian. By all accounts, the hit of the evening was John W. Alexander, who came as a mummy, "so natural he seemed to have stepped out of a case in the Metropolitan Museum." He remained propped up against a wall the entire evening, until supper was served.

Other guests whose names are still familiar were Mr. and Mrs. Cleveland Dodge, Miss Dorothy Roosevelt, Mrs. H. O. Havemeyer, Mr. Murray W. Dodge, Mrs. George W. Seligman, Mrs. Pierre Mali, Mr. Henry E. Coe and Mrs. Hiram Bingham. The name of Tiffany appeared in papers around the world, including, appropriately enough, the Egyptian *Gazette*.

There were a couple of hostile critics of the fete. Cholly Knickerbocker, who obviously had not been invited, got some satisfaction by writing that "all the best rugs were there . . . along with some of the best people, for it was held in Mr. Tiffany's rug store and the price tags added realism."

There are accounts of later Tiffany parties which hint at less innocent goings on. These are most improbable. There was not an affair, from the Egyptian fete to the last birthday party, where his children and grandchildren were not present, either as guests or, in the case of the younger ones, as supernumeraries. The beaming gentleman who never passed a child or grandchild without a pat on the head, and who had a most endearing habit of accompanying the gesture with a five-dollar gold piece (ten if you were older), would never have let them see anything that would damage their image of him.

Whatever society whispered about his private life, it was, after all, LCT's own business. He was a widower, his second wife having died in April of 1904, four months before Laurelton Hall was completed. Three pretty young nurses attended him during a protacted illness in 1908, and stayed on after he recovered. One, a vivacious Irish girl named Sarah Hanley, was his "constant companion" until his death; subsequently she continued to live in a cottage LCT built for her.

Laurelton Hall was the setting in 1914 for another lavish fete, restricted, so the press noted, to "Men of Genius." Grandchildren and their friends, dressed in long white robes, served the geniuses with, among other things, peacocks, skinned, roasted, and returned to the glory of their original feathers. Among the guests were Childe Hassam, Frederick Bok, Nicola Tesla, William Sloane Coffin and Charles Scribner.

Man-of-Genius Bok, as head of the Curtis Publishing Company, had commissioned LCT to collaborate with Maxfield Parrish in installing a mosaic of Parrish's "Dream Garden" in the company's headquarters in Philadelphia. The mosaic was fifteen feet high and forty-nine feet long, and composed of over a million pieces of glass. Bok praised it as a "veritable wonder piece, far exceeding the utmost expression of paint on canvas." Another of the glass mosaics was installed as the drop curtain for the National Theatre in Mexico City; this was a view of the valley of Mexico, with its background of mountains, as seen from the presidential palace. LCT's last commission was the decoration of the presidential palace in Havana; for this he received a fee of $1,400,000.

The early decades of the new century saw the vogue for LCT's work passing its peak. This was apparent at the birthday party in 1916 which LCT had felt "would be featured in the press as the artistic sensation of the social season." The highlight of the afternoon reception was a retrospective show of Tiffany's work. Instead of being greeted as a sensation, for the first time it evoked strong criticism. Certainly the great creative days were over, although the glass furnaces were kept in use until 1928, and the whole sorry end did not come until 1932, when Tiffany Studios declared itself bankrupt.

Louis's final project was to set up the Louis Tiffany Foundation, with an endowment of a million dollars for the preservation of Laurelton Hall and the operation of an art school there every summer for a dozen or so young artists.

Mosaic curtain, National Theatre, Mexico City.

LCT's winters were spent on Madison Avenue, with his children, grandchildren and great-grandchildren gathered around. The Christmas party was a highlight, as LCT, a true Santa Claus figure with his pure-white beard and mustache, handed out presents and the usual gold pieces.

His quest for beauty ended in 1932; he died in the Madison Avenue house at the age of eighty-four. Out of the fortune of $13,125,000 bequeathed him by his father he left an estate of $1,244,000. He had never heeded anyone's advice, not even that of his son Charles, who had become a vice president of the store and who had warned that LCT could not afford either his extravagant manner of living or his lavish projects "because you don't have the kind of money you think you have."

Laurelton Hall continued to operate for a time. But the expenses finally forced it to close, although the Tiffany Foundation still supplies scholarships for art students at various schools. The land and buildings, except for the Hall and four acres, went for sixty-five thousand dollars in 1939. The furnishings and art work were sold at the Parke-Bernet Galleries at one of their minor sales. Laurelton Hall itself was sold for ten thousand dollars in 1949 to Thomas H. Hilton, who had purchased it in the hope of living there all year around. He was soon disillusioned. True, Louis had installed that famous heating plant, but, as an engineer told Hilton, "it took a barge of coal to get the heat up and another barge to heat it for one day." There was still Tiffany glass in the windows, and murals still adorned the walls. Favrile glass was "prominent throughout the house"; Parke-Bernet had not thought enough of it to put it in the auction. An art dealer whom Hilton consulted was discouraging—no one, he said, would buy "that stuff" now.

In 1953 a fire so damaged Laurelton that it had to be torn down. Early in 1971 a family living next to the site of the old place was asked about Laurelton Hall. "Laurelton Hall?" was the puzzled reply. "I never heard of it. Are you sure it was around here?"

As for LCT's art, the Depression and changes in taste caused it to be all but forgotten. Much of the glass was given away by the heirs, who thought it hideous, or sold to second-hand shops, or destroyed. All the wonderful glass in the Mark Twain house simply disappeared. A contemporary of Louis Tiffany's, who had been given examples of most of his pieces, loaded them all in a station wagon one day in the 1940's and smashed the lot in the town dump. Another said candidly to a Tiffany descendant: "Thank God, I've finally gotten rid of all that Tiffany glass I got for wedding presents."

The renaissance of appreciation for Louis Tiffany's work has been slow but certain. It came out of the great swing of American painting to abstract expressionism. No one now questions that LCT was a forerunner of the movement, especially in those "accidentals" of carefully controlled abstract designs. For the artists of the fifties, and on into the present, Tiffany's lamps, dripping with their brightly colored fragments or rounded shapes of glass are expressionist pictures in themselves. As always, the appreciation from artists and critics came years before the public took notice. While price alone should not be a standard, it is a criterion of popularity. As late as 1958, prices for Tiffany pieces were still low. Lillian Nassau, of New York, the leading dealer in Tiffany glass, purchased a wisteria lamp that year for a hundred and seventy-five dollars—the same type that the Studios sold for four hundred dollars in 1904. She later sold the lamp for two hundred and fifty dollars. Then came the surge of popularity and prices—and such accolades as the LCT exhibit in the *Art of the XIX Century* show at the Metropolitan Museum in 1970.

In 1970 Mrs. Nassau attended an auction at Parke-Bernet, the same galleries which had refused to pick up the Tiffany glass and Favrile work thirty years before. She paid thirteen thousand, five hundred dollars for a wisteria lamp, and expects to sell it for twice the amount.

But exhibits in museums and specialty shops, no matter how skillfully the pieces are displayed or how carefully lighted, were not what Louis Comfort Tiffany had in mind. It would have pleased him to know there are still households where his Favrile glass and his lamps are part of the everyday living for which they were intended. After merely viewing the Tiffany creations at the exhibit at the Metropolitan, it is a delightful experience to visit a home where a Favrile ashtray is being *used* as an ash tray; to sit between two huge lustre lamps, whose bases shine with that iridescent blue "of a peacock's neck" that LCT so admired; to see roses in a vase designed for roses, the iridescence shading through all the colors of the rainbow, the top widened in the typical flowerlike folds of a Tiffany piece (there is further enchantment when the vase is seen under the light of the nearby Tiffany lamp: another of LCT's little surprises—shining through the translucent glass is a butterfly, etched on the inside of the vase). This practical use of his creations is what the tastemaker would have wanted, what his life was all about.

And as a tastemaker the rebel that he was in his youth is now recognized by the rebellious new generation of artists, with whom he had so much in common. During the Metropolitan show, one of them, schooled to scorn Victorian horrors, stood still for many minutes before the LCT exhibit and then said, "Why, it's beautiful."

Louis Comfort Tiffany on his eighty-fourth birthday.

The Lusks at Versailles, 1913: Louis, William T., Mrs. Lusk, Louise, Dr. Graham Lusk.

Mary Woodbridge Tiffany,
LCT's daughter.

LCT's Family Album

The Platt family.

(Right) Louise Lusk (seen as a child on opposite page) married Collier Platt. In group with her children, Thomas, Graham and Harry.

LCT with first wife and children: Hilda, in mother's lap; Charles and Mary.

Louise Lusk.

Louis Comfort Tiffany holding Harry Platt.

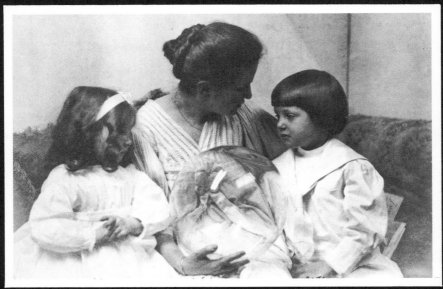

*Louise Lusk and her mother and brother, William,
later Tiffany & Co. president.*

Mary Noyes
(Mrs. Seldon Chapin).

Clarisse deRham
(Mrs. John Rutherfurd).

Charlotte Platt
(Mrs. Huntington Lyman).

The wedding party of Louise Lusk (Mrs. Collier Platt).

Betty Mosle
(Mrs. Charles Wight).

Anne Shiras.

Dorothy Moran
(Mrs. Karl Bricken).

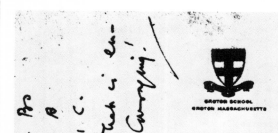

November 21, 1921

My dear Dr. Lusk:

        There is a new kind of candy called
"Lollipop". It is apparently a large lump of sugar *candy*
with some kind of flavouring. It is fastened on the
end of a stick, and takes about half an hour or more
in its consumption. This particular kind of confec-
tionery has become popular with the boys because it
is cheap and lasting. One of the dormitory masters
tells me that a great many boys have been nauseated
and have had digestive troubles this term which he
thinks probably due to the lollipop.

        Could you tell me anything about the nature of this
candy ? My instinct is to forbid its being used in the
School, but I should like very much the backing of an
opinion from you in order to avoid the suspicion on the
part of the boys of my being unreasonable.

        Incidentally, the lollipop makes a great deal of
itself and tends to spread itself over books and everything
that a boy comes into contact with.

                                Sincerely yours,

Letter to Dr. Lusk, with note about son's grades,
from Endicott Peabody, founder and headmaster of Groton School.

Donkey cart at the Briars with William, Louis and Louise Lusk.
Dr. Graham Lusk, who used to ride with Teddy Roosevelt.

Louis Comfort Tiffany
on the beach in Florida
—his last picture.

B

uild me a palace.'' The order, in the imperious style of Louis Comfort Tiffany, was given by Charles T. Cook, who had become president of Tiffany & Co. in 1903, after the death of Charles. Before Charles's death the project for a new building was well under way, and Cook's directive was given to the architects already chosen, McKim, Mead and White, who had built the house on Seventy-second Street, as well as other mansions for American royalty along Fifth Avenue. The land for the store, almost all of the east side of Fifth Avenue from Thirty-seventh Street to "within one door" of Thirty-sixth Street had been purchased for two million dollars, until then the highest price paid for a site by an individual or firm in the history of the city.

(Above) Charles T. Cook, second president.

*The Venetian
palace, Fifth
Avenue at
37th Street.*

The move uptown from Union Square was dictated both by the
need for more space and the change in the character of the Square.
The trees, grass and ornamental railing were gone; the fountains were
turned off. The houses that once surrounded Tiffany's had been torn
down or converted to serve trade—second-rate businesses at that.
"The aggressive tactics of the new merchants," as Tiffany's stated in
notices to customers announcing the move "have features so annoying
to our patrons that we conclude that a due regard for their comfort
and convenience make it expedient for us to seek another site."

For the new store, McKim, Mead and White took their instructions
literally: they copied a palace, one which had been hailed by Ruskin
as "a building without fault." This was the Palazzo Grimani, erected
in the sixteenth century on the Grand Canal in Venice by the famed
architect, San Michele, for Senator Grimani, who wanted "a palace
of noble proportions."

When the Tiffany copy was finished in 1905, at a cost of over six
hundred thousand dollars, it was hailed as a masterpiece in the press,
"the noblest of its kind . . . the highest mark of artistic excellence to
the present time. . . . a noble example of the second period of Venetian architecture." The shell of the building combined iron, marble
and terra cotta, and the fact that it was fireproof was still considered
worthy of note. From the outside, the building appeared to be only
three stories high, an illusion created by the three tiers of windows,
supported by terra-cotta pillars, but inside there were seven floors.

There was no name on the outside; the store felt that it had reached

The Paris office.

such an eminence that everyone would know that the palace had to
be Tiffany & Co., especially since Atlas and his clock were there, installed between the first and second floors. (The building still stands,
much degraded. The first floor, facing Fifth Avenue, has been chopped
away and large ''modern'' show windows installed. The great terra-
cotta columns were broken off during remodeling and only in the
back on Thirty-seventh Street is the building unchanged, still Venice
in Gotham.)

An artistically inclined reporter noted that the décor inside was
''better than Venetian; it is Whistlerian,'' meaning that the main
floor was done in the gray, foggy tones loved by the artist. The ceiling,
supported by pillars of purplish-gray marble was covered by that
wonderful new metal which once had been expected to compete with
gold and silver: aluminum. Huge silver chandeliers, made in the
Tiffany shops, hung from the ceiling; even the teak walls, inlaid with
borders of polished steel and brass, had been given a silver finish.
(One innovation would be a Godsend in present-day traffic-choked
Manhattan: delivery vans (electric and non-polluting) were loaded
and unloaded in the basement, then raised to the street level for exit.)
An uncanny phrase (for 1905) was used to describe the vaults in the
store: ''They are encased on all sides by gun metal and seem the
embodiment of a bombproof shelter.''

Cook did not live long to enjoy his palace; he died two years after
the store opened. His death brought a profound change in the policies
of Tiffany & Co. He was succeeded as president by John C. Moore, a

grandson of Edward C. Moore, whose silverwork had won so many awards. The new president was as different from his grandfather— and Cook and Tiffany—as granite is from a diamond. John C. Moore was solid but unimaginative. He never understood the masterly combination of salesmanship and publicity which Charles Tiffany had used to create the mystique of the store as a showcase of taste and elegance. The new president could hardly be faulted for not having the Tiffany touch for publicity, but he could be blamed for actively disliking the press which had helped bring fame to the store. Under Moore's regime, when the name Tiffany appeared in the newspapers, the story was usually about Louis Comfort Tiffany, who had inherited his father's talent for catching the fancy of reporters. Just as serious a flaw in Moore was his conservatism, which he inflicted on the firm, along with an inflexibility of policy which kept it from changing with

Tiffany salesmen drilling on roof during World War I.

the times. But these were internal matters which would not immediately affect the fortunes of the store; the momentum of years of success was too great for that. But the seeds of decay were planted in the palace on Thirty-seventh Street, and when they flowered many years later the very existence of Tiffany's was threatened.

A brief flurry of publicity occurred when Tiffany & Co. opened its new building in Paris in 1910. "Another American triumph," trumpeted the Paris *Herald,* which seemed to regard Tiffany's as an outpost of empire. "There is nothing in Europe which can compare with this establishment." (One customer of the Paris store, and a very good one, had always been J. Pierpont Morgan. His purchases during one six-week period in France: On April 30, one pair of diamond earrings, $105,000; June 4, a pearl and diamond pendant, $4,400; a ruby and diamond pendant, $10,000; June 6, a sapphire and gold toilette

de necessaire, $5,150; and three diamond and gold matchboxes for, respectively, $2,900, $3,000 and $2,900.)

Despite the fact that Moore seemed determined to run Tiffany's as if he wanted to forget the lively, adventurous past, the store continued to be incredibly profitable, coasting along on that legend. The story is best told in the fabulous earnings and dividends. The figures here, and in the pages to come recounting the ups—and the downs to come later —have never before been published.

In 1901, dividends were paid of 50 percent per share, or $500. For 1902, they were $350, then back up to $500 the next year. For each of the next seven years, Tiffany stock paid $250 a share, rising to $350 in 1911 and to $400 for 1913 and 1914. Only occasionally did a few shares of stock come on the market. A block of ten shares was sold in 1913 for $6,000 a share, a bargain in view of the dividends and the soaring sales of the company. From $7,000,000 in 1914, sales rose to a peak of $17,700,000 in 1919, a record that was to stand for forty years.

During World War I, Tiffany's did its bit, turning over part of the silver factory to the production of surgical instruments. Patriotism proved profitable, as it always has to American business. By 1916, the company was once more paying dividends of $500 a share and which it continued to do through 1920. By that time, the purchaser of those ten shares in 1913 had received $35,000 in dividends on the $60,000 investment—and the Golden Twenties were just dawning.

Profits were so high in 1920 that $9,600,000 was transferred to the capital account, i.e., reserves for the lean years that no one really expected. Two years later, another $4,000,000 was transferred to capital, and the stock was split five shares for one, as if to get ready for the heady stock market that was in the making. The split raised the number of shares to twelve thousand, an extremely small total for a firm of Tiffany's standing in the mercantile world.

In the light of these profits, despite the great changes which were sweeping the country, Moore became, if possible, even more conservative. There seemed to be no reason to change. The old familiar faces representing the (now) old established money—the Vanderbilts, Morgans, Astors, Belmonts, Rockefellers, Havemeyers, Mills—continued to be seen with highly lucrative results. Mrs. Rodman Wanamaker purchased a pearl necklace for one million dollars. And there was a new clientele: the stars from the stage and screen. Caruso made one of his last purchases at Tiffany's—a ruby bracelet for his wife. Geraldine Farrar, David Belasco, Mary Pickford and Douglas Fairbanks added glamor to the list of customers. When Reginald Vanderbilt became engaged to Gloria Morgan, one of the much-publicized and

beautiful Morgan twins, he took his fiancée into Tiffany's to choose a
16½-carat $75,000 diamond ring.

During the twenties, flapper daughters of the rich came in for
diamond headache bands in about the proportion that their grand-
mothers had picked up jeweled garters, paying as much as two thousand dollars for the trifles.

But there was a subtle change in atmosphere that scared away the
sightseers who once trooped through the store. Ads no longer emphasized that Tiffany's sold low-priced merchandise as well as $100,000
pearl necklaces. As early as 1916 the phrase "We invite a comparison
of our prices with our competitors" was dropped. One salesman,
known for his "$1,000 book," no longer bothered to be subtle. If he
started waiting on a customer and it developed that the person wasn't
interested in anything over that amount, he would haughtily signal a
younger clerk to take over.

A letter received by the management in the twenties could have
reminded him of an earlier tradition of courtesy and warmth. Mrs.
Rutherford Hayes, wife of a well-known watercolor artist, wrote a
charming note recalling the pleasant way in which she was introduced
to Tiffany's, in the year Moore became president, when she and her
fiancé purchased her engagement ring. Both she and the young artist
were in their teens; all the cash the young man had was three hundred
dollars in old bills, held together by a rubber band—Mrs. Hayes recalled that they looked as if he had just pulled them from under an
old mattress. She herself was almost too shy to go into the store, but
after he coaxed a bit the two went up to the ring counter. After much
trying on and whispered consultation she picked out a ring. Unfortunately the tag read three hundred and thirty dollars. More consultation. Could they give the clerk their three hundred dollars and
come back later with the thirty dollars? The clerk smiled on them
benignly and told the young man that he thought Tiffany's could
trust him for the thirty dollars. The young lady wore her ring out of
the store. "I thought it was so nice of them," she wrote. "They had
seen neither of us before. It was the first nice thing I ever had."

The store continued to hold its magic for the young, even for the
couple who came to symbolize idol-breaking youth, Scott and Zelda
Fitzgerald. In New York on their honeymoon, they received a wedding present from Tiffany's, a sterling-silver chocolate set. Zelda was
so impressed that she put the gift on the dresser, the most prominent
spot in their Biltmore room.

A story current at the time, less charming but possibly more typical
of the zany spirit of the Jazz Age, concerned a woman who hurried

(*Above*) *Mary Pickford and Douglas Fairbanks, Sr.*

(*Below*) *Mary Pickford in Her Spanish Lover.*

(*Above*) *Enrico Caruso, wife, and daughter*
(*Below*) *Caruso in* Rigoletto.

through the doors and up to the precious-stone counter. As the salesman came up to her she asked in a loud and slightly drunken voice,
"Where's the toilet?"

The salesman winced; it was not quite the word Tiffany customers
used. "The ladies' room," he emphasized, "is upstairs. Take the elevator."

While he was speaking, the woman was examining the rings in the
case on which she was leaning. She pointed to an emerald. "I'll take
that one," she said. "Have it wrapped up for me." And she walked
away, weaving slightly. On her return she asked for the ring and was
quite put out to find that it hadn't been wrapped. The salesman
pointed out politely that she had not paid for it. She pulled out a
checkbook and identification, and wrote out a check for $17,500.

Some two years later the same woman—either drunk again or still
—came in, hailed the same salesman, and made the same request. On
her way out this time, she stopped just long enough to buy a $12,000
diamond ring.

Telling the story later, the salesman consoled himself with the comment: "Anyway, she didn't pronounce it 'terlet.'"

Because they were handy to the door, jewelry clerks were schooled
in giving all sorts of directions. One day two men struggled in, drag-
ging behind them a huge bundle. "Where can we take this?" the
leader asked. The clerk recognized him as a customer, C. Whitney
Carpenter. "This" turned out to be (shades of Mr. Forepaugh) the
hide of an elephant shot in Africa. Carpenter wanted it made into a
set of suitcases (which Tiffany's still made), and he was politely directed to the custom luggage department.

Another time, Al Jolson, then at the height of his fame, came into
the store. Jolson liked to play the horses and he had heard about the
famous Tiffany timer, which the reader will recall, was an especially
accurate stopwatch. None was available (the price had been five dollars), but there was a Patek Philippe watch which Jolson decided was
suitable. He handed the salesman a check for a thousand dollars. The
check went to the credit manager for approval. But it came with a
note: "The check is good, but be sure of identification." When the
salesman asked Jolson to identify himself, the star fumed: "Tell that
manager to come out here and I'll sing 'Mammy' for him."

During most of the decade, sales ran about fifteen million dollars a
year. Dividends rose steadily. Starting at $100 a share in 1920 (the
equivalent of $500 on the pre-split shares), payments increased to
$125, to $135 and continued to rise, along with the price of the stock.
In 1929 the price of a few shares that came on the market was $6,000

John C. Moore.

a share. The reader will recall that this was the same price per share paid for ten shares in 1913, but with one great difference—because of the split, the ten shares were now fifty; by 1929, the owner had received close to $100,000 in dividends on his $60,000 investment and the shares were now worth $300,000.

The year 1929 was a turning point in the history of Tiffany's, as it was for the rest of the country. One unforeseen event was the way in which the crash affected the rising young executive Louis de Bèbian Moore, son of the president, who was working in the diamond department. He had made his first precious-stone buying trip to Europe two years before, and now was alternating in the job with LCT's son, Charles L. Tiffany II, a vice president and head of the department. It was Moore's turn to go to Europe in the spring of 1929, and, based on 1928 sales, the firm was confident that 1929 sales would break all records.

Young Moore's instructions were to buy more precious gems than usual, and he came home with over three million dollars' worth of diamonds, emeralds, pearls and rubies for the Christmas season. Unfortunately, Black Tuesday, ending the bull market, came in October before a white Christmas. Margins were wiped out in minutes, panic and suicides were very real. The Depression was on.

When the Tiffany directors met early in 1930 to decide about dividends, they went along with the experts from President Hoover down; the market's great fall was a temporary tumble. It had to go back up because, in those immortal words, ''The economy is fundamentally sound. Recovery is just around the corner.'' Tiffany's directors showed their faith in the American way by raising the dividend to a whopping $165 per share (or $825 on the pre-split basis).

But at the same time, sales were plummeting. In 1930 they dropped 45 percent to $8,352,977. Many old customers had reserves, but in that curious pattern of reaction that entrenched wealth follows during a recession, the rich became more tight-fisted than the truly stricken.

An anecdote from the early thirties documents the attitude. A small man came into the store and asked to see a silver pitcher for twenty dollars. The store did not have a pitcher at that price, but something in crystal might be found at twenty-five dollars. The man, looking anxious, hemmed and hawed and then asked to phone his wife. He was overheard by the sales clerk as he asked the butler to call her from the private tennis court. There was a wrangle and the man's ability to choose seemed to be in question.

"Why don't you try another store?" the wife was heard to ask.

"I don't have time," the husband replied: "You're forgetting I have to pick up the caviar." At last, he was given permission to spend the extra five dollars. He said he could not wait while the crystal pitcher was wrapped and would pick it up later. An hour went by and the pitcher was picked up—by a liveried chauffeur.

In 1930, for the first time since its founding, Tiffany's lost money. The directors, still bravely looking ahead, retrenched by cutting the dividend to $140 a share, but they refused to cut the advertising budget. The *Times* wrote with admiration of the spunk of the store: "Tiffany's knows that no one is buying now, but it continues its advertising schedule, thinking of the buyers of tomorrow. It may be one reason why Tiffany's is the most famous jewelry house in the world; it is always thinking of the buyers of tomorrow." The ads broke with tradition. The ad schedule itself, with its unprecedented use of illustrations, made six news stories in New York alone. It was fortunate that the firm's true financial status could not be known.

In 1931, sales dropped to $5,358,899; again the store lost money. Dividends were cut in half to $75. The bottom of the Depression was reached in 1932, although no one knew it at the time. Tiffany's sales collapsed to $2,941,305, less than the amount Louis de Bèbian Moore had invested for the Christmas trade of 1929. The company was forced to dip into the reserves built up in the twenties, transferring $4,800,000 to working capital. But when the time for dividends came around, the directors voted $60 a share.

No publicly held company could possible have justified this policy in the face of the drop in sales and profits, for Tiffany stock was as sick as the store's sales. A few shares came on the market in 1932 and fetched $600 per share, one-tenth of the 1929 peak. The heirs who held most of the shares were undoubtedly counting on the dividends to pull them through the Depression.

There was one note of cheer during the year: a victory in the first suit to prevent the pirating of the Tiffany name, which the firm may have come to feel was the most valuable asset left. The pirates were a Hollywood movie company, Tiffany Productions, which advertised in many ingenious ways, implying a connection with the jewelers. Tiffany Productions' letterhead featured a diamond with rays streaming from it; ads for movies used such phrases as "Twenty-three gems from Tiffany's" and "Tiffany, it's a gem." The moviemakers must be admired for sheer gall; they asked the patent office for the exclusive use of the name "Tiffany."

In ruling for Tiffany & Co.—and establishing a precedent that has deterred others from trying similar piracy—the judge succinctly summed up the mystique of the Tiffany legend: "The plaintiff has acquired both in the United States and elsewhere a reputation that is unique in character for exceptionally high quality of work . . . and also for integrity and commercial reliability." Since no one named Tiffany was connected with the movie company and "no explanation of any kind given on how the defendant had chosen the name," the court found the movie company in bad faith and barred it from using the name.

The "unique character and integrity" did help some during the lean years. When Edsel Ford wanted a collection of silver to give his father, he naturally went to Tiffany's. The bill was three hundred thousand dollars.

Tiffany's tried to increase sales by more changes in its advertising, including prices in ads for the first time in years and plugging low-priced items. For example, a pearl necklace was advertised for $50. But the effect was lost inasmuch as the same ad extolled the beauties of another pearl necklace for $470,000. The ad produced news stories, but all of the wrong kind; they concentrated on the fabulous $470,000 string, once more adding to the image of a high-priced store for the very rich. The image had to be changed, but how? This management did not have the answer. Amos Parrish, publisher of a business magazine, was genuinely puzzled by the performance. He wrote that "anytime Tiffany's wanted to go out and sell it could increase its business by 115%." With the store losing money, it appeared to be not a case of not wanting to sell, but of not knowing how.

One of the few laughs in those dismal years was provided by Harpo Marx. He came into the store one day and began wandering around so suspiciously that the store's detectives were soon watching him. As he left, five of them followed him to the sidewalk. Here, Harpo stumbled, and spilled what looked like a handful of diamonds, rubies and other gems onto the ground. Several detectives grabbed Harpo and held him as a nearby cop came over and began to pick up the gems—all the best that Woolworth's had to offer.

When the cop demanded what Harpo had to say for himself, Harpo gravely handed him a stone, saying, "Please have one of my diamonds." Harpo gave the Tiffany men "rubies," and he and the store got hundreds of lines of copy. The *Saturday Evening Post* claimed it

Harpo Marx.

was all a publicity stunt and that the caper never was pulled, but the Tiffany files do contain a letter from Harpo saying that it all really did happen.

Another story concerns Franklin D. Roosevelt. Reporters had noted an exceptionally handsome watch of heavy gold, intricately carved in a fox-and-hound motif, which F.D.R. consulted on occasion. Some time later, the President appeared at a press conference without the watch, and he was asked about it. F.D.R. explained that the watch had been presented to Andrew Jackson by Charles Tiffany, and Roosevelt had purchased the watch as a talisman. He thought that it had worked especially well in his overwhelming victory at the polls in 1936. However, he had decided that it was too valuable and historic a memento to wear every day, so he had put his Jacksonian watch in a safety deposit vault.

It was a nice story, and raised a cheer for Jackson, F.D.R., the Common Man—and Tiffany's—but there is no record that Charles Tiffany ever gave Jackson a watch.

George Washington Hill, himself a legend along Madison Avenue, played the lead in another episode. The mad mahatma of the American Tobacco Company was a very good customer of Tiffany's, particularly as a collector of pearls. He paid as high as forty thousand dollars for one pearl, and he had a collector's knowledge of all gems.

As the story goes, Hill, who was unhappy about his ads, called an executive from his agency into his office one day. Hill jumped up from his desk, curtly bade the man to follow him, swept out of the office to his waiting limousine, and without speaking a word on the way, drove to Tiffany's. Hill took his man directly to the diamond counter.

"Show me a hundred-and-fifty-thousand-dollar necklace," Hill directed the salesman. The necklace was handed to Hill. He inspected it carefully. In his gruff and penetrating voice he then proceeded to lecture his captive audience, which included not only the hapless ad man but all the salesmen and customers in the store. He informed his listeners as to how such necklaces were made, how the rough stones were selected, how they were finished and placed in their settings. The lecture concluded, Hill turned to the ad man and gave him the full power of his piercing eyes. "*That's* what I mean," he boomed, "give me finished copy, not rough diamonds."

The thirties brought one great change to the jewelry business that could not have been avoided, although the damage could have been easily lessened if Tiffany & Co. had not become so determinedly conservative. Tiffany's queen of gems, the Oriental pearl, was dethroned by the cultured pearl. The favored jewelry of the twenties—ropes that cost from a hundred thousand dollars to a million—became poor investments. The first cultured pearls from Japan had been no threat; rough and misshapen, they were no more than an amusing novelty. One dealer sold oysters in cans for two dollars, each one guaranteed to contain a genuine pearl. The pearls were scarcely prettier than the cans. But as the Japanese improved the quality, jewelers gradually gave in. Eventually, Tiffany's was the only jeweler in the country that did not sell—or even handle—cultured pearls.

The collapse of the Oriental-pearl market is best illustrated by a story concerning a competitor, Cartier's. In 1916 a millionaire named Morton Plant noticed an extraordinary string of pearls at Cartier's, and M. Cartier, who knew Plant, took the string out of the case.

"No one has anything finer," he told Plant.

"And the price?"

"One million dollars."

Plant suggested a trade. He and his wife owned a house on the southeast corner of Fifth Avenue and Fifty-second Street, an area which was becoming too commercial for their taste. House and land were valued at $925,000. Why not exchange the pearls for the real estate? Since Cartier's was not satisfied with its space across Fifth Avenue above Fifty-fifth Street, the exchange was made. (Sometime later, Mrs. Plant had Cartier's make her a diamond necklace, with the help of Tiffany's. Cartier's got the commission for the chain of diamonds; but not satisfied with any of the large stones in the store, Mrs. Plant sent over the large center drop stone, a 16-carat diamond, which she purchased from Tiffany's.)

In 1956 Mrs. Plant (who had become Mrs. John E. Rovensky) died. The million-dollar pearls, restrung into two strands, were auctioned off at Parke-Bernet. The larger string brought ninety thousand dollars, the smaller sixty-one thousand dollars, a drop in value of about 83 percent, most of it attributable to the introduction of the cultured pearl. As for the property at Fifth Avenue and Fifty-second Street, which Cartier's still occupies, the tax valuation in 1956 was $1,500,-000, an increase of close to 60 percent. The actual value today is far higher. (The year 1956 also saw cultured pearls finally on sale at Tiffany's; naturally, they were Burma pearls at ten thousand dollars and up.)

This blindness, or stubbornness, in refusing to face the changing times, kept the company in the red to the tune of about a million dollars a year all during the thirties, but it never stopped paying dividends. In 1937 the firm was forced to dip into capital reserves to the extent of $3,800,000; stockholders got twenty-five dollars per share but the cutbacks continued to be made, reluctantly, until the dividends reached their lowest point in 1940 at five dollars a share.

Despite the decade of staggering losses, Tiffany's again decided to move uptown, for the sixth time, and leased land on the corner of Fifth Avenue and Fifty-seventh Street from the Astor estate, to which it sold its old building. This time there were no grandiose instructions to the architects, Cross & Cross. What Tiffany's wanted was a severely functional building which would make the most of its space, and that is what it got: a seven-story building of pinkish granite and limestone with not a single curlicue. It still was the most expensive building Tiffany's had put up, costing $2,484,079.09 (for the first time Tif-

Fifth Avenue and 57th Street in 1863.

fany's was counting the pennies), more than triple the cost of the palace at Thirty-seventh Street. Atlas and his clock came along, and continue to look very much at home over the Fifth Avenue door.

Another time signal, however, was left behind, the steam whistle installed on the roof at Thirty-seventh Street which used to be blown promptly at twelve noon and 1 P.M., the lunch hour for employees in the manufacturing departments. The whole neighborhood was accustomed to setting watches by the two-toned blast. Tiffany's decided this might not sound the right note in the ears of its new neighbors, Bonwit Teller and Bergdorf Goodman, so the whistle was sold to *Cue* for five dollars, a few days before the New York Historical Society indicated that it would have liked to buy the whistle. "The directors of Tiffany's store were in a quandary," Geoffrey Hellman reported in *The New Yorker* in 1940. "They didn't want to offend *Cue* which had made the prior offer, but they weren't sure whether it was in the tradition of a 133-year-old firm to put a six-year-old magazine in the position of being able to say it owned the Tiffany whistle and to blow it at will. Moreover, they had always blown the whistle exactly on time, being guided by a Western Union ticker announcement sent out by the Naval Observatory in Washington, and weren't convinced that *Cue*, with all the good intentions in the world, would be as accurate. The thought that Tiffany's whistle might not blow precisely at noon depressed them. They finally settled the matter tactfully by keeping the whistle." After a "tactful" wait, Tiffany's presented the whistle to the Historical Society, where it is still on exhibition.

The new building was finished, and the move was made in October 1940. The movers were good. Out of the thousands of fragile articles

The new store, 1940.

—and millions of gems—the only losses were three inexpensive cups and two glasses. Unlike the occasions of the previous moves, there were no huzzahs from the press. Lewis Mumford, architectural critic and high priest of taste, did not like the building at all. "Compared to the old building," he wrote, "the new Tiffany's is an improvement. That is not saying much because it is hard to think of a stiffer, duller piece of architecture than the old pile." *Architectural Forum* was kinder: it praised the functional display counters and the physical comfort of the new store (Tiffany's was the first completely air-conditioned building in New York).

It is possible that Louis de Bèbian Moore had special talents for design that were never properly given expression. He planned the first floor, something of a wonder, in that its 8,500 square feet are not broken by a single pillar or column; the high ceiling is suspended from the same great steel trusses which hold up the building. Moore worked for a whole year on the lighting which *Architectural Forum* admired; even today the effect is astonishing. Looking up from below, it resembles nothing so much as an enormous geometrical pattern of hundreds of the wooden maze puzzles made so popular by another New York institution, Abercrombie & Fitch. The sides of the mazes protect the customers' eyes from any glare. Enclosed are over two hundred spotlights, aimed at many different angles, so that each important ring or brooch can sparkle in its own individual lighting.

When the store opened, John C. Moore stepped up to the chairmanship of the board and turned over the presidency to his son, Louis de

Bèbian. At the same meeting, LCT's son Charles II was elected vice
chairman. The latter's first suggestion was that he and Chairman
Moore have their salaries cut from twenty-four thousand dollars a
year to eighteen thousand dollars. It was not done.

Louis de Bèbian had been well trained by his father in the conservative tradition. His genuine dislike for publicity was fortified by an
intense personal shyness; only with close friends could he relax, and
then he was a warm and entertaining companion. He was one of the
founders of the Creek Club; in 1970, at the age of eighty, he purchased his usual four foreign sports cars, continuing the pattern of
many years in pursuing the passion of a lifetime.

To employees (all of whom Charles had called by their first names)
he was a cold and distant figure. In the light of his traumatic experience in 1929, the chances which Charles had taken were not for him.
Moore believed in keeping extra cash in government bonds, and not
investing it in famous jewels, which would have brought publicity,
sales and profits. Shortly after the new store opened, the working
capital of the store was so tight that it was necessary to transfer a
further $3,600,000 from reserves; in 1941 the capitalization stood at
$4,800,000, precisely what it had been in 1919. If Tiffany's policies
did not change rapidly, it would soon be bankrupt.

World War II turned the tide temporarily. The country boomed
and business everywhere improved, Tiffany's along with the rest.
Tiffany's also made a small but vital contribution to the war machine.
The silver factory had turned to making precision parts for anti-
aircraft guns and fitting blocks for airplanes. Its moment of drama
occurred as Colonel James Doolittle, preparing for his raid over
Tokyo, discovered that the engines were overheating; the trouble lay
in defective baffles used for cooling the motors. There was no time to
go back to the mass producers. So he turned to Tiffany's skilled craftsmen: Could they make new baffles by hand? They could and did. The
raid was a great success at a time when the nation needed a lift. Stories
of the raid raised headlines and hearts across the country; Tiffany's
part, in accord with the store's policy, was never mentioned.

Tiffany's had its own brief brush with the Germans when they took
Paris in 1940. There are two versions as to what happened. In one,
the manager of the Paris branch, A. A. Southwick, hastily loaded the
most valuable gems and jewelry in his car, and reached the south of
France, putting his treasure on one of the last boats leaving Marseilles for New York. In the other version, Southwick managed only
to stash almost everything in the vaults of the Societé Générale bank.
Obviously, everyone was very close-mouthed at the time. The Nazis

put their own man in charge of Tiffany's, a Luxembourger, who happened to be an honest man. He also gloried in the nickname *le Crocodile,* which he obtained, harmlessly enough, from the shape and enormousness of his nose. Wherever the Tiffany millions were, there was only about four hundred thousand dollars' worth of stock in the store itself. *Le Crocodile* never went near the vaults of the Societé Générale. Every night he took the valuables from the store to the safe of Morgan, Harjes, entrusting the key to an equally honest official. Thus he could say truthfully, when questioned by any jewel- and/or art-loving Nazi: "I do not have the key to Tiffany's." Tiffany lost not a single ring to the Germans.

This good fortune was reflected in the profits of the store in New York. The old days appeared to have returned, the lack of publicity notwithstanding. Barbara Hutton was adding to her large collection of gems. Mrs. Walter Chrysler, Jr., was photographed with big clips of Tiffany diamonds and pink beryls at each temple anchoring a mantilla, to set a new style for readers of *Vogue.* Later, the Duke of Windsor, who loved gems, would drop by for an occasional jewel and to talk shop, bringing with him the magic of his name.

Those who came into the store found that the firm still catered to the whims of its rich customers. An Indian prince and his ranee, enchanted with the idea of having identical bracelets fastened permanently around their ankles, caused no one to lift an eyebrow. Asbestos pads were brought out, the solder heated, and in moments the whimsy had become real.

A young man confided another problem to an attentive clerk: his spaniel played an important part in the ritual of his owner's esoteric religion, which prescribed that the pet wear a jeweled collar at an especially sacred moment. Could Tiffany's make one? It was like a return to the 1890's for the store. The dog's neck was measured, the clerk went away to return with the perfect collar, a blaze of rubies. The pleased young man paid cash and disappeared, and the clerk discreetly discarded the box in which he had found the "collar," an expensive ordinary bracelet from the stock on the first floor.

In 1946 the profits were $1,068,134, and the directors celebrated by paying out $45 a share in dividends. Like many celebrations this one was premature. By 1949, the dismal Depression pattern had reestablished itself. Tiffany's made $19,368, scarcely enough to buy one of its own medium-priced necklaces.

Changes in policy were made. The firm attempted to broaden its market by franchising stores around the country to sell its flatware. This helped, but it was too little too late. Some of the young men who had come to work after the war thought that they knew what the trouble was—Tiffany's complacency and conservatism.

"I told Mr. Moore that our competitors were running away with our market," one of them recalls. "I see the jewelry that my friends are buying and they're not buying it from us. We lost the pearl market and we're losing the diamond market. We should be out buying stones, big stones, at every auction and every sale that comes up. We should be putting our cash in stones, not keeping it in government bonds. We need to be talked about; we need publicity."

As an example of what he meant, he cited the story of the large diamond Tiffany's had bought in 1946, a human-interest story which under Charles Tiffany would have been run by all the newspapers in the country. A Mrs. Pellie Howell, of Searcy, Arkansas, sent Tiffany's a pebble which she had found twenty years before, as a child of ten, while picking cotton with her father. The pebble turned out to be a perfectly crystallized diamond of 27.21 carats, the third largest stone ever found in this country. Tiffany's paid her "several thousands of dollars for it." The story did not come out until years later under a new regime.

"I told Moore we should have new designs for the new people who are buying," the young executive continued. "Our jewelry was old-fashioned. No one under fifty would be caught dead in it."

He and the other young men were right. There was new competition. Cartier's had been around a long time and, fortunately, remained as conservative as Tiffany's, but there was a difference: the New York store was a branch of Cartier's Paris and London offices, while Tiffany–New York, was Tiffany's—the Paris branch had closed in 1952.

Europe was again the center of design. Van Cleef and Arpels was showing great imagination. The style and wit of a newcomer, Jean Schlumberger, had captured the favor and money of the international set. China and silver from Denmark, with its clean, simple lines, appealed to the young New York market, and Georg Jensen was reaping profits from their sale.

Harry Winston, who had begun as a wholesaler, was hurting Tiffany most of all. It was Winston who was laying out millions for famous gems at the important auctions and jewel sales, as Charles Tiffany had long ago, and receiving the same worldwide publicity. Beyond the publicity, Winston's ads were masterpieces of style and direction. He had no appeal for the masses and indeed never pursued them. But readers of *The New Yorker, Vogue* and other slick magazines pored over his full-page ads, which might feature a single magnificent necklace of diamonds and emeralds, shown full size; or the small type, beneath the picture of the jewelry, instead of reading "enlarged to show details," would read "reduced in size to show the whole piece." It worked. Winston knew his postwar market.

It also was good publicity that no one was invited to browse at Winston's. There was a certain éclat in just being seen entering the dignified old mansion east of Fifth Avenue on Fifty-first Street. The same holds true for his new building on Fifth Avenue and Fifty-sixth, across the avenue and one short block from Tiffany's. For insurance reasons, Winston has never permitted his picture to be taken, and no one can recall that one was ever printed by the press. Somewhat incongruously, while he built his reputation as the jeweler to see for important stones, he has kept his wholesale business and he still sells engagement rings wholesale for as little as twenty-five dollars.

At Tiffany's, by 1952, things were gloomy enough for even Moore to consider relaxing his restrictions on publicity. He agreed to a series of articles in *The Saturday Evening Post*. Negotiations between the store and the magazine were so ludicrously drawn out that one would have thought the security system at Fort Knox was being cautiously revealed. The magazine's "Keeping Posted" page announced its coup with the headline "The Writer Who Got Into Tiffany's." Henry La Cossitt, a respected professional journalist, had to make his advances through a friend in an advertising agency which handled the Tiffany account. An elaborate dossier on La Cossitt was submitted. Weeks went by, until he was summoned and passed upward through a chain of executives into the presence of Moore and William T. Lusk, the executive vice president. La Cossitt had to promise not to mention any living customer or to publicize any officer of the store, but he could not help musing aloud that readers might wonder what kept the store in business—perpetual motion? Finally the whole thing was put down in writing and formally signed. As the *Post* commented, "tradition always weighed heavily at every turn. For example, President Moore could not be referred to as president of the store."

But the store's ultraconservatism was coming to an end. At last, Moore and his directors had to admit that things could not drift on much longer. Stockholders were displaying signs of restlessness, and Moore's first move was to offer to buy all the stock of the malcontents, offering $40 a share or under, if the market price was less (the stock had been split sixteen for one in 1949). He acquired 32,109 shares in this manner. This left most of the 164,560 shares outstanding in the hands of heirs or friends, and he was certain that they would cause no trouble. In this, he could not have been more wrong.

R evolt against the re-
gime of Louis de B. Moore began in a small way, and the cause went
back many years, to the incorporation of Tiffany & Co. in 1868,
when ninety-one shares were allotted to Charles M. Cook. Eventually a small number of this block were inherited by Anna C. Marsh,
who had married a New York real estate man, Allen Watts. In the
course of business, Watts dealt with another real estate man, Irving
M. Maidman. Watts admired Maidman's sagacity, and one day in
1954 he called on him with a story to tell. His wife was unhappy about
her Tiffany stock; dividends had been reduced and some of her friends
who also owned stock shared her dissatisfaction. In recalling the conversation later, Maidman said: "It was paying dividends that had not

(*Above*) *Irving Maidman.*

been earned, and it looked as if the company was going out of business.'' The first statement was true, the second a possibility. Maidman did not weep for Tiffany's troubles or for Mrs. Watts's stock; he was instead, transfixed by the vision of a wonderful opportunity.

Maidman conceived a grandiose scheme, something William Zeckendorf might have maneuvered in his salad days. The land on which the store stands is one of the choice plots in New York; ''The property was just too valuable to have only a seven-story building on it,'' was the way Maidman put it.

He visualized a building soaring to the clouds and covering the entire block between Fifty-sixth and Fifty-seventh streets, from Fifth Avenue east to Madison Avenue. The keystone of the dream was the Tiffany land, which was tied up in a long-term lease from the Astor estate. Bonwit Teller, too, leased its land, but any immediate move against Bonwit was out because the store was owned by the Hoving Corporation, and 65 percent of the Hoving stock was safely tucked away in the hands of the Bankers' Acceptance Corporation, owned by Albert Greenfield, a Philadelphia real estate millionaire. There seemed to be no way for Maidman to get his foot in the Bonwit door, beyond going in to buy an expensive present for his wife.

Tiffany's was something else. The stock was selling well below its book value of sixty-five dollars, and that was composed of government bonds, jewelry, gold and a fine building, all of which could easily be turned into cash. In a word, Maidman saw Tiffany's as worth more dead than alive; even the legendary name could be sold for a nice sum.

Maidman charted his campaign. If other Tiffany stockholders could be found who were as dissatisfied as Mrs. Watts, it should be easy to get a foot in *that* door and follow it with his whole body. Maidman quietly began to buy stock over-the-counter, and in the name of a broker, so that Tiffany's would have less chance of finding out who was doing the buying. At the same time, he went to see Thomas J. Watson, who was still running IBM, which occupies a large building on the corner of Fifty-seventh Street and Madison Avenue, a site necessary to Maidman's plan.

''Watson told me that he didn't think the plan was possible,'' Maidman has recalled, ''but I could see from the expression on his face that he was receptive to the idea. If I could assemble the land for one big building, IBM could have all the space it wanted.''

What about Tiffany's? ''At the time, I planned to keep a small portion of space for Tiffany's.''

Maidman kept buying stock, and by the time of Tiffany's annual meeting in January of 1955, he held approximately 30 percent. That would have been enough for control in many companies. Full of confidence, Maidman felt he should be put on the board of directors at the forthcoming meeting. As a preliminary, he visited Moore in his office on the mezzanine floor to acquaint him with the facts. When Maidman told Moore the extent of his stock buying, the latter countered with: "What do you know about the jewelry business?"

"I was brought up in the jewelry business," Maidman replied. "My father owned a jewelry store, but he went bankrupt before World War I. The first job I ever had was in the jewelry department of Gimbels. When I married my wife, I bought her a Tiffany ring. It was the strangest thing, but the Tiffany ring cost less than what you could buy at a retail store. If people only knew about this you could sell millions of rings. You could sell them all over the country. You could sell them by mail."

"What else do you know?" asked Moore.

"I also bought a chest of silver and it was cheaper in Tiffany's than anyplace else. But people don't know this. Now, take your silver polish. It's the best polish made and you only charge fifty cents or a dollar. If you go into a department store or super market, silver polish costs twice what you are getting. Nobody knows about the silver polish, either."

"Do you have any more ideas?" asked Moore.

"I've got other ideas for the company and I own thirty percent of the stock. I think I should have a seat on the board of directors."

"Well, no," Moore replied quietly.

Maidman was not a quitter. He attended the stockholders' meeting and made another try. "I told them that their expenses were way out of line," Maidman recalled many years later. "I also raised some questions about the inventory. I thought they were carrying it above cost to make a better showing on the balance sheet. I told them how much stock I owned, but they turned me down, too." Maidman was outraged. After the meeting, he talked to reporters, and the press duly reported the fact that a struggle had started for the control of supposedly impregnable Tiffany's; this was the first hint the public received that all was not right under the marble and granite and the clock of Atlas. Maidman told the press that the management was "rapidly dissipating" the firm's capital reserves, that dividends had been reduced to a dollar a share and "that was not earned. The present management does not realize that the era of Diamond Jim Brady and J. P. Morgan is over."

When the stories appeared in the newspapers the day after the meeting, Maidman received a telephone call from Stanley Simon, executive vice president of the Bulova Watch Company. It developed that Arde Bulova, the president who also controlled the company, was interested in Maidman's Tiffany stock. Now the whole complexion of the battle changed. Bulova had made a success of his company by starting out with lower-priced watches and gradually upgrading them in quality and price. But no one had ever referred to Bulova as the Tiffany of watches. Bulova, too, could dream, and he could see himself acquiring the Tiffany name, putting out the Tiffany watch and becoming the top watchmaker of the world.

"Bulova was not interested in the real estate," Maidman has since confirmed, "only the name. I don't know what they wanted to do with the rest of Tiffany's. They would continue to run the store, but not the way it had been—not in the Tiffany tradition."

With Maidman interested only in the land, and Bulova only in the name for his watches, it looked like the end of Tiffany's as an institution. However, for all his strong talk to Moore (and much of it made sense), Maidman was in a weak position. For one thing, his assault had frightened Moore into taking action. He wrote to all the stockholders; he soothed them, telling them, correctly, that Moore, the Tiffany heirs and "close associates" between them owned more than 55,000 shares of the 132,451 outstanding and that none of them intended to sell to Maidman. He asked that no one sell to Maidman "without first discussing the matter with me," since there had been "a great improvement in our business in the past fifteen months."

This letter effectively blocked stock sales to Maidman. More important, Maidman was at the limit of his resources. He had borrowed two million dollars from the Manufacturers' Trust Company to buy the Tiffany stock, and the bank was pressing for repayment. Reluctantly, he made a deal with Arde Bulova to sell him his stock; in return Bulova signed an agreement under which Maidman would get the lease on the Tiffany site if Bulova got control of Tiffany's.

About this time, Walter Hoving again became interested in Tiffany's. Bonwit Teller was doing very well and he thought it was time to expand. He would have liked to buy Lord & Taylor, his old store, but it was not for sale, nor were any of the other specialty stores around the country of the caliber he wanted. His mind turned next door, to Tiffany's.

"I knew the company was not doing well," recalled Hoving, "and it occurred to me that it would make a good addition to the Hoving Corporation. I tried to get in touch with Moore whom I had met only once before, but he was not in good health." In line with Tiffany policy, no one made it easy for Hoving to reach the president or gave him any information. Hoving finally got Moore's unlisted number in Oyster Bay from an old friend. He phoned Moore, said he was sorry to hear that Maidman was harassing him about Tiffany's and asked if he could be of any help.

"I don't see how," Moore replied. He may have been short with Hoving at the time because he was in bed with diverticulosis, a particularly painful intestinal disorder.

"Why don't I come down to your home and see you there," Hoving suggested, "let's say, the day after tomorrow at three o'clock in the afternoon; that would be Saturday." Moore may have been surprised that Hoving would not be put off. At any rate he assented: "All right, come along."

It was August, and Hoving and his wife left at once for their summer place in the Berkshires to relax for the intervening two days. But matters speeded up. On Friday the officers of Tiffany's received the news that Maidman had sold his block of stock to Bulova. They knew that Hoving had been talking to Moore. Vice President William T. Lusk, a grandson of Louis Comfort Tiffany, was detailed to get in touch with Hoving to tell him of this new development. Lusk located Hoving in the Berkshires, found that he was out playing golf, and left word for him to call back as soon as possible. Hoving was handed the message on the fifth hole; he did not know Lusk but he knew he was an officer of Tiffany's. Hoving went back to the caddy house and phoned Lusk, who gave him the news that Maidman had sold out to Bulova.

Lusk and his fellow directors had been relaxed, since they knew that Maidman was being pressed by the bank and could not buy any more stock. Bulova was a far more serious problem; he had the money to buy and could afford to keep a few million dollars tied up. The way things were going, eventually enough stockholders would sell out and Bulova could gain control.

Hoving and Lusk arranged to meet at the Moore house at 12 o'clock on Saturday. After lunch, the three men sat down to talk over the situation. Hoving had already made up his mind. He told Moore and Lusk, "If the heirs will sell me their stock, I am prepared to buy enough to get control. I will pay fifty dollars a share to the members of the Tiffany and Moore families, whose members are active in the business. I'll pay fifty-five dollars to members who are not active." (The market price of the stock was then sixty-five, helped by Maidman's buying and the news around Wall Street that a fight for control was on.)

NEW YORK, N. Y.,
·c. D. 509,171, S. 404,992,

Maidman Offering His Tiffany Shares

Parcel, Including Bulova-Optioned Stock, Said to Equal 33% of Total

By Max Forester

Irving Maidman, the New York real estate man who last summer figured in a shift of rights of a substantial parcel of stock in Tiffany & Co. to Bulova Watch Co., offered his shares

NOV 3 - 19

Ceramic Sculptures

A special exposition works of Edward Boehm, noted American ist-sculptor, goes on Monday at Tiffany for During the first few da Boehm, who is her h

SETTLEMENT: Genesco places two directors on Tiffany board

GENESCO, INC., and Tiffany & Co. Tuesday announced settlement of their long-standing dispute over two seats on the Tiffany board. The settlement permitted Tiffany to go ahead with its scheduled annual meeting. Two Genesco representatives were elected to the Tiffany board

W YORK TIMES, FRIDAY, OCTOBER 5,

Genesco Wins a Round In Court Fight to Keep 2 Tiffany Board Seats

Judge Bars Tiffany Stockholders' Meeting Until Tiffany Accepts Genesco Claim or Court Rules

By a WALL STREET JOURNAL *Staff Reporter*
NEW YORK—Genesco, Inc., won a round in its legal battle to keep two seats on the 15-member board of Tiffany & Co., New York jewelers.

Judge Nathaniel T. Helman, of New York County Supreme Court, granted a motion by 721 Corp., a Genesco subsidiary, temporarily stopping Tiffany from holding an annual or special meeting of stockholders to elect a new board of directors. Such a meeting can't be

The newspapers kept score in the battle for Tiffany's:
1. Walter Hoving.   2. Arde Bulova.   3. William T. Lusk.   4. Louis deB. Moore.

Two Representatives Of Genesco Are Kept On Tiffany & Co. Board

They Get 1-Year Terms, Settling Long Dispute; Tiffany to Open A Branch in Houston on Oct. 1

By a WALL STREET JOURNAL *Staff Reporter*

NEW YORK—Genesco, Inc., and Tiffany & Co. announced settlement of their long-standing dispute over two seats on the Tiffany board.

The settlement permitted Tiffany to go ahead with its annual meeting yesterday. Earlier, Judge Nathaniel T. Helman of the New York State Supreme Court granted Genesco's motion prohibiting the meeting until a settlement was reached.

Under the settlement terms, two Genesco representatives were elected to the Tiffany board for one-year terms. They are Douglas Brooks, president of Brooks Instrument Co. of Hatfield, Pa., and Philip A. Williams III, a vice president of International Commercial Equities, Inc., Houston.

They replace two other Genesco representatives who have been serving on the Tiffany board—W. Maxey Jarman, Genesco chairman, and Ben H. Willingham, Genesco president.

The settlement announcement didn't say whether Genesco had won the right to the two board seats "in perpetuity"—its original object in bringing the suit. Neither Tiffany nor Genesco would comment on this.

Genesco's claim to the two seats was based on terms of the sale of controlling interest in Tiffany in 1961 to a group headed by Walter Hoving, Tiffany chairman. The interest, amounting to some 52%, had been owned by a Genesco subsidiary, 721 Corp., which operates Bonwit Teller stores.

At the annual meeting Mr. Hoving outlined further expansion plans for Tiffany, which has already announced plans to open a branch store in San Francisco on Sept. 4. A second branch will be opened in Houston Oct. 1 and future stores are planned in some five more locations, Mr. Hoving said.

Wall Street Journa; - July

Business Milestones
General Shoe Buy Control From Ba

Transaction for 65% Interest Understood to Involve Over $10 Million Cash

By a WALL STREET JOURNAL *Staff Reporter*

PHILADELPHIA—Bankers Securities Corp. has sold its 65% interest in Hoving Corp. to General Shoe Corp., according to Albert M. Greenfield, chairman of the Philadelphia-based merchandising and real estate operating and holding company.

Exact terms of the sale were not immediately disclosed. However, it is understood the sale was a cash transaction involving in excess of $10 million.

Banker Securities had owned approximately 470,000 shares in Hoving, including 15,000 class B common shares. Hoving has outstanding 652,000 common shares and 30,000

Maidman Turns Over Tiffany Stock

Gives Bulova 33,000 Shares in Loan Repayment

By Max Forester

Irving Maidman, the New York real estate man who last summer figured in a shift of rights of a substantial parcel of stock in Tiffany & Co. to Bulova Watch Co., offered his shares for sale yesterday.

Mr. Maidman's offer apparently included all the stock in the Bulova deal, which was viewed as possibly foreshadowing the capture of control of the 119-year-old jewelry concern by the watch manufacturer.

He offered 43,500 shares "for sale subject to immediate acceptance," and said this comprised "33 per cent of total outstanding capital stock."

Package Sale

Reached at his offices yesterday, Mr. Maidman said he could not name a price on the stock. He noted it was to be sold "as a package," that he was receiving offers, and that the sale "would have to made the sale "would have to be made price."

The 43,500 shares offered by Mr. Maidman included the 33,000 shares which Bulova was

Bonwit Teller, Inc., the women's specialty store chain whose Fifth Ave. headquarters is a Tiffany & Co. neighbor.

Previously, officials of Bulova had hinted that the summer-born romance was over. A year after its optioning of the stock, the management of Bulova told the watch firm's stockholders, at their annual meeting last July, that the company stood to get back all of its commitment in the transaction, which was placed at $2,240,000.

Bulova Plans Noted

Stanley Simon, a Bulova vice-president, was asked at that time whether Bulova intended to negotiate with General Shoe Corp., which in the meantime had bought control of Hoving Corp., for the stock that it con-

Moore had 13 percent of the stock, the largest single block. He and Lusk agreed to Hoving's terms and also agreed that they would help persuade the other heirs to sell. Hoving decided to ask Lusk to do the buying, in order to keep the matter a secret as long as possible. None of the terms was put into a formal contract; the verbal agreement between gentlemen was sufficient.

On Monday, Hoving assembled his own board and told them what he had done. During the meeting he received a call from Bankers' Trust, which said it would sell him four thousand shares held by outsiders, but the price would have to be the market price, which was sixty-five dollars a share. Hoving took it, telling his board, "I know the Tiffany heirs will stick by their agreement to sell at fifty dollars and fifty-five dollars because that is the kind of people we are dealing with."

Bulova's agents and Lusk scurried around the country chasing stock. It was a case of finding the heirs and getting there first with the most persuasive words, and, with the outsiders, the most cash. The price was slowly rising, higher than it had been for years, bringing out sellers. Hoving suffered a blow when Bulova located first, and bought one block of two thousand shares. Then, despite the agreement, Moore could not force any heirs to sell. Going down to the stretch, Hoving needed only some thirteen hundred more shares to get his 51 percent. It seemed possible that neither side would win control.

Finally, Lusk located a thousand shares owned by a Mrs. Ralph Laighton in Portsmouth, New Hampshire, a distant relative of Gould Remick, a friend of Hoving's. Lusk failed to persuade her to sell. The stock had been left to her by her husband, whose uncle had once been head of the watch repair department at Tiffany's, and the shares had a great sentimental value to Mrs. Laighton.

Hoving now decided to try using his own considerable persuasive powers. Phoning La Guardia Airport, he chartered a small plane, but when he arrived at the field a fog had closed in and the control tower was not letting any planes take off. Hoving waited in the hangar for a time and then went outside and looked up at the gray sky. A genuinely religious man, who believes in the power of prayer, Hoving recounts how he prayed, "Oh, Lord, if you want me to go up and see this lady, please see that the control tower releases me." Some minutes after, the control tower called Hoving's pilot and said there had been a partial clearing and asked, "Are you going north? If so, you can take off, but we're not releasing anybody else."

Without further difficulties, Hoving tracked down Mrs. Laighton, who was ninety-two but very spry, "with good New England manners," as Hoving recalled. She invited him in, but after he told her what he wanted she said she did not want to sell her stock.

There was more talk and then Hoving said: "I'm paying members of the family at the store fifty dollars and fifty-five dollars a share. I'm going to pay you the highest price, seventy dollars a share, because we need your stock so badly."

"I don't want to sell," Mrs. Laighton repeated. "Mr. Bulova has been after me and I told him that, too. I just don't want to sell."

"Don't you think it would be better to have the store in our hands rather than Mr. Bulova's?" Hoving asked. Mrs. Laighton thought for a minute or two, then replied, "Yes, I do. I'll sell."

Hoving told her he would write out what she needed to do. Mrs. Laighton left the room and came back with an old laundry ticket; he told her that this was too small. She went out again and this time handed him a wrinkled brown-paper grocery bag. Hoving wrote on it how she should transfer the stock.

Shortly thereafter, in September 1955, Hoving was able to buy a small block in Boston, to give him exactly 51 percent of the stock. Unfortunately, although 51 percent had been promised him, only about 20 percent had actually been sent in to the Irving Trust Company, which was acting as depository, and until the stock was in the bank's hands, Bulova might reach the stockholders, offer more money and win it away. It was time for a bold move.

Hoving called the press and at 4 P.M., announced that the Hoving Corporation had bought control of Tiffany's. An hour later, Hoving's phone rang. Bulova, whom he had never met, was on the line. "Are you the Hoving that bought control of Tiffany's?" Bulova asked.

"Yes," replied Hoving.

"That's very interesting."

"I agree with you. It's very interesting. I hear that you have been buying, too, and paying pretty good prices," Hoving said. "As near as I can figure out, you've been paying about sixty-five dollars a share."

"What have you been paying?"

"We've been paying an average of about fifty-six dollars a share."

Bulova paused for a moment and then said, "I tell you what I'll do. I'll give you ninty-five dollars a share for the stock."

That price would have meant a clear profit to the Hoving Corporation of about $3,500,000, more than Tiffany's had made in the past ten years.

"I'm sorry," Hoving replied. "It's not for sale."

That ended the conversation, but it did not end the matter. The possibility of such a large profit came up shortly at a meeting of Hoving's directors. One suggested that the Tiffany stock be held for six months and then sold to Bulova so that the Hoving Corporation could take a long-term capital gain. But after Hoving explained that the heirs had sold the stock to keep the store out of Bulova's hands, the directors agreed that they were honor-bound to keep their end of the bargain: the Hoving Corporation would run Tiffany's.

Thus ended the reign over Tiffany & Co. by the heirs of the founding fathers. However, as far as Moore was concerned, the change in ownership did not make any difference. He continued to appear every day in his office and to operate the store exactly as before. Six weeks went by, and the man who now controlled the firm was not even asked to join the board of directors. However, Hoving was not a man who could be ignored; he wrote a letter to Moore, requesting that he be asked to attend the next meeting of the board. At the meeting he "suggested" that he be elected chairman of the board. Moore and his directors had no choice but to do as asked. Hoving then "suggested" that he be given office space in the store, and was given a small office next to Moore's. Like the original deal made in Moore's home, it was all done in a quiet, well-mannered way.

Hoving began his operations at Tiffany's by calling in key people and trying to find out how the store was run. When he had a good idea of what was wrong in some area, he discussed his ideas with Moore; he also sent him memos on what he thought could be done to help business. Moore paid no attention to the memos, but Hoving persisted.

Finally, after a month, Moore, then sixty-five, came into Hoving's office.

"I think it's about time I retired," Moore said. "I don't see how your views and mine will ever be compatible; I'd like to retire on a dollar a year."

Hoving, who admits to a weakness for the facetious, then asked Moore, "Do you want to be paid in a lump sum each year or would you rather take it quarterly?" Moore did not see anything funny in this. Hoving admitted later, "I really didn't blame him."

William T. Lusk, great-great-grandson of Charles, was elected president. "We always had good luck when a Tiffany was president," explained Hoving. He was now firmly in control, but he still had one large, unhappy stockholder: Arde Bulova. He not only owned Maidman's stock, but he had bought more on his own during the fight; in all, he had some forty thousand shares worth about $2,500,000. Bulova now took his turn in trying for a seat on the board and was turned down.

Hoving's job now was to reorganize Tiffany's into the kind of store he wanted. As he said, "I had worked for Macy's and Montgomery Ward. And in those stores the policy was to give the customer what he wanted, to suit his tastes. Now, for the first time in my life, with Tiffany's I had a chance to give the customer what *I* wanted, to suit my taste."

Hoving began his regime—while also running Bonwit's—by getting rid of everything that did not conform to his taste in what employees called the Great White Elephant Sale, the first such store-wide advertised clearance in the memory of employees. Invitation cards (printed, not engraved) were sent to all charge customers "announcing reduction in prices in certain of our stock." The reductions were flaunted, marked with bright-yellow price tags.

There were bargains—and news stories once more—galore. A lady's gold cigarette case with sapphires and diamonds was reduced from $14,000 to $8,000; a diamond-and-emerald brooch with the emerald from a Sultan's belt buckle, was cut from $52,000 to $29,700; a sterling-silver tea set from the nineteenth century was $12,000, down from $32,000. Low-priced items were also reduced: silver matchbox covers to $6.75 from $9; stemmed goblets from $22 to $11.

"You don't see women clawing and pushing to get at the counters," said one salesman, "but we have a sprightly traffic in handbags."

With the store cleared of much of what he did not like, including the silver plate and all leather handbags, Hoving put into operation Phase II: finding designers who could produce what he did like. First to be hired was Van Day Truex, who was retiring as head of the Parsons School of Design in New York. Hoving persuaded Truex to postpone his dreams of leisure to paint in southern France and set up design criteria for the china and silver departments. Next recruited were Nicolas Bongard and his partner, Jean Schlumberger, the latter to design the store's finest and most expensive jewelry. Schlumberger was firmly established as a jewelry designer, turning out pieces for such notables as Mrs. Byron Foy, Mrs. Mario Pansa, Angier Biddle Duke and Mrs. John Barry Ryan, who were also among the backers of the shop Schlumberger and Bongard had opened on East Sixty-third Street in 1947. Tiffany bought this business, but the partners kept a store in Paris. (The partners paid off their wealthy investors, giving them a 20 percent capital gain, once more proving the truth of that old saw that "them as has . . .")

The Schlumberger department found ample separate quarters on the mezzanine, with an elevator to the left of the Fifth Avenue en-

trance for its exclusive use. Hoving also brought Gene Moore into the
store to decorate the Tiffany windows. His ''decorations'' have been
hailed as works of art ''not to be missed on a visit to New York.''

To provide the proper background for the renaissance, the store
was completely redecorated. The rows of glass coffins on the second
floor which had contained the silver displays for more than fifty years
were replaced by tables. As for the china and crystal department on
the third floor, ''We got rid of that awful yellow,'' as Hoving remarked. Everything became a pale mauve. Hoving gave identical instructions to all his new tastemakers: ''Design what you think is
beautiful and don't worry about selling it. That's our job.''

Truex, a dapper man with bright-blue eyes, a pink face, iron-gray
hair and inexhaustible energy, ruthlessly weeded out everything in
china, glass and silver that *he* did not like. As the *Herald Tribune*'s
Priscilla Chapman said, ''When it comes to the question of taste, he's
spendidly opinionated, emphatically outspoken and dead right.''

This also could be said of Hoving, if his standards of taste are
judged by one important if worldly criterion—what happens to the
sales and profits of the store. In 1952 and 1953, Tiffany's had lost
$147,787 and $24,906 respectively. The store was in the black in 1955,
when Hoving took over, but profits dropped slightly when Hoving re-
organized the store, taking losses on most of the articles sold off in the
White Elephant Sale and spending money redecorating the store.
Then the improvement in taste, plus Hoving's merchandising skill,
began to pay off. Sales and profits rose steadily until, in 1961, profits
were $570,080. By that time, the image of Tiffany's had also changed,
from the high-priced store for the very rich to a high- and low-priced
store for all. At the annual meeting that year, Hoving held up before
stockholders a half-carat diamond ring with a Tiffany price tag of
$243.

''If you can find this ring anywhere at a lower price,'' Hoving told
stockholders, ''I'll give it to you.'' There were no takers.

The year 1961 produced not only a rosy balance sheet; it was also
the year that Walter Hoving gained unchallenged control of Tiffany's,
which he had not really had heretofore. Hoving did not own the Hoving Corporation. Control remained in the hands of Albert Greenfield
and his Bankers' Security Corporation, which owned 65 percent of
the stock. While Greenfield had always backed Hoving and given him
a free hand in running his corporation, there remained the possibility
that he might sell his block of stock.

That is precisely what happened, and a new character appeared
upon the stage. This was M. W. (Maxey) Jarman, president of Gen-

eral Shoe Corp. (later Genesco), a mammoth company which operated
eight hundred shoe stores throughout the country. Jarman, a Baptist
who has taught Bible classes on Sunday, is a Southerner, and so proud
of it that he always carries Confederate bills in his wallet. Jarman was
looking for a Fifth Avenue store to carry his new line of Christian
Dior shoes. He had tried Bonwit's but, having no luck, went over
Hoving's head to Greenfield, who also was cool to the idea. However,
Greenfield, who had a nice profit on his Hoving Corporation investment, had another thought: How would Jarman like to buy control of
the Hoving Corporation, and obtain control of Bonwit Teller and Tiffany's as well?

Jarman did not think twice. The shoe business is peculiar in that
it is spread out among many stores and many manufacturers. Genesco
had only 5 percent of the market. To increase his business, Jarman
was already selling men's and women's clothing in his shoe stores.
The acquisition of Bonwit's fitted in with his plans for expansion. The
deal was made, and control of the Hoving Corporation passed to
Genesco, along with Tiffany's, "almost by accident," as a Genesco
officer said.

Hoving and Jarman turned out to be personally incompatible.
Their disagreements came out into the open when Hoving resigned
from Bonwit's and announced that he was going to devote all his time
to Tiffany's. Then, when Huntington Hartford, the A&P heir, announced he was going to donate $862,000 for a café to be built in a
corner of Central Park at Fifth Avenue and Fifty-ninth Street,
Hoving filed suit in the name of Tiffany's to block the project. He felt
strongly that "no one should be allowed to encroach on the Park to
build monuments to themselves. If this café is allowed, where do you
stop?"

In the midst of the civic battle, Hoving received instructions from
Genesco to drop the suit. As the New York *Post* put it: "The stylishly
shod foot of the massive Tennessee corporation has booted Tiffany's
right out of the court fight." Hoving promptly filed another suit, this
time as an individual, and Jarman did not like this at all.

As Jarman put it, "Tiffany's did not fit into the Genesco operation," and to rid himself of both the store and the troublesome Hoving
he put Tiffany's up for sale, offering his stock at eighty dollars per
share. There was no rush of buyers, for the price was much too high,
and as Jarman had found out, the store could be run well only by
someone with sure taste as well as merchandising skill.

Hoving, who knew he had the combination, quietly began to put
together his own group to buy the stock. Among the investors were

W. Alton Jones, president of Cities Service Oil Company, and a collector of Tiffany jewelry; Mrs. Merriweather Post, another collector and the breakfast-food heiress; and pollster Elmo Roper, a one-time jeweler, who had always regarded Tiffany's as the most desirable company in the world.

The arithmetic went like this. The newly formed Hoving group bought the 51 percent from Genesco at the comparatively high price of eighty-four dollars a share. The company made an offer for Bulova's stock at sixty-five dollars a share. With the block of Bulova stock retired, the Hoving group's interest in Tiffany's rose to 78 percent, in effect lowering the original price the investors had paid per share. Baffled by Hoving's high-wire act, *The New Yorker* could only comment on the Genesco–Hoving feud that "Tiffany's was the consolation prize." Maybe so, but it was one of the fanciest consolation prizes in the world. True, no one but Hoving had wanted it, but that was because no one else knew what to do with it. Hoving did, since Tiffany & Co. was what he had wanted all along.

Hoving gambled on how much his customers would like his taste, and from 1961 through 1970 sales almost tripled and earnings per share (the stock was split until there were 1,729,000 shares), went from twenty-three cents to $1.40, a greater increase even than in the fantastically profitable years of the past century when the store was run by Charles Lewis Tiffany.

All of this seems to prove one of Hoving's favorite remarks: "Aesthetics, if properly understood, will almost always increase sales."

"Give Them What We Want"

alter Hoving could be the descendant of Charles Tiffany, if character alone were the genetic link. Like the first Tiffany, he is a superb merchandiser of unimpeachable integrity and strongly held, often iconoclastic, convictions. He has the same flair for publicity as Charles and is never at a loss for an answer to the press when one is needed.

In 1970 a columnist wanted to know who had designed the famous old six-prong setting. The question was passed up to Hoving, who said, "Tell him Charles Tiffany designed it." The story duly recorded this fact, and when Hoving was later reminded that there is no evidence that Charles ever designed anything, he replied smoothly, "Well, maybe not the actual drawing; but he probably said, 'I think the set-

(Above) The Tiffany Award.

ting ought to go like this,' '' gesturing with his fingers bent like a prong setting.

Hoving's dictum that Tiffany's was going to give the customer what *it* liked because what *it* liked the public ought to like was widely spread by the press. Also carried as news was Hoving's pronouncement on most American design: bad. It was implied that good design, as exemplified by Tiffany's, was synonymous with good taste. All this was not only good publicity, it was good business.

Unlike his predecessor, Louis de B. Moore, Hoving wanders about the store, listening to what customers have to say. He likes to tell about the day when he "ran into a very nice woman who was registering her daughter for wedding presents. She said she and her husband had scrimped and saved and sent their daughter to college and now that she was being married they wanted everything to come from Tiffany's, because if it did they were sure it would be all right. I asked her what her husband did and she told me, 'He's a mailman.' So we start with mailmen and go right up to millionaires. We are not interested in a person's social standing or anything else. If they like the same things we do, it's a love affair from then on."

There are those who do not make it a love affair ("All those jeweled bugs and things, ugh!"). But no one has quarreled with Hoving's basic tenet—that taste and design should play a more important part in what America makes.

Hoving keeps a folder in his desk filled with ads for products which he thinks are badly designed, adding a new horror from time to time. What makes him particularly indignant is a reference to Tiffany's (without permission, of course) to add glamor to a product. This always brings a sharp note from Hoving, such as this reaction to an ad of the Kimberly-Clark Corp., which headlined its "Tiffany Taste." Hoving wrote to the president, Guy M. Minard:

Dear Mr. Minard:
I am rather surprised that you would use our name in this advertisement without permission. Especially so since we wouldn't be seen dead with a jewel box that even had the slightest resemblance to the one pictured.
Nor do I think that the merchandise used in the background does credit to your great company. I think that, too, is just god-awful.

Hoving is so sincere in preaching his gospel of good taste that he might be said to be a fanatic on the subject, but there is doubt as to whether his edicts are as strictly observed as they are supposed to be. The rule that the store will not sell diamond rings for men, because

Tiffany's considers such rings in poor taste, is an essential part of the Hoving credo.

Nevertheless, the following is an example of what can happen.

A strapping Texan in a ten-gallon hat stopped at the diamond counter one day. With him was a small, pretty young man, wearing earrings and bracelets. They looked at all the rings, and the young man finally selected one for seventy-five thousand dollars and tried it on his little finger.

"We'll take that," said the tall Texan, "but it's too small."

"I'm sorry," said the salesman politely, "but we do not sell diamond rings for men." The customers were nonplussed, but only momentarily. The younger man spoke up: "Oh, no. You have it all wrong. It's for his girl and she wears the same size I do."

With that assurance, the salesman tapped for a messenger and the ring was sold. Sometime later, word drifted back from Neiman-Marcus in Dallas that N.M. had enlarged an expensive Tiffany diamond ring to fit a young man's finger.

Unlike the Tiffanys, who trace their ancestry in the United States back to the seventeenth century, Walter Hoving is an immigrant, whose parents are from Viborg, Finland, where his grandfather was a banker and a member of the Finnish Parliament. Hoving's father, Johannes, was a leading heart specialist. At the time of Hoving's birth, Finland was a duchy of Russia, and the Finns did not like the Russians any better then than they do now. Just before her son was born in December 1897, his mother, who had been a Danish star with the Royal Opera in Stockholm, went to Stockholm so that Walter would not be born a Russian.

Dr. Hoving had stayed out of politics, but when the Russian governor-general of Finland was stricken with a heart attack, he refused to treat him. Threatened with exile to Siberia, he prudently departed for the United States and, a year later, sent for his family. Ten years later, when Walter was just fifteen, that magic age when Charles Tiffany had entered the business world, he left school and took his first job, selling soap from door to door; he stuck it out for ten months before he decided this held no future, and returned to school.

After graduating in 1920 from Brown University, Hoving went to work, and out of his first five jobs he was fired from three. He decided to try merchandising and was put on the training squad at R. H. Macy & Co. He moved up fast, as if to make up for lost time, going from the research department to the job of assistant to the manager of the rug department, and then of assistant to a merchandising counselor, who supervised buyers. In 1928, at the age of thirty, he

(*Above*) *Helga Hoving, Danish opera star
and mother of Walter Hoving
(right) Board Chairman of Tiffany & Co.*

was made executive vice president and merchandise counselor in charge of buyers on the main floor at a salary of twenty thousand dollars a year.

Despite his fast climb, Hoving felt a great lack in his education; he knew nothing about design. He matriculated at New York University, which was then holding evening classes in design twice a week at the Metropolitan Museum of Art. He went to school for three years, studying historic textures and, as he says, "color and design of furniture, old silver, rugs, various paintings and things of that sort.

"While I was a vice president of Macy's," he recalls, "I had a table in my office which had a hundred small articles on it, covered by a cloth. When I interviewed people for the job of buyer or assistant buyer, I would often take the cloth off and say to them: 'Why don't you put the ones that are well designed on the right side of the table and the ones that are badly designed on the left side of the table.' Then I'd go out and take a walk around the store for fifteen minutes and come back and see what they had done. This not only evaluated what they knew about design but it quickly got out around the staff that you really had to have a very professional view of things of this sort. Many of the young people who had come to Macy's began to go to design classes."

After Hoving had been at Macy's for several years he went to Montgomery Ward in Chicago as vice president in charge of sales and advertising. One of his first actions was to organize a design department; at one time, there were thirty-two designers on the staff, who redesigned everything from packages to manure spreaders.

The aesthetic changes had commercial results. Hoving recalls: "I remember that one group of packages we made over was for harness oils and all the different kinds of things farmers keep in their barns. We designed a label that was bright red on the upper half and black on the lower half; the lettering on the red was black, while the lettering on the black was red. It was very startling but also simple and attractive. We did no special advertising for these products, but in the first year the sales increased some eight hundred per cent. We felt that it was entirely the aesthetic quality that sold it, even though the farmers had never heard about aesthetics."

Hoving stayed at Montgomery Ward's four years before he moved to the Associated Dry Goods Company, which owned Lord & Taylor, where he was named chairman, president and chief executive officer. He had finally moved from mass to class in merchandising.

The nation was still haunted by the tail end of the Depression, and the war boom had not yet started. There were more job seekers than jobs, and looking back on his own experiences, Hoving wrote his first book, *Your Career in Business.* "Face yourself, stop your eternal pampering of yourself . . . use your mind" was Hoving's advice.

By 1946, Hoving was ready to leave Lord & Taylor and be his own boss. He quit his $135,000-a-year job and set up the Hoving Corporation, raising $2,500,000 in capital from friends and $6,500,000 in a public stock issue.

Hoving looks as if he had been sent from Central Casting for the job. Now in his mid-seventies, he looks ten years younger and has no thought of retiring. "After all," he likes to remind people, "Charles Tiffany worked until he was ninety." Hoving talks easily and well, and tells a funny story with superb timing. One of his best involves the time the owner of the largest topless restaurant on the West Coast called him with an idea he thought would be good business for both his restaurant and Tiffany's. "I want to have the finest pasties in the business," he told Hoving, "and I want Tiffany's to make them." He had forty waitresses, with five reserves on call. Hoving said, "That makes forty-five." Pause, eyes withdrawn for an instant. "Doubled, of course." Hoving finishes the story: "He was willing to spend up to three thousand dollars on each pastie, whatever we suggested. When I told him we wouldn't fill the order he refused to believe me. 'You're throwing away nearly three hundred thousand dollars' worth of business,' he kept telling me."

In 1926 Hoving was married to Mary Osgood Field, a pretty and popular New York debutante. They had two children, Thomas and Petrea (nicknamed Petie), before they were divorced in 1936. A year later, Hoving married Pauline van der Voort Rogers, widow of Colonel Henry H. Rogers, the son of one of the founders of the Standard Oil Company.

The Hovings are in the Social Register, and Hoving belongs to the proper clubs—the River, Brook, Racquet and Tennis, the Pilgrims and the Creek; Mrs. Hoving is a member of the Colony Club and the National Society of Colonial Dames.

In one way or another Hoving's name was often in the news both before and after he took over Tiffany's. He was a man of opinions and he was not reluctant to voice them. As the long-time head of the Fifth Avenue Association, a group of the avenue's merchants, he fought the various city administrations on sales taxes and anything and everything else that he thought would adversely affect Fifth Avenue business.

Once, in a squabble with Mayor Fiorello (Little Flower) La Guardia, Hoving irked the mayor into remarking: "Hoving? Why,

Mayor Fiorello LaGuardia and wife with Jacob Ruppert.

I'm not going to turn this city over to a floorwalker.'' To which Hoving replied blandly: ''May I remind his Honor that every floorwalker wears a little flower in his buttonhole?''

One fight lost by Hoving and his group was to keep Fifth Avenue from being turned into a one-way street. Hoving called the advocates ''the lunatic fringe'' who would ruin the avenue. The ''lunatics'' won, but some still wonder if their victory has not helped in the march of real estate men bent on changing Fifth into another characterless avenue.

Hoving was so well-known as a merchant and civic do-gooder that he was asked several times to run for mayor. He always declined, explaining with tongue in cheek that as a native of Sweden the job would be a dead end; he could never be President. It was reported that once in the *Daily News* straw vote on possible mayoral candidates Hoving was elected. He himself laughs and says, ''I got three votes.'' Although he never became a city official, his son, Thomas, did; he became commissioner of parks in 1966 (he is now director of the Metropolitan Museum of Art).

When it comes to his basic interest, design, Hoving is always delighted to share his opinions, cheerfully unmindful of the shower of chips that may fall on the heads of his fellow merchandisers. He wrote an article for the Sunday *New York Times Magazine* with the premise that the backwardness of American design came from the

American tendency to copy European fashions "down to the last buttonhole." He wrote:

That the European businessman is usually aware of good design is not surprising. Living in cities like Rome, Florence, Venice, Paris, has meant that he has literally "walked in beauty" all his life. . . . such surroundings influence all who work with him.

The Roman ceramic manufacturer . . . has an excellent staff of designers, and is himself a man with a highly developed critical judgment. Compare this with our approach . . . When the designs are finished they are submitted to the vice president in charge of production . . . After which the rest of the company's executives review them. . . . Men who would never dream of expressing an opinion on law unless they were lawyers . . . cheerfully deliver themselves to judgments on color, form and style.

Hoving is also the author of a best seller, *Tiffany Table Manners for Teenagers*, which was inspired by his own experience in teaching manners to his children Tom and Petie.

In the book, which is still selling, Hoving says in a foreword: "It is dangerous to have one system of manners for home consumption and another for dining out. This is apt to cause dinner-table insecurity in later life."

Walter Hoving and President Truman.

Hoving's rules make the ritual of eating simple and natural. "First of all," he says, "let's get straight which fork or knife to use. Make a mistake? Just continue eating. *Don't* put the silver back on the table. Be nonchalant."

Other pointers: "You don't have to wait for your hostess to start eating, but don't leap at your food like an Irish wolfhound."

The soup spoon: "Don't hold it like a mashie niblick; this is not par for the course." The reason for spooning soup away from you? "If you spill some, it won't splash your clothes."

Asparagus: "If it is long and thin, cut off the ends . . . you will then avoid imitating a trained seal."

If a boy spills water on a girl, "don't start mopping her. It might be misunderstood." Book sellers believe that the little volume is as much read by adults as by children.

On questions of taste, Hoving brooks no compromise, not even when the President of the United States is concerned. President John Kennedy asked the store to make some small calendar plaques showing October 1962, the month of the Cuban missile crisis, to give to his aides. The President wanted the plaques done in Lucite. Hoving declined politely. He suggested silver.

"We do not make anything out of plastics," he told the President. "If you want them, you'll have to go somewhere else, although I don't think you'll like them in Lucite."

Kennedy did go somewhere else for his plaques. When they were delivered he did not like them. Somewhat sheepishly he went back to Tiffany's and had them redone—in silver.

Hoving, an old friend of Ike's, likes to tell the story about the time Eisenhower, when he was President, came into the store to see about a gold medallion he had designed to give his wife. It was to be quite simple: on one side, a star in a wreath, and inside the wreath the words "To Mamie"; on the other side the inscription "For never failing help since 1916—in calm and in stress, in dark days and in bright. Love, Ike, Christmas, 1955."

With Tiffany president William Lusk joining Ike and Hoving, the conference over the medallion took place in Hoving's teak-paneled office on the fifth floor.

After Ike had explained what he wanted, he asked, with his famous grin, "As President of the United States don't I get a discount?"

Hoving swung around in his chair and looked at the picture of Mary Todd Lincoln, wearing her Tiffany pearl necklace, which always stands on a low window shelf behind him in the office.

1. Don't forget, the finger bowl is not a bathtub. Don't dunk hands.

2. An artichoke is eaten with fingers.

3. Cut off ends of asparagus. Avoid imitating a trained seal.

4. If you spill water, don't start mopping your partner's dress.

5. Don't leap at food like a wolfhound.

6. If you drop your knife or fork don't dive for it. Pick up another.

Tiffany's Table Manners for Teen-Agers turned out to be also a best seller among parents.

Mary Todd Lincoln wearing her pearl necklace and earrings.

"I really haven't been here long enough to know," said Hoving. "Perhaps Mr. Lusk can tell you what the practice is."

"Well," said Lusk, "we didn't give any discount to Lincoln."

It amused Ike, and certainly did nothing to strain the Eisenhower-Hoving relationship. (On the occasion of the state visit of Queen Elizabeth II and Prince Philip in August of 1957, Mr. and Mrs. Hoving were among the very few guests from outside the administration.)

The picture of Mrs. Lincoln had been a nagging reminder to Hoving of a gap in the Tiffany legend, because, following the pattern of historic jewelry, the necklace disappeared in the last century. On Lincoln's Birthday in 1970, Tiffany's ran an ad showing only a copy of the picture of Mrs. Lincoln in Hoving's office. Shortly after, Executive Vice President La Bar Hoagland received a phone call from Mrs. Melvin Dichter, of Stamford, Connecticut. She said she believed she had the Lincoln necklace, and would like to check with him. Always interested in tracking down a historic piece, Hoagland asked Mrs. Dichter to bring in the necklace.

She told an interesting story. Her great-grandfather, an auction buff, attended an auction at the time Mrs. Lincoln's jewelry was sold, and it was his understanding that he had purchased the Lincoln necklace and earrings. Since the necklace was too tight for his wife, he had the earrings set into the string to lengthen it. Upon examination, Hoagland could see where the earrings had been attached without any change, except that the fasteners on the back had been removed. Comparison of Mrs. Dichter's necklace, which has the Tiffany mark, with the Tiffany picture proved that the necklace is indeed the Lincoln pearls.

Another story told about Hoving concerned what one paper referred to as "Hoving's 24-carat gold heart." In December 1964, Tiffany's advertised a $176,000 square-cut diamond ring. The ad caught the eye of David Jablonski, the eleven-year-old son of author Ed Jablonski, who wrote a letter to Tiffany's.

Dear Tiffany's:

I saw your ad about the $176,000 ring. I would like to buy it for my mother. But my allowance is fifty cents a week. Could we work out some kind of arrangement?

Sincerely,
David Jablonski.

The letter ended on Hoving's desk, as such things usually do. He answered this one:

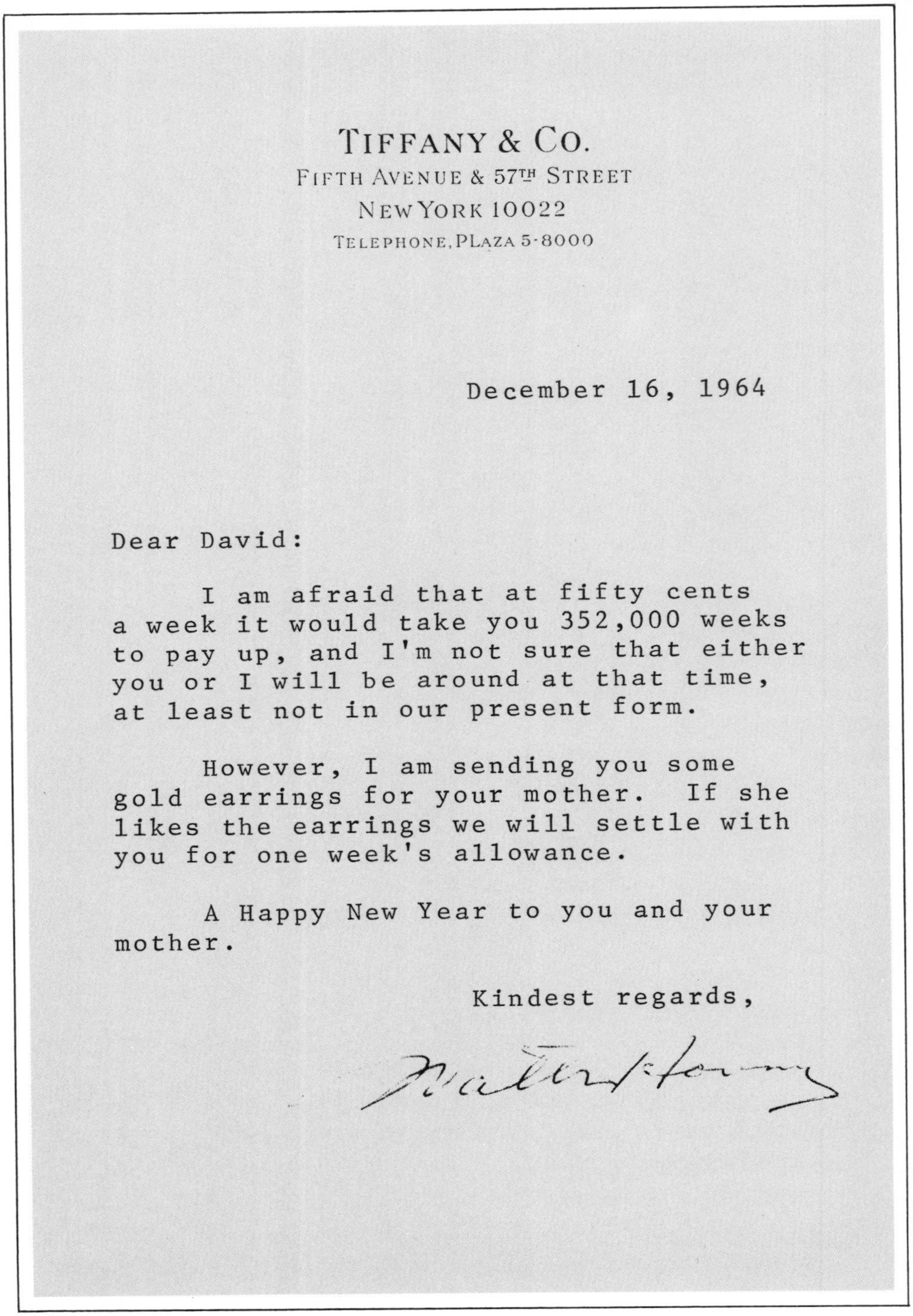

TIFFANY & CO.
FIFTH AVENUE & 57TH STREET
NEW YORK 10022
TELEPHONE, PLAZA 5-8000

December 16, 1964

Dear David:

I am afraid that at fifty cents
a week it would take you 352,000 weeks
to pay up, and I'm not sure that either
you or I will be around at that time,
at least not in our present form.

However, I am sending you some
gold earrings for your mother. If she
likes the earrings we will settle with
you for one week's allowance.

A Happy New Year to you and your
mother.

Kindest regards,

A present of earrings.

Another letter was written to Tiffany's current president, Farnham Lefferts, a nephew of Mrs. Louis de Bèbian Moore, in 1967. Like David's, this letter, too, was considered to be in Hoving's province.

Dear Mr. Lefferts:

In 1887 the Missouri-Kansas-Texas Railway Company was building south through Oklahoma and down through Texas. My grandfather was in charge of building bridges and trestles. In Texas he met and fell in love with Grandmother. On his next business trip to New York he bought their engagement ring at Tiffany's—a center sapphire (her birthstone) circled with 12 pearls, a turquoise at top and bottom of circle, set upon an engraved band of gold.

Down through the years the ring became much more than an engagement ring. It was a talisman, a good luck charm, a worker of "miracles." When Grandmother's children were ill, she would place the Tiffany ring on a little thumb and say, "This ring will make you well, but you must believe in it. Take your medicine, stay in bed, do as the doctor says or the ring can't work to make you well quickly." As my uncles and aunts grew older, many times an excited young aunt would dash in with, "Quick, Mother, the Tiffany ring. I want to wear it so Joe will take me to the dance," or, "I'll get the lead in the school play," or, "I'll be selected for solo in the concert."—The Tiffany ring never failed. It always brought about the desired "miracle."

Grandmother died and Mother inherited the Tiffany ring and it retained all its "magic" qualities. When I was a child my mother and I were on a train going from Texas to Oklahoma City. A flood washed out the bridge over the Canadian River. Our train was stopped for hours. Long past midnight word came that an engine and cars had been sent from Oklahoma City and was waiting on the opposite bank. The women and children were loaded in wagons and hauled to the edge of the water. The men walked carrying torches of bound cornstalks, dipped in oil and ignited. The pitch-black night, the roaring waters, the flaming torches made an eerie and frightening scene to a child. I cried and Mother said, "Nothing can harm us, I have the Tiffany ring in my purse." She felt in her lap; the purse was gone. She hopped out of that wagon and ran back the path we had traveled. She found the purse squashed in a muddy wagon rut. Back she came, and we were put into the boat. The swift current made rowing agonizing for the men and at times the boat tipped perilously. The women screamed, the children cried. Then Mother shouted, "SHUT UP! every one of you! I have a good luck charm in my purse that has never failed. We will get safely across but every one of you be silent and believe." Then, not another whimper or scream and of course we landed on the other side without incident.

At Mother's death the ring became mine. The 12 little pearls had blackened. I took the ring to a jeweler to have them replaced. In the conversation I mentioned the ring came from Tiffany's in 1887. He snorted, "Impossible! They probably were not in business then, but if they were, the ring does not have the Tiffany mark and all their merchandise bears their mark." I was stunned. I had the same feeling as if someone had told me my child was not really mine.

All this leads to a request, please. In view of this marvelous ring's long history of good deeds and its "magic" qualities, would you be kind enough to overlook the argument whether it did or did not come from your place of business in 1887 (I am still convinced that it did), and have your engraver place your mark on it so my child who will inherit this ring will not be hurt as I was.

If this can be done, I will send the ring and a check promptly if I may know the engraving charge.   *Sincerely,*

K—— H—— L——

The lady mailed her letter on October 5. Hoving's answer was in the mail four days later.

Dear Mrs. L—:

I have your letter with the incredible story of the magic properties of your Tiffany ring. You can just tell that jeweler that Tiffany is 130 years old and had been in business just exactly 50 years in 1887. I would say that there isn't any question that the ring came from Tiffany. Your grandfather certainly knew where he bought it.

You just send the ring on in care of me and we'll be very glad to put Tiffany's name on it free of charge. I would also like personally to see such a remarkable ring.   *Kindest regards,*

Walter Hoving

If incidents such as this are a reminder of the "magic" of the Tiffany legend, there are other anecdotes which illustrate why the legend has to change with the times. One afternoon, a young man in Levi's and an old army coat walked barefooted into the store, carrying his shoes. He stopped at the watch counter, where the salesman asked him politely if he would mind putting on his shoes.

"I'd rather not," the young man replied politely. "My feet hurt."

The young customer pored over the cases for some time and bought a watch for a thousand dollars. When the incident was later related to Hoving his comment was: "Good, that proves we're getting the younger generation."

N ot only was the store
"getting the younger generation," but it was attracting customers
from a generation which had not ventured inside its doors for the past
twenty years. This was the rapidly growing affluent middle class,
where the merchandising future lay, the class on which so much bad
design had been inflicted. In the words of Van Day Truex: "The designers . . . often lack taste because they think they were born with
it. They sit in a dark room trying to create something original. It's a
misspent effort. Outside of scientific advances everything has been
done and I think there is so much bad design as there is because the
designers try to be original rather than selective."

Truex himself was "selective," looking everywhere for new ideas,

(Above) Benjamin Franklin.

Van Day Truex (left), George O'Brien (right).

from the Museum of Natural History in New York to the Pitti Palace in Florence, and in the fashionable houses where he was invited to dinner. In the Pitti he saw an ivory pagoda from the Far East; Truex had it duplicated in silver for Tiffany's, and it remains one of the store's handsomest and most popular centerpieces. One morning he arrived at the china department, bubbling with excitement. Under his arm was a package which contained a Japanese porcelain bowl with a blue-and-white design.

"I borrowed it from my hostess last night," Truex explained to the staff. "Can't you just see this as a ravishing plate, keeping just the center and eliminating the rest?" Not only was a plate made, but Truex's enthusiasm turned the creative mind of the department back to Japan, that excellent source of wares in the first days of Charles Tiffany.

Truex told the china department, "China should look like it is made for an individual rather than being based on statistics that supposedly show mass taste." His idea of a "personal design" was a plate pattern with a strawberry and blossoms in the center.

"George Washington had it in his house and it's just as delightful now as then," he said. "It's timeless. Quality is aloof from fashion. Fashion will change, but an article of the right design will remain in fashion forever."

There were endless news stories when Tiffany's introduced vermeil (pronounced vair-may) in 1956. As a matter of record, the proper word would be "reintroduced" since Tiffany's had sold French vermeil for a time after 1845. The ware had been a great favorite with the French nobility, for whom gold plate was a chancy luxury at a time when the Sun King, and the rulers who followed, were apt to confiscate such ware and melt it down to pay for the greater *gloire* of

France in wars or the boudoir of La Pompadour. The smiths of the day had a clever method of coating silver with gold, giving a luxurious effect but one less likely to tempt a monarch. Unfortunately, vermeil workmen tended to go blind, and in the early 1800's scientists discovered that they were being poisoned by the mercury in the process. The nineteenth century proved more enlightened about mercury pollution than the twentieth—the manufacture of vermeil by the mercury process was banned by law (and it still is).

The beauty of the old pieces had always appealed to Truex, and after months of experimenting, the Tiffany factory finally found the solution: the secret lay in two separate plating processes, the first with 18½-carat gold, the second with 22½-carat gold. The result was a rosy glow, virtually identical with the mercury-process vermeil.

A certain amount of nonsense has been written about vermeil—for example, that it should be washed in champagne. It can be, of course, if one wants to waste champagne. Mild soap flakes and warm water do the job better, if not as romantically.

"Everyone should have one set of pure white china before anything else," is one of Truex's dicta, and he chose a set made by Wedgewood. This took a bit of negotiating, since Tiffany's had dropped all Wedgewood several years before, claiming the designs were not popular. Wedgewood says that Tiffany's had cut prices and was dropped by Wedgewood. In any case, although the white china was stocked and some other designs as well, Wedgewood blue never came back. If a customer asks for it, he is told the name of a shop where it may be found.

The Truex tradition has been continued by his hand-picked successor, George O'Brien, who came from *The New York Times*, where he was home furnishings editor. The responsibility for design decisions, however, has been broadened. They are now made by six boards which "edit" all Tiffany designs. The boards take their duties seriously, meet often and consider every new piece of merchandise. For example, at a recent session of the silver board, which lasted two hours, much of the time was spent examining a small silver bell which had a buttonlike appendage on top. Everyone felt that the shape was not quite right—either the button was too big or too small or there should be something instead of the button—but no one had a better idea. Finally, the bell was put aside for the next meeting.

Asked whether Tiffany's tries to cater to the woman's point of view, George O'Brien said, "Generally the thing we try to keep in mind is the quality—so it will be right for our women customers, so she won't ever be ashamed to own it. Suppose every woman in the country decided she wanted something, and we decided it was bad design. We're under no obligation to make it or sell it to them. The principle back of this isn't arrogance; we believe that sooner or later the customer will discover what she has bought is bad and she won't like it; we'd rather she got mad at somebody else.

"There is a large plate sold [at other places] that comes with a well in the center to hold a cup and a sandwich. There are a lot of women who don't know any better who think that this is an absolute necessity. But it's bad design; it's like a blue-plate special. It's precious and we will not have it in the store."

"There is a certain amount of stuff that we put out there that will never sell well," says La Bar Hoagland, executive vice-president, "but it creates an atmosphere that enables us to sell a hell of a lot of other stuff." This gets back to the old museum idea; women come in to look at articles they could not possibly afford, and then they see something within their own price range.

Some of the tasks of the design board are more glamorous than others, though it isn't every day that any store is called upon to turn out the flatware and china for the king of Morocco or to design new china for the White House; in fact, the set Tiffany's did for the Johnsons was the first to be ordered since the Truman administration. The association between Tiffany's and Morocco began in 1956, when the father of King Hassan II shopped in the store, and recommended it to his son. When Hassan decided to refurbish his favorite hunting lodge, he turned to Tiffany's. The company has an international department, headed by Anthony Holberton-Wood, the very model of a British major (which he was) and a veteran of the British diplomatic service. With his clipped accent and his Briticisms (he always refers to Hoving as "the Chair"), he gives the correct note of formality to

La Bar Hoagland.

Tiffany's dealings with heads of state, ambassadors and lesser fry from the embassies, all good customers.

When Holberton-Wood heard that the King was in a shopping mood, he hustled abroad and found that the hunting lodge was in the Atlas Mountains, abounding with lordly stags. O'Brien suggested that the handles of the knives, forks and spoons be in the shape of a stag's hoof, with enough of the foreleg added so that the whole would not be too bulky. The drawings were sent to the King and approved; a model was made and also approved.

In working on a design for the King's china, Holberton-Wood discovered that the monarch's favorite tree was the cedar of Lebanon; in fact, he was so fond of it that he had a grove planted around the hunting lodge. This time, Holberton-Wood took the subway to the New York Botanical Gardens in the Bronx and got a snippet from a cedar tree, from which a simple pattern was devised: four leaves forming a cross in the center of the plates—pale green against stark white. All told, Hassan bought forty-eight settings of the vermeil, and the same of the china, adding the correct number of service plates in vermeil and matching candelabra and ash trays. The order took two and one half years to complete.

The design and manufacture of the White House china took even longer: three years from the first drawing until the last plates were delivered after President Nixon was in office. New china for the White House is no luxury; when LBJ moved in, there was not enough of any one service for state dinners, and the china supply was eked out by mixing in remains of services of three or four preceding administrations. China has always been one of the minor problems of the highest office in the land since the time when Old Hickory's supporters smashed a few pieces. Some Presidents, like Washington, brought their own. Buchanan had to use china from the Jackson through the Pierce era, and the different designs of eight administrations caused a reporter to note that the dishes were ''more or less odd.''

All the sets were imported until Woodrow Wilson insisted that a United States firm have the business. Wilson's service was bordered in a deep cobalt-blue, rimmed in gold and bearing the Presidential seal. Harding, Coolidge and Hoover all used the Wilson china, making do when necessary. F.D.R. added a new service, much like Wilson's but with a border feather from his family's arms. Truman also was forced to buy a new set, because of breakage and the steady growth in the size of the state dinners. Eisenhower made do with Truman's, but added service plates with a wide buff-and-gold border; and the Kennedys went along with what was on hand.

When the Johnsons took over, they found a strange mixture: there were pieces of historical value, almost too precious to be used at all; quite a lot of the Wilson-through-Truman period remained, but not enough for a complete state dinner. For smaller affairs Mrs. Johnson liked to use the Rutherford B. Hayes service, a handsome collection portraying vegetables, coon dogs, buffaloes, Indians, bears and turtles, along with wild turkeys and other fowl shown flying into melodramatic sunsets.

At first, LBJ wanted the china done in his native state. It took some time for him to convince himself—or be convinced by Ladybird —that no one in Texas was up to the job. Mrs. Johnson chose Tiffany's, and the immense amount of research and work began. The First Lady wanted to break with the cold formality of the past; besides the Hayes set, she had the precedent of Washington's charming flowered pattern. Dignity, she felt, did not have to be solemn or pompous, and she thought of the nature of Americans as happy, friendly and outgoing.

Truex himself took over the assignment, with Holberton-Wood serving as liaison with the White House. He worked up a dozen or so conventional and fairly formal designs; they were rejected. Then he asked Mrs. Johnson to consider a series based on the country's wild flowers. Ladybird was delighted; the concept fitted her own beautification program.

Ninety of our native wild flowers appear in the service. The paintings are so delicate that many of the pieces are done in twelve or fifteen colors. As a bow to tradition, certain plates are adorned with the American eagle, copied from Monroe's china. The service plates are centered with the eagle, bordered with wild flowers, and both the eagle and wild flowers are worked into the borders of the dinner plates. The dessert plates each carry a different state flower in the center. Tiffany artist André Piette gave the service an early American yet modern look; instead of painting only the blossom he painted the whole plant—flower, stems and roots—in the style of books on botany in the eighteenth century.

The 2,190 perfect plates were manufactured by Castleton, of Newcastle, Pennsylvania. Fortunately for the special fund given by private donors who footed the bill for the $80,000 service, the dinners themselves—and, therefore, the china requirements—no longer match the ones given by President Grant. In the Grant regime, dinners of twenty-nine courses, with services for each, were commonplace; a twenty-minute promenade and a glass of Roman punch at mid-meal perked up appetites for the second half.

As a final test before the White House china was approved for manufacture, Mrs. Johnson gave a candlelight dinner, with Major Holberton-Wood among the guests. The question was whether the background of the plates should be the then chic dead-white or the more old-fashioned cream. By candlelight the flowers proved too startling on white, so cream it was.

White House dinners during the Johnson regime averaged a hundred and ninety guests, so a service was made for two hundred and fifty. As further insurance, six duplicates were made, but not painted, for each piece in the service.

Scarcely had the last of Johnson's service been delivered when word came from the White House that Mrs. Nixon wanted a new service. The reason, said Mrs. Helen Smith, then director of press relations for the First Lady, was that "every President chooses his own new set of dishes." When White House reporters pointed out that this was not true, Mrs. Smith tried again. "I think sometimes they didn't have enough of the Johnson china." She said that some had been broken before the Johnsons left office and more had disappeared when the settings had been flown to Paris for Nixon's reciprocal dinner honoring De Gaulle. Reporters informed her that only two pieces had been broken (one under the Johnson regime, one under Nixon). Furthermore, it was the Truman set that had been flown to Paris. The truth is that the Nixons do not like the Johnson china, which the columnist Eugenia Sheppard noted was "much gayer and less loaded with protocol" than older patterns. (If ordered, the Nixon china would undoubtedly be "loaded with protocol," in line with other moves toward formality of the Nixon administration.)

While the Johnson service is the most recent one made for a head of state, it is not the most expensive. That honor belongs to the Royal Copenhagen set made for Catherine the Great of Russia which was reproduced and is sold by Tiffany's.

The price for this regal set starts with $350 for a five-piece place setting, although any hostess will tell you that a nine-piece setting would be a better estimate of what would be needed for the sort of dinner at which the china might be used. There are egg cups at $87 and pot-de-crèmes for $187, each pot with its own separate tray (quite unusual, making the individual pots a favorite gift). The complete service, with dessert, fish and fruit plates, platters, tureens and covered serving dishes, costs thousands of dollars. Most people stand away from the open display on the third floor—to replace the tureen alone would cost over $1,100. As might be expected, in the light of Catherine's known preferences, it is also the most ornate pattern in the department. Imperial taste ran to a great deal of gold, with enamels and hand-painted centers. The half-inch rim of rippled gold on the dinner plates is ornamented with raised dots of gold. Flowers and leaves were not considered too informal for the Court of St. Petersburg. The dinner-plate flowers are as botanically detailed as the Washington, Hayes and Johnson services, the backs of the plates even noting the Latin names of the flowers.

The fish service is painted with breathtaking fidelity to nature, and visitors always stop before it. The plates are in muted marine colors, and the fish seem to swim underwater, beneath sea plants, or to leap over an incoming wave. There are twelve different pictures, so that in a service for a dozen not a scene is repeated.

The workmanship is so detailed that it takes three years to deliver the complete Catherine the Great service after it is ordered. This is not a record. The odd piece of china that is primarily decorative can take even longer. In 1965 a customer admired a pair of tall branched candelabra, with a price in the thousands. Regretfully the salesman told her that this item was made to order in Germany and that Tiffany's could not promise that she would receive it within a period under five years. The customer was agreeable, and Tiffany's man was accurate almost to a day. The candelabra arrived in May 1970.

Nautically minded purchasers who wish to drop another royal name (and who can afford $215 per plate) can have copies of the china Queen Elizabeth II uses today on the royal yacht. The pattern leans heavily to cobalt-blue with ropes in heavy gold, coiled and braided around the rim.

Looking around the floor today, it is hard to find that set of plain white china Truex ruled so important. The place is a rainbow—Tiffany's arranges its displays by color—and the prevailing impression is that the design board likes its china bright and decorated with anything that crawls, flies or grows.

Occasionally, all this botany can be confusing. Two or three years ago the china department received a call from a woman in Texas who had seen a picture of Tiffany china in "some bride's magazine, with vegetables, insects, flowers and that sort of thing." Her husband was building her a French provincial house in a town in the middle of some oil fields (the husband owned both); she had no idea of the name or date of the magazine but she simply had to have that particular china. Tiffany's public relations department tracked down the magazine and phoned the woman: the plates were special German imports at two hundred dollars apiece. Delighted that she would be receiving her two dozen plates, the customer confided: "They're just the thing I need for my kitchen.'' (The designer of these plates had his little German joke. The pattern includes very lifelike lady-bugs; on one out of every six or seven plates, a ladybug seems to have escaped and can be found hiding on the underside of the rim.)

Tiffany's two most illustrious designers from the eighteenth century are a nobleman, the Earl of Coventry, and our own Benjamin Franklin. Franklin had his set made by Royal Worcester when he was our man in Europe. The pattern, in rich cobalt-blue and gold, features an American eagle in the center of the plate.

In 1770 the Earl ordered a set of china to be decorated with a pattern of one of his own rosebushes. Soon after, he was blinded in a hunting accident, and to ensure that he would get what he had ordered, the Earl had the set made with a raised design, a sort of early Braille, so that he could trace the leaves and buds with his fingers—hence, the Blind Earl pattern.

The Royal Worcester assortment of porcelain flowers (dogwood, daffodils, tulips, etc.) is exclusive with Tiffany's—only because no one else has the courage to carry it. The reason for this is that, although breakage in the store is great and the problems in shipping greater, the store guarantees to deliver every flower undamaged—thus, the store's uneasy monopoly.

Oddly enough, bone china, which looks the most fragile, is the strongest. In the seventeenth century, the English discovered that porcelain, first imported from China in 1470, could be made finer and stronger by mixing the clay with the ashes of bones. A new salesman had his lesson in applied science on his first day at Tiffany's. Told to ''look around, touch all the patterns, get acquainted with them,'' he was in the process of doing so when he knocked over a complete place setting. As the china came tumbling down, the alarmed young man grabbed wildly, helped by two nearby shoppers. They caught everything but two plates. With visions of his new job gone before it started, he managed to make himself look down—not a chip.

Strong it may be, but bone china is not impervious to the greatest enemy of expensive dinnerware: the electric dishwasher. Delicate, hand-painted patterns fade after repeated washings with harsh dishwasher detergents. Some wealthy customers who feel that they cannot live without the appurtenances of gracious dining, but who cannot find the help willing to clean up afterward, have solved the problem by buying three identical sets of china and rotating them. Eventually all the design comes out in the wash, but much later.

''In our silver department,'' Walter Hoving says, ''some of our articles are created by the foremost designers in the world, and some are designed by God.'' What he means is that the most imaginative silver pieces are blown-up copies of tiny seed pods and microscopic plants, less than a quarter inch long in their natural state. Enlarged to scale, they are eight to eleven inches in diameter, and made by skilled workmen in Mexico with great patience. A small cactus, for example, is covered with ten thousand tiny spines, each soldered separately by hand.

"What on earth do you use that for?'' a browser asked a salesman, pointing to a vermeil seed pod.

"To look at, to feel, to enjoy,'' the salesman replied. Two were given by President and Mrs. Eisenhower to the King and Queen of Thailand during their state visit here in 1960. Another White House favorite is the vermeil rose, which the City of New York gave to Princess Margaret. Mrs. Onassis is given credit for making these eight-inch roses "growing'' in clay pots such popular gifts, since she ordered them in large quantities when she was First Lady, but it was actually Mamie Eisenhower who started the custom when she chose them as presents for wives of illustrious visitors.

The question "But will it work?'' is often asked about another article, a frying pan of sterling silver, bottom and all. It is guaranteed not to melt over the hottest top-of-the-stove flame. A French chef was so fascinated that he bought ten of them (at $415 apiece) to take home as gifts.

Once in a while, an article will sell beyond merchandising reason. Several Christmases ago the store imported a stag of brushed silver from Italy. He was a noble beast, with magnificent antlers—handsome, but not particularly practical. One assistant decided that the appeal lay in the creature's warm eyes, which contrasted with his majestic whole. The stag was placed in a window as part of the holiday décor. The store had imported ten, the price was twenty-two hundred dollars; all were sold within a week.

Tiffany's likes its little conceits, like the berry boxes, which duplicate (in silver at $350; in vermeil, $380) the cheap wooden ones on every roadside stand, down to the rough grain and the cracks in the wood. The silver is so heavy, the empty boxes weigh a great deal more than the fruit-laden variety at the stands.

Tiffany's brings its china, silver and vermeil together in its fashion show of table settings, given at different seasons of the year. What makes the displays notable is the cooperation of rich and prominent Tiffany customers who are happy to put their concepts on view. The displays are something of an illustrated Amy Vanderbilt of the table: what Mrs. Vincent Astor has done, a person not sure of her own taste

1. *Johnson White House service plate.*

4. *Catherine the Great plate.*

2. *Independence plate by Benjamin Franklin.*

5. *Old Spode pattern.*

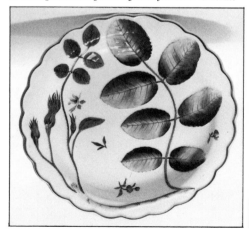

3. *The blind earl.*

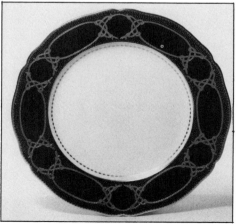

6. *Royal yacht of Elizabeth II.*

1. *Silver objects d'art.*

4. *Vermeil rose.*

2. *Silver seed pod.*

5. *Nine-sided coffee pot.*

3. *Berry basket.*

6. *Silver open-work tureen.*

Flatware: Audubon, Rat Tail, and Olympian patterns.

would feel she also could do. Mrs. William Woodward, one of New York's *grandes dames*, Mrs. Mellon Bruce, Mrs. Lytle Hull, Mrs. John Pierrepont, Mrs. Ogden Mills and Mrs. Gordon Douglas are among those who have participated. Clare Boothe Luce set her table to show off her lace place mats, which were especially made for her in Venice when she was ambassador to Italy. Mrs. John R. Drexel III achieved a ''country look'' by combining a bare table, fruit in green and pink, and three vermeil boxes in the shape of an artichoke, a lemon and an orange. Mrs. William S. Paley chose to do ''Breakfast at Tiffany's'' with easy chairs, crewel pillows for the back, and brioche in a silver mesh basket.

When the series started in the 1950's, President and Mrs. Eisenhower graciously lent the antique vermeil collection willed to the White House by Margaret Thompson Biddle, the pièce de resistance being the footed tureen which Louis XV had given to the Prussian ambassador. The most elaborate service displayed was that of Mrs. William Randolph Hearst when she recreated a turn-of-the-century dinner. The silver service plates were the ones Tiffany's had made for her with a deep, sculptured wreath, an inch and a half wide, around the rim. The flatware, of sterling inlaid with copper, and appropriately named Aztec, also was designed for Mrs. Hearst by Tiffany's. Each handle of the forks and spoons has a different Indian motif, some so elaborate that they extend outward from the stems more than an inch —handsome but spiky in the hands. The knives are conventionally smooth with the sun disks of the Aztecs in graduated sizes of copper embedded in the silver. The stemware was Louis Comfort Tiffany's Favrile.

It is the Tiffany flatware which indicates that, as in generations past, a start has been made toward setting up a proper household. Engaged girls select their patterns from twenty-nine on display and note their choices in the store's ''Bride's Register,'' together with preferences in china and crystal, for the convenience of gift-giving friends and relatives.

The popularity of Tiffany silver is largely due to the fact that, ounce for ounce, it is among the lowest-priced silver sold and no one likes a bargain better than the rich. Even the critical Mr. Maidman bought his flatware at the store.

The grandest designs are the oldest, and oldest of all is the Rat Tail, generally considered the first matching place setting made, which is an import from England. The name came not from the curl at the end of the knife handle, as some customers believe, but from the way the spoon is made. Early craftsmen could not make a spoon that would not break under pressure at the joint between the handle and the bowl, unless it was given extra support. They invented a supporting spine on the back that looked like a rat's tail. Science has long since learned how to make spoons without the spine, but it still can be found on the back of the Rat Tail spoons.

The most elaborate patterns are the Olympian and the Audubon, both designed by Tiffany's before 1878. If anything happens to the dies, they will not be made again; the intricate designs are beyond the capabilities of modern craftsmen. The Audubon, naturally, is based on the bird paintings, with eight species represented. But it is the Olympian which is the Zeus of the lot. There are seventeen different designs for the front of the silver, and each has its complementary smaller design on the back. To be really appreciated, Olympian needs a magnifying glass and some time. Also, as a salesman pointed out, the bas-reliefs, for that is what they are, show up better if the piece is slightly tarnished—not advocated, but true.

All the flatware, except the Rat Tail, is made in the factory in Forest Hills, New Jersey, which the firm built in 1897. The press of the day described it as "a fine brick structure, without any attempt at ornamental effects." An article written in 1968 saw it as "a castle straight out of the Middle Ages, complete with turrets and spire." A huge two-story structure, built around a hollow square, the main entrance is in a four-story tower, topped by a Norman spire. The building resembles a fortress in more than looks; it was designed to be almost completely self-sufficient. The Norman tower is utilitarian; it holds a

The silver factory, Forest Hills, N.J.

Silver etching, enameling and finishing department (1897).

23,000-gallon water tank, in case of fire; an artesian well in the court-yard adds another 87,000 gallons of water. The only material which has to be brought in to operate the plant is coal, used both for heat and to make electricity. The castle was the first factory in the world to have machinery entirely electrified.

With minor modifications, the firm's silverware continues to be made by the "new method" invented by Charles Tiffany and Edward Moore in the 1850's, when they applied mass production to what had always been a hand art. The process of manufacture was described in the 1870's at the time it was used to make Mrs. William Vanderbilt's $25,000 fish service: "The plates of the fish service are like small salmon, all fashioned with covers and provided with handles, so that they can be kept hot . . . the ice cream plates are made like clover leaves, with special spoons shaped like shovels."

In effect, what Tiffany and Moore did was to take a potter's wheel, set it horizontally instead of perpendicularly on a lathe, and run it by steam. Excepting that, since 1897, the lathe has been turned by electricity, the following account in the press of the 1870's is accurate today.

The silver ingots, already tested for purity, are crushed between two steel rollers . . . drawn closer and closer together, until it comes out a wide, smooth sheet, from $\frac{1}{16}$th to $\frac{1}{8}$th inch in thickness. From this, a chip is cut to go to the mint for assay . . . no silver is allowed to go to the workmen without this ceremony. The workman [making a bowl]

*consults the plan from the designing room and cuts two circular pieces
for the bowl and its base, and sends them off to the spinner. The spinner takes the larger circular piece for the bowl and fastens it to the
axle of the lathe between two pieces of wood, one of which is shaped
like the inside of the bowl. Then comes a surprise; the lathe begins to
whirl; outlines of the wood and silver dim. With a long, blunt-pointed
steel lever, the workman brings a steady pressure upon the edge of
the plate furthest from the block. It begins to curl up at the edges,
gradually taking on the shape of a huge saucer . . . the pressure is
continued, the softened metal flows up under the instrument, and
when the lathe at last stops a symmetrical bowl is removed from the
block. Until the spinning process was introduced by Tiffany & Co.,
all the shaping was done by hand. One hundred thousand blows were
sometimes expended on the body of a tea pot.*

The pieces are finished by hand, in 1971 as in 1870. Having been
cut and spun, the parts of a more complicated piece, such as a tea or
coffee pot, are given to a craftsman to solder together. The parts are
all carefully numbered (the work is custom-made to the extent that
the spout of one pot would not fit the body of another). The final step
is the polishing, first on a wheel covered with walrus hide, and then
by hand to what is called the butler's finish.

Engraving silver takes a highly skilled hand. After outlining the
letters in white chalk, the engraver boldly carves—virtually free hand
—the inscription, a thin sliver of silver curling up from under the
point of the tool. And if he makes a mistake? What happens was noted
by another jeweler: ''The policy of the store has always been one of
absolute integrity in little things as well as big ones,'' he wrote. ''If a

Stationery department brochure.

Tiffany engraver makes a slip while cutting an inscription on a watch cap, he is not allowed to cover up the scratch by making some fancy flourishes such as we all have done. At Tiffany's if the defect could not be burnished out perfectly a new cap would be made, regardless of expense.''

Engravers are long-lived. Some ten years ago Harry Illavac retired at seventy-one, after fifty years. He was so skilled that once he put a full page of writing on the face of a locket that measured exactly one inch each way. He also did Chinese ideographs for Mme. Chiang Kai-shek and invitations for the White House. His favorite was a pair of gold buckles for a lady's garters. One buckle read, ''You've Gone Far Enough''; the other, ''This Belongs to Me.''

The store's favorite sentimental note was requested by a pretty young woman who did not bat an eye as she asked that a key ring with a gold heart attached be engraved on one side ''To Darling Basil'' and on the other side ''From his neighbor, friend and mistress.''

Most of the key ring engravings are more conventional: ''Please Return to Tiffany's if Found.'' When customers began buying the disks to wear as identification bracelets, Hoving's macabre sense of humor got the better of him: ''I suppose in case of accident, they'll ship the body to Tiffany's.''

In the stranger-than-fiction department, a disk did save a customer's life. This gentleman left home to walk down the block to have his shoes shined and collapsed in the shop from a heart attack; the only identification on him was his key ring. The shop's proprietor called Tiffany's, who identified the man and phoned his home for his doctor. In short order the customer was in a hospital under emergency care. About this incident, Hoving murmured, ''We do all we can to keep a customer.''

The factory furnishes Tiffany's with almost all its stationery. Buying writing paper at Tiffany's is an old New York tradition. The stationery department survives from the original store, where, as Charles Tiffany once noted, it was one of the most successful departments in the house. He said: ''Later, our stationery department developed so that we took orders for stamping paper and envelopes; our facilities were for a long time limited to a little hand press with a set of block letters. The whole outfit very much resembled a toy printing press. Today [1898] this branch of the business is as well known throughout the world as our dealings in precious stones. Orders from Japan, Hawaii, Venezuela, and remote parts of the world are a frequent occurrence.'' They still are. The department is considered so important that no less a person than Tiffany president Farnham Lefferts came up through Stationery.

In the last century, a party, no matter how grand, was not official until the invitations were ready. The *Tribune* of January 20, 1885, reported: "Society is excited at the prospect of Mrs. Astor's ball. The invitations are now at Tiffany's, soon to be delivered by the faithful Johnson."

In the spring of 1907, for use on the *Corsair* alone, J. Pierpont Morgan ordered five hundred cards and envelopes, engraved with his house flag and the name of the yacht; three hundred correspondence cards and three hundred dinner cards, with the flag alone; thirty quires of paper and seven hundred and fifty envelopes, with the name of the boat and the flag; six hundred half-sheets and envelopes, engraved with both; seven hundred and fifty menu cards, with the flag alone; thirteen hundred sheets of paper and thirteen hundred envelopes, with the flag and the name of the yacht. The bill: $428.90 (paid promptly).

This order makes more amusing a running skirmish carried on between the Morgan office and Tiffany's from July 14, 1906, until July 7, 1907. Remember that Morgan had spent millions for jewelry and his collections at Tiffany's. In the most elegant script, a 1906 note from the store reminded Morgan that a bill for paper and envelopes amounting to $3.75 was past due. The Morgan office replied quite as politely that it had no record of such a purchase. Tiffany's responded with a copy of the order; Morgan's said it would have to check. Eight exchanges later a Morgan secretary found the original order and paid.

Until the Bureau of Engraving took over the job, Tiffany's for years did all the White House invitations, including the ones for Grover Cleveland's wedding on June 2, 1886, to Miss Frank Folsom. For this first wedding in the White House, Tiffany's also supplied many of the presents, including a solid-gold horseradish dish, on which was traced in diamond dust a garden picture representing the opening scene of the third act of the opera *Faust*. Tiffany's also supplied the boxes, covered with white satin, for the wedding cake. The most remarkable characteristic of the boxes was the size: six and a half inches by one and a half inch—it was a time of larger appetites. Painted on the satin was the monogram of the bride and bridegroom, beneath a linden leaf, the old-time emblem of marriage. Inside, the cake was covered with a fringe of thread lace.

If engraving is a dying art, so are some of the other methods used

*Great Seal of
the United States.*

to turn out stationery. The factory glues its own envelopes, using two kinds of glue: one for the three sides, where strength counts; and the other for the flap, for taste.

The store's insistence on perfection awed one customer in 1916. A Mr. James B. Wasson was so impressed that he told the press about his experience. Tiffany's had made up an unusually large order for him—cards of all sorts, writing paper and envelopes in many sizes. They were delivered and Wasson was completely satisfied. A few days later a letter came from Tiffany's: "Would Mr. Wasson please destroy the entire shipment?" On looking over the order, a slight imperfection had been found in the die (Wasson never did find it, even with a magnifying glass), and Tiffany's would prefer to do the lot over again.

If a baby wasn't born until Tiffany's had sent out the announcements with the improbably tiny bows, and a girl wasn't "out" or married until Tiffany invitations heralded the event, the heavy cream-colored cards and folders also seemed a prerequisite for events of more universal importance: the dedication of the Statue of Liberty in 1886; the opening of the new Stock Exchange in 1903; the inauguration of Belmont Park; the launching of the battleship *Florida* in 1910; the visit of Queen Marie of Rumania in 1926; the opening of the George Washington Bridge in 1931. A sampling of these events is kept in a display in the stationery department on the first floor.

Tiffany's engraved the Great Seal of the United States in 1885, when Secretary of State Frederick T. Freylinghuysen discovered an error in the original seal; the eagle was holding the wrong number of arrows. Scholars on heraldry also decided the eagle was clutching the arrows the wrong way (in heraldry, not necessarily for an eagle), and both mistakes were corrected.

Not all business is on this rarefied plane. An ingenious insurance agent used Tiffany invitations as a piece of direct-mail selling. The

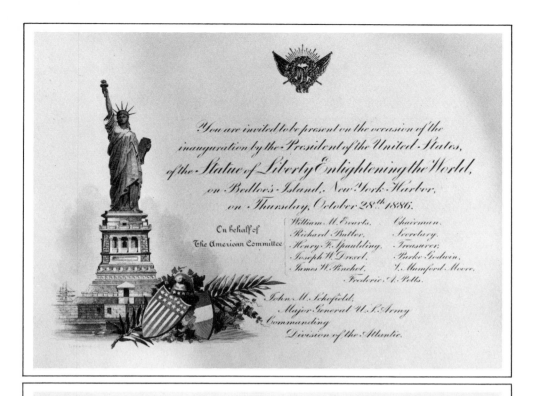

You are invited to be present on the occasion of the
inauguration by the President of the United States,
of the Statue of Liberty Enlightening the World,
on Bedloe's Island, New York Harbor,
on Thursday, October 28th 1886.

On behalf of
The American Committee

William M. Evarts,	Chairman.
Richard Butler,	Secretary.
Henry F. Spaulding,	Treasurer.
Joseph W. Drexel,	Parke Godwin.
James W. Pinchot,	L. Mumford Moore.
Frederic A. Potts.	

John M. Schofield,
Major General U.S. Army
Commanding
Division of the Atlantic.

The Secretary of the Navy
requests the pleasure of your company at the launching of the
United States Battleship Florida
on the morning of Thursday, the twelfth of May
One thousand, nine hundred and ten
at half after ten o'clock
at the Navy Yard, New York

*Public events seemed more official
with cream-colored invitations from Tiffany's.*

agent, Ed Hanlon, of Akron, Ohio, realized one day that while he knew almost everyone of importance in Akron, many of his acquaintances did not know that he sold insurance. How could he let them know "without becoming a pest on the golf course?" as he put it. He prepared a list of two hundred and thirty-five friends, "inviting" them to do business with him. An enclosed card had a box under "Go Away" to check if they did not wish to. To add the proper business note, Tiffany's mailed the invitations from the Wall Street substation to obtain the Wall Street postmark. Ninety-seven friends sent back the card; only a few checked the "Go Away" box. One sent a dollar to help defray the cost; when Hanlon told him the per capita cost was two dollars he sent along another dollar. Hanlon was delighted with his gimmick. "Nothing I had done in my thirty-nine years in the insurance business caused so much comment."

A

mong the innumera-
ble silver articles which Tiffany's turned out in its early years, there
was nothing quite like the sporting trophies and memorial vases (as
they were called) made for prominent citizens. These developed a
style all their own, what might be called "testimonial ostentatious."
As the custom of bestowing presentation pieces grew, so did the
number of committees and other delegations charged with approving
the designs. While conceived as a token of esteem, the ornate vase or
bowl was also expected to demonstrate its costliness in a plutocratic
society bent on conspicuous show.

These objects did not reflect that purity of design on which the
firm rested its international artistic reputation. Certainly present-

(Above) August Belmont in 1852, shortly after his marriage to
Caroline Perry.

day management would like to forget all of them. However, there is no evidence that Tiffany's ever turned down a single commission. Business was business, and the store had a virtual monopoly on making the important pieces. If the excesses helped shape the taste of the times, Tiffany's must take the blame as it took the profits.

A notable example of "testimonial ostentatious" was presented to William Cullen Bryant at a huge civic testimonial dinner in 1876, on the occasion of his eightieth birthday. The solid-silver vase was, in effect, the biography of the poet. The committee paid Tiffany's five thousand dollars and the committee received its money's worth.

The poet thought so too. After the presentation (to the strains of "Lo! The Conquering Hero Comes"), Bryant responded, overcome with emotion: "My friends, we authors cultivate a short-lived reputation. One generation of us pushes another from the stage. We cease to be read. But a work like this is always beautiful, always admired."

There was a lot to admire, as reported in the *World*.

[*The vase was*] "*covered with a fretwork of apple blossoms, beneath which are the primrose and amaranth. The body displays elaborate medallions of the poet, presenting prominent features of his life. The principal of these is the portrait bust; above his head is the lyre, symbolizing his art; below the printing press suggesting his work as a journalist [Bryant had been editor of the New York* Post] *and below this is the waterfowl, a reminder of the poem of the same name. On the opposite sides of the vase are two female figures, representing Poetry and Nature . . . on the sides medallions presenting scenes in the poet's life. The first is with his father, who points to [John] Home [a forgotten Scots writer "pushed aside" by Bryant's generation] as a model of poetic construction. The next represents Mr. Bryant as a student of nature as he appears in "Thanatopsis." The lower part is ornamented with cotton and Indian corn, staples of American agriculture; the neck is encircled with primroses and ivy. The line 'Truth crushed to earth shall rise again' forms a border inlaid with gold . . . at the foot of the vase is a water lily, symbol of eloquence . . . the handles are decorated with fern, Indian corn, and a bobolink . . . the crossed pens and broken shackles represent the poet as the emancipator. . . .*

Testimonial dinners were not always such models of good feeling and euphoria. Tiffany's stepped into a battle royal over the "costly silver" testimonial vase for Queen Victoria's three-time prime minister, William E. Gladstone. (Victoria never pretended that she didn't detest him.) If Tiffany's was naïve about what sort of reception the "graven image" would receive, Joseph Pulitzer, the brilliant owner of the New York *World* and St. Louis *Post-Dispatch,* who promoted the enterprise, was not.

Pulitzer had started the campaign to raise funds for the testimonial in the fall of 1886, at the height of the ruckus over Gladstone's bill to give Home Rule to Ireland. Emotions among conservative Britons were at high heat, and roughly can be compared in modern terms with the way Republicans in the United States would feel if the Democrats were courting an invasion of revolutionaries from Cuba. In England of the 1880's the American Fenians were the equivalent of the Reds.

The bill was defeated, and Gladstone fell with it. When Pulitzer arrived in England in July of 1887 to present his vase, Gladstone was Ireland's hero but a traitor to his countrymen. Most of the funds to pay for the testimonial had been subscribed by Irish-Americans; Gladstone's acceptance speech poured oil on the waters, and then set a match to it. "Give us your money," said Gladstone, referring to U.S. citizens' help to Ireland, "for our landlords, take away our emigrants of whom we want to be rid, bear the cost of their famine for which we ought to provide, and we will not complain. But assist our fellow subjects to fight the battle of liberty in accordance with our law and constitution and immediately we indignantly expostulate and complain to the world that you are interfering with British institutions."

The London *Times* led the savage attack against Gladstone, and referred to Pulitzer as that "Bavarian, who conducts a New York newspaper largely dependent on the Irish for support"; it also attacked the American system, "Mr. Perry Belmont who lacks promotion" and the amount of money raised, which it sneered at as "a paltry $3,382.09."

The Pall Mall Gazette took up the gauntlet for Pulitzer and the Americans against its rival, the *Times,* replying that "the *Times* is becoming . . . too silly and too enraged in its editorial opinions to be tolerated . . . it has evidently no idea that most people have come to take no notice whatever of its rabid utterances on the Irish question . . . the *Times* account is mostly bosh."

The uproar, which delighted Pulitzer, was a two-week sensation. "Presentation Roils the British Soul," the *World* trumpeted. "Savage Attack on Grand Old Man and his American Friends."

Nevertheless, the "memorial vases" were staid compared with the sporting trophies. A prime example of the latter was the James Gordon Bennett Cup, donated for a New York Yacht Club race. One member grumbled that it would be more fitting for the losers in the French and Indian Wars. Another wit suggested that the motif demonstrated what Bennett would like to do to his competitors. Set on a wide base, the trophy included the model of a war canoe being paddled by Indian braves through some extremely rough waters; above the canoe were emblazoned shields, bows and arrows, and other weapons. The whole was topped by an exuberant Red Man executing a war dance and holding aloft a scalp.

Tiffany's has made so many trophies for the New York Yacht Club that the Race Committee would probably cry "Foul" if an outside trophy turned up. What the firm did not make—although it is often credited with having done so—is the America's Cup. Possibly the reason for the misunderstanding is that in the 1890's Tiffany's printed a descriptive booklet about the race, displayed the cup in the store's windows and stored it between challenges until the cup was given its own niche in the New York Yacht Club. (In fairness, Tiffany's must be exonerated of any part in designing this English atrocity.)

Tiffany's *is* responsible for another ornate and famous cup, the one awarded in the Belmont Stakes. The race, inaugurated in 1867, was run at the old Jerome Park track until 1890. It commemorates the three horses from which all thoroughbreds have descended: Eclipse, Matchem and Herod. Two of them are carved into the base, the third crowns the trophy. However, when Belmont Park suggested to Hoving a few years ago that it would be a nice gesture to display the trophy in a Tiffany window, on Belmont's 100th anniversary, Hoving said "No. It's just too homely."

As *Sports Illustrated* has also pointed out, Hoving's comment could apply to "lots of Tiffany's period pieces for sport. On exhibit at the Aqueduct Race Track is a trophy made in 1902, showing a thoroughbred and Winged Victory sprinting wing and hoof toward a photo finish. Victory never looked so close to defeat."

But this piece was made long after the great period of Testimonial Ostentatious. The golden age is exemplified by the Preakness Trophy. This started out as the Woodlawn Vase, a trophy awarded for a number of horse races, including one at Coney Island. One of its early winners, according to *Sports Illustrated*, buried the vase on his plantation in the South "to keep Union soldiers from melting it down into bullets" (or bullion?). Not until 1917 did the vase become the Preakness Trophy. Now, despite, or because of, its intricate design of horseshoes, galloping horses, horses standing still and various other equine symbols, it is valued at five hundred thousand dollars.

Gradually the growing simplification of public preferences invaded the sporting world. The Best in Show for the Westminster Dog Show is a huge, plain Tiffany silver bowl, ornamented only by an etching of Sensation, the great English pointer.

The testimonial-gift design that Hoving himself endorses is best shown by the Tiffany Design Award, which he inaugurated in 1963. This is nothing more than a cube of silver, three inches each way, which weighs five pounds five ounces. (''Careful, it's heavy,'' Hoving warned Dr. Frank Stanton, president of the Columbia Broadcasting Company, when he handed it over at the presentation luncheon in the spring of 1970.) On the top is engraved ''The Tiffany Award''; on one side, the name of the winner and why he won. It pleases Hoving because it is simple and it is functional—it can be used as a paperweight or for exercising the wrists, or both at once. The Tiffany Award is not an annual one; it is given only if and when the firm (Hoving) finds a worthy recipient: an executive who ''has best initiated and carried through a comprehensive design program.'' In the first eight years there were only four winners: Frederick R. Kappel of A.T.& T.; Thomas J. Watson, Jr., of IBM; Dr. Stanton; and Irwin Miller of Cummins Engine Co.

Out of these hit-or-miss commissions over the past one hundred and twenty years, a very important and not at all casual department has been established. Even before Hoving initiated his own award, he realized that at some time nearly every business firm or executive is faced with choosing awards and testimonial gifts. For them, the contract department was established; it now accounts for 15 percent of the firm's business. The department will advise a client, whether he is an ambassador or a sales vice president for a toothpaste company on what he can give that is in good taste and within his budget. Usually, the object is available on the store's shelves; if not, the gift will be made to order.

The Department has customers from nine thousand firms, who are the only outsiders to receive a discount from Tiffany's; 10 percent when the amount is under twenty-five hundred dollars, 15 percent if the total is higher. The selection includes presents at every level— $5.25 to eighteen thousand dollars. Goldman Sachs & Co. spent as much as seventy-two thousand dollars in one year. Shell Oil and Pan Am are other companies which use the department. Tiffany's makes the J. P. Stevens Co.'s Golden Linebacker Fabrics prize. It also designed the 14-carat gold bowl which Cone Mills presented to Levi Strauss to mark that company's fiftieth anniversary as a customer.

Because of Tiffany's reputation as an authority on protocol, many customers are from the U.N. and not at home in English. Edward Bower, head of the contract department, has employees who can conduct business in ten languages, including Yiddish. Major Holberton-Wood, who handled the Johnson china service and outfitted the King of Morocco's hunting lodge, performs the same negotiations for U.N. missions and various governmental agencies, aided by Liselotte van Falkenhayn, a German baroness, and Mme. Ayako May Tanaka, who was born into the Japanese aristocracy.

The White House has retained its rating as a very good customer.

Super Bowl football trophy.

The store guarantees to deliver a gift suitable for a visiting head of state at the lifting of the White House phone. President Kennedy was always in a rush. A call would come to the contract department: sometimes a specific article was wanted; in other circumstances the choice was left to Major Holberton-Wood, who would fly to Washington with the gift or gifts. The selection would be made, and Holberton-Wood would be on the next plane back to New York to have the present engraved. Next day, the major would be back at the White House, the gift ready for presentation. Even though Kennedy usually created a last-minute flurry, the department always found him, as well as Eisenhower, easy to work with. Ike's only demerit in the eyes of the store was his affection for Steuben glass—an admiration not shared by Hoving, who refuses to stock it. Eisenhower's gift to President De Gaulle on his state visit was a handsome set of four silver branching candlesticks, with a matching square centerpiece, in bamboo design. And when Ike left the White House, the staff came to Tiffany's for his going-away present—a 14-carat gold liqueur goblet.

When Lyndon Johnson took office, calls from the White House

1. Bryant vase.
2. International Challenge cup, steam yachts.
3. Bennett trophy.
4. Gladstone testimonial.

stopped abruptly. It wasn't that LBJ had anything *against* Tiffany's; he just thought that a true-blue Texas firm could produce more suitable gifts than a Northern outfit. For a time, gifts came from Texas firms, but before long, the little flags of battle had begun to move northward. By the time LBJ had invaded Baltimore, Tiffany's figured it would not be long before it got that phone call.

Once President Johnson began to order from Tiffany's he proved as easy to work with as his predecessors, except for the familiar LBJ mannerisms. For example, when the Punta del Este Conference was held in South America in 1966, the President took along a Tiffany engraver, who had been born in Argentina, as well as a collection of silver boxes, bowls, and cigar and cigarette cases. LBJ was a man of impulse and he wanted to be ready when the impulse struck. The President would come back from a meeting and say, ''I just met a delegate from Brazil and he's certainly a fine fellow. I'd like to make him a little present. What have we got?'' The engraver would lay out his stock; LBJ would make his selection; the engraver would carve the name of the recipient and the good wishes of the President, and off it would go. Such prompt gifts never failed to surprise and delight LBJ's newest friends.

When Pope Paul VI announced his visit to the United States, the White House considered the occasion so special that it went beyond Tiffany's; a number of firms were asked to suggest a gift. All met in Washington with their suggestions. One was a real eye-popper: a design, in plaster, of a life-size figure of the Pope seated on the papal throne. Tiffany's Major Holberton-Wood arrived with a little box in his hand.

The major's sales pitch was brief. He opened his box and brought out a silver globe, three inches in diameter, engraved with a map of the ancient world, the lettering in Latin. ''The Pope is not coming primarily to visit the United States,'' said the major, ''he is coming to address the United Nations. The gift should represent the whole world, without modern boundaries.''

President Johnson chose the small globe, a standard item at Tiffany's selling for about three hundred dollars. However, the one presented to Pope Paul is unique: Tiffany's put on a vermeil coating, and will not make another vermeil globe.

There is one gift which the major selected for Lyndon Johnson that he was not allowed to give. The story begins in a castle in Belgium when Tiffany Vice President Hoagland stopped off to see a private silver collection. Included among the treasures was a nine-sided coffeepot, the first—and the only one—he had ever seen. Hoagland was so taken with the handsome piece that he obtained permission to copy it for Tiffany's. The copy eventually was placed on the special shelf in the silver department reserved for the "museum pieces."

It was there when Major Holberton-Wood came roaming through the store to find a suitable gift for LBJ to give to the Shah of Iran. The coffeepot was the sort of unusual article that only Tiffany's could supply. But when the major approached Mrs. Elizabeth Willard of the silver department, he found unexpected opposition. Mrs. Willard told him flatly, "No." She wants the special pieces to find proper homes, where they will be appreciated.

"LBJ will give it to the Shah," she told the major, "and he'll take it home and throw it in a closet with all those other presents which are given him on these tours. No one will ever see it again and that would be a great waste. No, I won't let you have it for the President."

Word of a dispute on this level quickly reached Hoving and he came down to the silver department.

"Mrs. Willard," he reminded her, "you are here to sell these articles, not keep them on the shelf to admire."

"We went to a lot of trouble to get this coffeepot," she answered, "and it should be owned by someone who will love it as much as we do. I still believe what I told the major: it just shouldn't be tossed in a corner somewhere and you know that is what is going to happen if we give it to the Shah."

Hoving looked at the pot, raised an eyebrow at Mrs. Willard, and turned to Holberton-Wood.

"All right," he said a bit wearily, "what else do we have for the President?"

The "what else" turned out to be a handsome covered bowl, especially vermeiled. Later, Tiffany's was commissioned to make a much more elaborate bowl of solid 18-carat gold, a gift to the Shah from oil companies who were glad to pay the eighteen thousand dollars.

In due time, President Richard Nixon also came to Tiffany's for his official gifts. Nixon prefers severe, masculine-looking pieces. A favorite gift to heads of state is a reproduction of a covered sugar urn made by Van Voorhies & Schanck, eighteenth-century silversmiths in New York. The Nixon version is in 14-carat gold and costs eighteen hundred dollars. Another item on Nixon's list is a silver tea service which he gave to the crown prince of Nepal.

A Nixon favorite was not *from* him but *to* him: the gift of the White House photographers. They came to Tiffany's for something for the President's desk—at a price of five hundred dollars. The contract department designed a memo pad of vermeil and leather which looks like a book. On the back is an etching of the White House. Nixon was so pleased that he not only keeps the present on his desk to remind him of appointments but asked that it be added to the official list of governmental gifts. Tiffany's has since made ten for the State Department.

Offbeat requests are frowned on unless there is sentiment or humor attached. One day a staffer from *The New York Times* came in with an old brick. He and other *Times* writers had procured the brick from the old Metropolitan Opera House when it was being torn down, and wanted to present it to an opera buff who was retiring from the paper. Tiffany's mounted the brick on a crystal base, with a silver plate engraved with the name of the recipient and sent it over to the *Times*. The bill: fifty dollars.

On another occasion a man bought a silver box and asked that it be sealed shut, with a copy of a cedilla (the squiggle under the *c*, in French, as in *façade*) entombed. On the top was to be engraved: "There's a cedilla inside." "This guy is going to go crazy wondering if there really is a cedilla inside," said the donor, laughing fiendishly.

A good customer in the garment district once ordered a gift for a shifty competitor: three vermeil walnuts and a pea, mounted on a base. Recently, the heads of three management consultant firms all bought the same article—a crystal ball, mounted on a silver base.

Corporations have had such a sizable number of women employees for many years that the department has become an expert on what —and what not—to give the ladies. The department will never suggest earrings. "When a woman tries on earrings," John Brown, the department's designer explained, "she looks at her face, not the earrings, to see if they are perfect for her. It is impossible to make a large number of earrings of the same design that will be wearable for a large number of women in one group."

Often a client will start out with a budget and end up spending a much larger amount. When J Basil Ward, whose hobby is fishing, was president of Addressograph-Multigraph, he wanted Tiffany's to design something around a muskellunge, the fighting fish of the Middle West inland lakes. Tiffany's came up with a pair of cuff links and a tie bar in vermeil, for fifteen dollars, but they were not very impressive. The artists kept designing, and evolved cuff links with a muskie in relief, trying to shake off the fisherman's hook. The department made a model instead of drawings. Addressograph was so pleased that it changed the order for the metal to 14-carat gold, adding a ruby eye to the fish—and ordered more than seven hundred pairs at over ninety dollars a pair.

Tiffany's can be uncooperative if it does not approve of a project. In the Navy, all officers need a card tray; the custom, when an officer is sent to a new post, is to place the tray in a designated spot so that other officers can leave cards as a gesture of hospitality. Friends of a young woman who had just received her commission as a nurse wanted Tiffany's to make a tray in the shape of a sterling-silver bedpan. Tiffany's did not consider this in good taste, but rather than have the young woman embarrassed if her friends carried out their project elsewhere, the salesman did not mention aesthetics. He simply quoted a price so high that the idea became impractical. He then suggested a miniature hospital bed and this was accepted.

When the New York Jets became football champions, the management wanted Tiffany's to make diamond rings for each of the players. "No," said Hoving, "no diamond rings for men, not even for certified he-men like halfbacks." Tiffany's supplied the trophy for the champions, a full-sized football in silver mounted in the kick-off position. But when Tiffany's wanted to engrave it for the "Super Bowl Champions," Commissioner Pete Rozelle said, "No, bad taste, you know. 'Super Bowl' is only a slangy newspaper phrase." The trophy is inscribed "World Professional Football Championship."

Corporate gifts are often expensive. The most costly given by one company is the gift that the board of directors of RCA gave to Chairman David Sarnoff on his seventy-fifth birthday. General Sarnoff, a dedicated cigar smoker, received a cigar box of 18-carat gold, resembling an old book; the RCA emblem on the cover is of diamonds, and the spine of the book is encrusted with diamonds. The value: "around" ten thousand dollars.

While Tiffany's appreciates high-priced orders, it also enjoys the challenge of a worthy cause and a tiny exchequer. A small Catholic organization wanted a prize for the best religious television show; its budget was two hundred dollars. The contract department found a silver bowl with slightly squared sides. It was a simple matter to etch on one side the semblance of a television screen, with the name of the winner. Budget accomplished. In another case, the College of the Pacific wanted an award for an outstanding faculty member. Again the budget was two hundred dollars. A designer wandered through the store until he saw a pair of silver candlesticks in a flame motif—of course, "education enlightening the world." One was mounted on an ebony base, and the college had its award for $175.

The least expensive item in the department is "the screwball key ring"—not as screwy as it sounds. The ring is in the shape of a three-quarter hoop, with balls at either end. One is permanently attached;

the other unscrews so that the keys can be slid on. The price is $5.25 and the department sells thousands every year. Big spender David Merrick gave the key rings to the cast of *How to Succeed in Business Without Really Trying* to celebrate the first anniversary of the show.

Not all of the commemorative pieces made by the department are for recording happy occasions. One of the most unusual silver articles is a memorial to a tragedy, the drowning of three people during the qualification races for the national championship regatta of Thistle-class sailboats. This is the Mac Luff Trophy, a gallon-sized silver goblet in the shape of a brandy glass, donated by George A. Dornin, Jr., of Sewickley Heights, Pennsylvania, as a perpetual trophy; it is awarded annually to the winning skipper of the first three races at the national championships. An unusual condition is attached to the award: "It shall be the obligation of each recipient to fill the goblet with a one gallon mint julep which he shall share with all other trophy winners at the banquet following the last race. This julep shall be made pre-cisely according to the following recipe [which was supplied by Dornin]." All of this has meaning in the tragedy in which Dornin's son, George A. III, was drowned, along with his wife, Priscilla Reily Dornin, and the other member of the crew, Richard John Nagy. The accident occurred July 5, 1969, several miles off Santa Cruz, Cali-fornia, because of an incredible chain of events. The light breeze in which the race had started suddenly increased to a shifting thirty-five miles an hour, creating big waves and capsizing so many boats in the race and nearby that rescue boats and helicopters had their hands full rescuing sailors from the 50-degree water. The *Mac Luff* capsized once and was righted by skipper and crew and continued the race. When it capsized a second time, they could not right it and they were out of sight of rescue boats. The bodies of Mrs. Dornin and Nagy were found the next day; the body of skipper Dornin was never found.

As for the julep ceremony, donor George Dornin has this to say: "My son was a friendly, gregarious person who loved sailing, people and parties. He would have wanted his friends, particularly those in the Thistle class, to have remembered him with happiness. When he was in college I used to make mint juleps for him and his friends in a fifty-two-ounce goblet that I once won sailing a Raven boat and it seemed fitting that a trophy in his memory should be used in the same way. I'm sure that Jay would heartily approve. By a happy coinci-dence the trophy was won in both 1969 and 1970 by close personal friends of Jay's; in 1969 by Jim Miller of Oyster Bay, who my younger son, Chris, crewed for in the 1970 Nationals; and in 1970, by Dave Minton of Columbus, Ohio.

While the contract department has turned out to be a brain child to be proud of, Hoving has had less luck with another department he hoped to set up: an international division. The Middle East is filled with oil-rich sheiks and other rulers, who are always passing out gifts which they buy from French and British jewelers. Hoving thought Tiffany's should get its share of this business.

The obvious head for the department was right in the store. The redoubtable Major Holberton-Wood had spent five years as a British diplomat stationed in Jaffa, Jerusalem and Istanbul, and speaks what he calls "kitchen Arabic." Tiffany's decided to work with the Bankers Trust Co., since it had many officers in the Middle East. Holberton-Wood went off on his first selling trip, taking an assortment of beautifully colored slides and a projector. He was welcomed by all; his slides were admired. But the mysterious East was not that ready for the mechanized West; Tiffany's had mistakenly assumed that, like Texas oil millionaires leafing through the store's Blue Book, sheiks would buy from looking at pictures. On Holberton-Wood's next trip, he took along some million dollars in jewelry, but not without an insurance problem. The mere mention of the turbulent Middle East set insurance companies quaking. Finally, a deal was worked out to send a guard with the jewels on one plane, on which Tiffany's took out insurance, and Holberton-Wood on a second plane, the thought being that in this way the major would not be kidnapped for ransom.

Holberton-Wood first displayed his jewels in Beirut, then flew on to Kuwait. Success seemed certain. The brother of the Emir was shopping for presents for his thirty-third wife, a German woman. The prince selected three pieces worth about thirty-five thousand dollars and then dismissed Holberton-Wood, telling him to leave the million in jewels behind. Unfortunately, King Hussein of Jordan chose this moment to pay a visit to Kuwait, and all thought of jewel buying was put aside for diplomacy. All the jewelry came back.

The next stop was Dubai, a very primitive town on the Persian Gulf. The flight was made in a small plane with the jewels and two guards, whose rifles were on the rusty side. As the major's plane descended at the airport, he noticed that the runway was lined with sandbags—at least they looked like sandbags, but this seemed a strange place for them. An ambulance with an agent from Banker's Trust drove up and the chest of jewelry was loaded into it.

"What are all those sandbags for?" Holberton-Wood asked.

The man from Banker's Trust laughed. "Those aren't sandbags," he replied. "They're bags full of gold bullion. It's bought from the Bank of England and landed here and loaded into fast dhows and smuggled into India, where the price is much higher. Lots of men here are getting rich off the business.''

''But isn't it risky leaving the gold lying around like that?''

''Not here it isn't. No one would dare steal. The old law still prevails; they cut off the hands of thieves.''

A meeting was set up with Emir Rashid, and Holberton-Wood laid his jewelry out on a rug before the ruler. The Emir glanced at the display and then he, too, dismissed Holberton-Wood: ''You will please leave now. I want my wives to see the jewelry and you are not permitted to be here.'' So Holberton-Wood again had to leave his million dollars in jewels on the floor. He was called back in half an hour, and found everything as he had left it. He was packing up when the word came that Rashid's father would like to see the jewelry. He was led into the old man's bedroom, where he found the prince, a fierce-looking Arab with a great aquiline nose, sitting up in bed.

The first article Holberton-Wood showed him was a ring with a canary diamond. The old prince looked at it, said, ''I'll take it,'' and stuffed it inside his djellabah.

''Your Majesty,'' said Holberton-Wood, ''that ring sells for sixteen thousand dollars.''

''I'll give you twelve thousand,'' said his Majesty, and that was the end of the bargaining.

While Holberton-Wood was worrying about how he was going to explain this business to Hoving, the prince said, ''Now I'll give you something.'' He handed the major his amber worry beads, a highly appropriate gift under the circumstances. In the afternoon, a check for twelve thousand dollars was brought to Holberton-Wood. A problem of doing business in the Middle East is the custom of bargaining. If Holberton-Wood had asked for twenty thousand dollars he undoubtedly would have received his sixteen thousand dollars.

So Holberton-Wood returned to New York with something less than a dazzling story of success. After listening to him, Hoving agreed that the Middle East was no place for a one-price, straightforward Yankee trader.

Having given up on the East, Hoving turned to the West, opening branches in San Francisco and Beverly Hills. Since then, Tiffany's has gone to Houston, Chicago and Atlanta. More branches are planned, but none in the suburbs of New York.

''After all,'' President Lusk once observed, ''you don't buy fifty-thousand-dollar diamonds in Manhasset.''

N ew York on that Sunday
morning in August 1958 was quiet, as usual in midsummer. The downtown streets were empty. The only signs of activity were around St.
Patrick's Cathedral, where worshipers were entering the church for
the 6 o'clock mass. As the services began, a single car cruised up Fifth
Avenue, past the cathedral, and continued on for six blocks, stopping
in front of Tiffany's. A man got out, walked leisurely to the corner
and glanced along Fifty-seventh Street. It, too, was without signs of
life.

The man went back to the car and lifted out a heavy sledge hammer; at the same moment a second man jumped from the car, carrying
a second sledge hammer. They walked to the display windows, glitter-

(*Above*) Painting in window.

ing with diamonds, which flank the Fifth Avenue entrance to the store, lifted the hammers and swung them in wide arcs. The heavy blows broke holes about five inches across in the centers of the windows of the five-eighth-inch-thick, supposedly shatterproof glass. The men thrust their arms through the holes and plucked out two diamond necklaces, a diamond pin and a diamond ring. Not more than a few minutes passed before they were back in the car and on their way up the avenue with $163,000 in jewelry.

The armed guard and a detective inside the store heard nothing. Not until 6:15 A.M., when a patrolman walked by, was the incredibly bold robbery discovered, and the method reconstructed by the police. The robbers had been lucky, as well as meticulous, in timing their coup. The corner of Fifty-seventh Street and Fifth Avenue is what the police department terms a "post"; a patrolman is always kept there, since across from Tiffany's is a branch bank, and near another corner was Van Cleef and Arpels.

But at 5:45 that particular Sunday morning, the officer had been sent to the Waldorf-Astoria to supplement the guard awaiting the arrival of Soviet Foreign Minister Andrei Gromyko, in the city to visit the United Nations. Ironically, the policeman was not needed; Gromyko had stopped off at the Russian embassy.

The daring robbery highlights the overall security problem which haunts stores like Tiffany's, which, as the press noted, "had been regarded as being as invulnerable as Fort Knox." The window smashing revealed a grave flaw in the security system; since no one had conceived of such a robbery the windows had not been wired into the central alarm system. After the fact, this was done, and the glass replaced with planes which were proved to be shatterproof in the best possible test. A second robbery attempt was made several months later, this time by firing two bullets into the windows, but the only damage was two small holes on a corner.

The jewelry taken in the first instance was never recovered. Nevertheless, Tiffany's did not change its policy and follow the practice of most important jewelers who replace displays at night with inexpensive articles or artificial stones. Windows with phony diamonds would not be genuine Tiffany windows.

Chairman Hoving felt the same as a long-time customer who said, "After all, when do couples go strolling along the avenue on a window-shopping spree? At night and on Sundays. Where do they pause? At Tiffany's. And where do they return next day to buy a part of the dream? Tiffany's."

The biggest loss in the history of the store took place, not in New

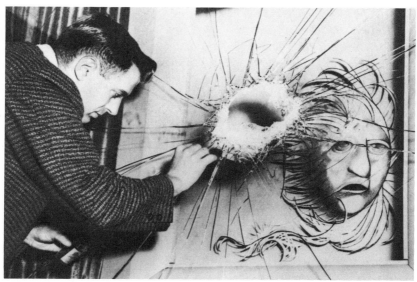

Smashed window after Fifth Avenue robbery.

York, but in Chicago in 1966, one month after that branch opened. This robbery also was perfectly timed, at 8 A.M. on a Saturday. As the first seven employees, including three guards, entered the basement of the building, they were confronted by four gunmen wearing ski masks, and were locked in a storeroom. When the manager and his assistant appeared, they were forced to deactivate the night alarms in the store and open the vault before being put in the storeroom. The robbers walked out of the store with eight hundred thousand dollars in loose gems and jewelry. Again, robbery at that hour of the day had been thought "impossible"—and once more, Tiffany's made a change in security. Now no one can deactivate the alarm system until a coded signal has been sent the Burns Agency that all is well. And if all is not well, if a robber should be standing beside an employee with a gun thrust into his side as the signal is sent, that too can be coded into the signal.

Tiffany's came to its complicated, expensive and comprehensive system of security the hard way, as the robberies prove. The security method in the old store on Union Square was somewhat elementary, but it was effective in the case of one thief. As the *Times* told the story, it was a fine June day in 1885—fine weather seemed to bring the light-fingered fraternity to Tiffany's—and a man came into the store and said he wanted a diamond engagement ring. He showed proper identification—manager of the well-known Hoffman House. The first diamond did not suit; as the clerk turned his back to find another, he could still see the customer in the mirrors installed back of the counter (the security system at that time) and he saw him slip the diamond into his pocket. The clerk, a Mr. Snell, "an athlete in strength," as the paper noted, jumped over the counter in a second, grappled with the thief and extracted the diamond from his pocket. Mr. Snell collared the thief and started to haul him off to the precinct station. The criminal managed to pull away, and drawing a gun, shot at Mr. Snell. By this time, in 1885 even as today, "the commotion finally attracted the police, a constable arrived and the thief was overwhelmed."

The most mysterious theft took place on Union Square, just before the store moved uptown to Thirty-seventh Street. The firm had acquired three stones from the famous Excelsior diamond (the second largest diamond ever found), which were put into settings in the workrooms on the fifth floor. The gems, worth about eighty thousand dollars, were placed in the "out" cage, to be taken to the first-floor jewelry department. They never got there—and another improvement was made in the security system. A strict control, which is still in effect, was placed on the movement of all jewelry within the store.

The workshops on the seventh floor of the present store in New York are caged in, and all doors on the floor are always locked and controlled within the alarm system. Precious metals and stones are checked in and out again; the fifteen skilled workmen do not mind; the security shields them from harm as well as protecting the millions of dollars in jewelry.

On the top floors, electronic eyes beam across each space where there are windows, and if a spider web should break the beam, the alarms ring. While entering the store from the roof seems as impossible as, say, stealing from a Fifth Avenue window, that eventually was also guarded against, long before *Topkapi* and the Murf the Surf caper at the American Museum of Natural History.

The security system is like an iceberg; only a small part is visible, but like a single berg on a wide expanse of ocean, that part is very visible indeed. The most casual browser who walks into the first floor is soon aware of the men with big shoulders and small hats lined up against the walls, sometimes only two or three, often as many as seven or eight on a busy day. There is always a man near the diamond counter and another beside the private elevator to the Schlumberger shop. This elevator operates on an automatic sequence. If a person enters the elevator and it does not return to the first floor in the allotted time, a detective hustles up to the mezzanine to make sure that everything is in order. The Schlumberger shop, as a matter of fact, for all its swagged brocade draperies and antiqued walls is a large, air-conditioned safe.

The too small hats of the detectives are part of the scenario: they make the men conspicuous without giving them the sinister look of the snap-brim Dashiell Hammett private eyes. The hats and the watchful faces ("Stay around a while and you'll get that feeling of tenseness; it never leaves and pretty soon you'll feel it, too," a guard remarks) are a deterrent to thievery as carefully thought out as the stainless-steel safes behind every showcase. The men are there, not primarily to prevent daylight holdups, for that *is* inconceivable, but to watch out for new shoplifting tricks or clever sleight-of-hand artists. There are always other armed security guards, both men and women, around the store, not in uniform and indistinguishable from customers or salespeople.

Tiffany's also has had its share of loss through trickery. One of the most successful frauds was engineered at the end of the last century by a "lady Detroiter," as Jack Manning, a civically proud Detroit columnist has recalled. This was Sophie Lyons, who achieved global notoriety during the eighties and nineties, abetted by her devoted husband, Billie Burke. Sophie, who reformed and devoted her time to "rehabilitating criminals, especially youthful ones," told a police official about the time she took Tiffany's.

As the columnist wrote:

Sophie swept regally into the store and demanded to be shown an assortment of rubies and diamonds. She was a superb actress and could dress and talk like a patrician. She examined this stone and that and finally announced there was nothing suitable and rose to leave. Then the clerk noticed to his chagrin that seven expensive stones were missing, worth about fifty grand. She and the clerk were the only persons within touching distance. Was it possible she had dropped them into her handbag? The lady drew herself up in haughty indignation. The clerk called a store detective . . . and she was escorted into a room and searched by a matron. Nary a stone was found on her, and she threw the place into an uproar, threatening damages for humiliation, false arrest, etc. . . . eventually, she exited, the management apologizing. As Sophie said, "the most sullen and baffled apology you can imagine. They were not stupid. They knew I had taken the stones but they were helpless." . . . The next day her husband strolled nonchalantly into Tiffany's, bought a diamond ring from the same clerk his wife had tricked, and paid cash. While the clerk was making out the receipt, Billie slipped the seven stolen gems from the gum under the counter where Sophie had stuck them and walked out a happier and wealthier man.

The detectives remain on the alert for the gum trick, but there is always something new. Only a few years ago a young woman approached the diamond counter, which is just inside the Fifth Avenue doors. She tried on rings, occasionally stepping back from the counter and holding out her hand, as most women do, to get a better look. As she stepped back toward the door, she suddenly turned and dashed out. A security man took after her. Outside, the traffic was stopped on Fifth Avenue by a red light, but as the woman dashed across the avenue, the light turned green. Traffic suddenly filled the street, stopping the pursuing detective at the curb. By the time the light changed, the woman had disappeared. As the outsmarted guard said ruefully, ''She had that light timed perfectly.''

The trick of the beautiful blonde in 1950 was quite as ingenious. She examined a tray of engagement rings and finally narrowed her preference to two, one for $2,550 and one for $3,250. She finally said she couldn't make up her mind; could she please show the rings to her mother who was sick in a nearby hotel? Naturally, the salesman could come along. The salesman did, and also a detective. Would they mind waiting in the sitting room of the suite while the customer went in to her mother in the bedroom? Always gentlemen, the Tiffany men sat down to wait. They waited, and waited, and waited. The same idea occurred to both at the same time. They ran into the bedroom. It was empty—an open door leading into the hall showed where the blonde and the rings had gone.

The most audacious trick of all was performed by another woman, again described as ''a perfect lady.'' She pulled off her remarkable coup in 1965, under the eyes of closely watching detectives and salesmen. What is more, she was able to defraud both Tiffany's and Harry Winston's in the space of fifteen minutes. The razzle-dazzle started at Tiffany's. As she approached the diamond counter, the clerk noticed she was wearing an expensive marquise diamond ring. She asked to see something in higher-priced marquise rings. Impressed by the customer's gem, the salesman brought out several rings, leaving them on the counter while the lady tried on first one and then another, comparing the stones. Eventually, she said she simply could not make up her mind and left the store.

She walked down a block to Harry Winston's and asked to see their more expensive rings, laying her own ring on a table. Again, the suitably impressed salesman brought out a number of marquise rings.

Nevertheless, since the customer was not known, she was more closely watched than usual by a security guard, an ex-FBI man. Eventually, as she had at Tiffany's, the woman said she could not make up her mind and left the store. It was not until later, when they checked over their stock and talked to each other, that the salesmen at Tiffany's and Winston's learned what had happened.

At Tiffany's the "perfect lady" had exchanged the 2.75-carat diamond worth $7,500 that she had worn into the store for one weighing 3.69 carats, worth $19,800, which she wore going out. She walked into Winston's wearing the Tiffany ring, and with two men closely watching, managed to exchange it for a Winston ring of 5.30 carats, worth $38,500. The daring and nerve of the woman who had tricked the two most closely guarded stores in the country aroused the grudging admiration even of Winston. "She was not a professional thief," he said, "just a woman who wanted a more expensive ring to wear." As might be expected, the slick switch brought another new rule at Tiffany's: never more than two rings on the counter at the same time.

While this and other thefts are covered by insurance, they cost Tiffany's far more than the actual cost of the article. Every robbery of any consequence causes a rise in insurance rates.

The widespread increase in jewel robberies has caused a crisis in jewelry insurance. Stage and movie stars find that insurance is well-nigh prohibitive or impossible to obtain. It is not that they are less honest; it is because their jewelry is so publicized that it is a special target for thieves. Life was made more difficult for all owners of jewelry in New York City in 1970, when insurance companies changed their regulations. Hitherto, jewelry was covered under a general household policy; it is now covered under such a policy only when it is not worn outside the home—which is not what most owners had in mind when the jewelry was purchased. Coverage outside the home comes under a special, and very costly, policy.

This is why Cartier's gives free insurance from Lloyd's on pieces bought there, but only for one year. Tiffany's could do the same, but it feels that it is just a method of discounting the price of a piece.

The problem is not new, only magnified. For several years, residents of certain sections of New York City—along parts of Park Avenue, for example—have not been able to insure their jewelry. New York is not unique. In 1969 a customer of Tiffany's who lives in a wealthy suburb of Boston bought his mother-in-law a $55,000 necklace. He was surprised and dismayed to find that no company would insure jewelry in his neighborhood. He took his problem and the necklace back to Tiffany's. The store could do nothing for him but take the necklace back and refund his money.

Many top-income-bracket owners of jewelry carry no insurance on their jewels. If they are stolen, the loss can be written off on taxes and the savings are greater than the insurance premium would be. There is one not-so-minor problem; Internal Revenue insists that the taxpayer provide evidence that the jewelry actually was stolen, that a house or apartment was actually burglarized. The government is a trifle cynical about such matters since many "stolen" jewels are simply lost or left carelessly lying about to be taken. Such thefts as those which are engineered with passkeys in hotels or apartments are often difficult to prove to Uncle Sam's satisfaction.

T

he Cellini of the twentieth century." This is the way that Jean Schlumberger (rhymes with Fabergé), the store's top jewelry designer, is described by Chairman Walter Hoving, no man to minimize the talents of his staff. Schlumberger himself disagrees. "Cellini was a goldsmith and a sculptor in his own right," he says. "He worked with the metal himself. But I do not. I am what you might call a draftsman or a jewelry designer, much as Fabergé was."

But if Schlumberger wishes to designate himself as only a latter-day Fabergé, it is quite true that he is, at least, the equal of the great Russian. "Johnny," as Schlumberger is known to his friends, is the most famous—and considered by collectors the best—jewelry designer

(Above) The master: Benvenuto Cellini.

in the world today. His designs have set styles and trends, and he has a large and loyal following among the great and rich of the world. Many of his customers consider his jewelry works of art, to be displayed in their homes, along with their Picassos or Monets. He never designs to follow a particular fashion; he creates on the assumption that his jewelry will always be in fashion.

As an example, in 1940 he designed a Pegasus pin for Mrs. DeWitt Wallace of the *Reader's Digest* when the flying horse was carried on the magazine's cover as its trademark. The Pegasus has long been removed from the cover as being old-fashioned, but Mrs. Wallace's pin still looks extremely stylish.

For Mr. and Mrs. Paul Mellon, Schlumberger has done some beautiful pieces, more art than jewelry, which he likes to call fantasies. One such fantasy started out with a phone call from the widow of a mining engineer to Nicolas Bongard, who manages the business side of the Schlumberger department. Her husband's hobby had been collecting gems, she explained to Bongard, and now she wanted to sell some of them; was Tiffany's interested? Bongard went immediately to her hotel room. Rarely had he seen such a magnificent sapphire as the one which the woman took from her purse and handed him. The stone, weighing 100 carats, was bigger "than the end of a man's thumb" and the widow would sell it for $160,000. Bongard thought it a bargain and bought it immediately.

The sapphire was just the type of rare gem that Bongard knew that the Mellons, who have a notable jewel collection, would want. They did, and they commissioned Schlumberger to make a proper setting for such a prize gem. This posed something of a problem. The stone was too big for a ring, and almost too big for a brooch, except

Pegasus pin of Mrs. DeWitt Wallace.

one to be worn on special occasions. The Mellons wanted to be able to enjoy their magnificent gem at all times and not keep it in a jewel box or vault most of the year.

Schlumberger decided the stone could best be used in one of his fantasies, in this case, a sunflower. The result is a bloom, eight inches tall, on a gold stem with leaves sprinkled with emeralds. The heart of the flower is the sapphire surrounded by a sunburst of gold leaves; the back is pavé with diamonds. The flower grows out of an ordinary clay pot from the Mellons' greenhouse made extraordinary by a latticework of thin strips of gold. The ''dirt'' is black garnet dust. (Later, Schlumberger redesigned the flower slightly so that the sapphire could be detached and worn as a brooch.)

When Jacqueline Kennedy became First Lady, the President-elect had Schlumberger design a strawberry clip in rubies and diamonds for her, coming into the store himself to choose the design ''in December, before he was enthroned,'' Bongard recalls.

Schlumberger once made Aristotle Onassis a piece that was neither jewelry nor art, but an exact copy of the ''shoe'' used in dealing cards in baccarat. The shoe, which resembles an old-fashioned sugar or coffee scoop, holds a deck of cards so that they can be dealt out from the front, one by one. Onassis, who controlled the gambling at Monte Carlo, wanted the shoe to present to his Fiat friend Gianni Agnelli, because he was such a good customer. The shoe was made of ebony, covered with ivory lozenges held in place with crosses of gold. The handle was of gold. Both Onassis and Agnelli were delighted with the $15,000 shoe that worked just as well as an ordinary one.

Schlumberger was born in 1907 in Mulhouse, Alsace, the son of a wealthy textile manufacturer. His father was opposed to his artistic bent and sent him about the world to various jobs in an effort to turn him to business. None of these exposures took. In the early thirties, Schlumberger was in Paris, where—in the Flea Market—he finally found what he really wanted to do. There he picked up some china flowers and designed an assortment of clips for his elegant lady friends, including the Duchess of Kent, the Honorable Mrs. Reginald Fellowes and Elsa Schiaparelli. Schiaparelli was so pleased that she hired him to design costume jewelry for her. Before long, the great world of Paris wanted him to design for them, but now in real jewels.

During World War II, Schlumberger fought as a corporal with the French army, and was with the forces that were evacuated to England; he then made his way to New York, broke but not friendless. Mrs. Sophie Shannard, one of the owners of Chez Ninon, a fashionable custom dress house, got in touch with him and announced that the firm needed three evening dresses to complete its fall collection.

"But I've never designed any clothes," he protested.

"You must have learned something from Schiaparelli. We've got to have the dresses."

Schlumberger agreed to do the job and was paid on a royalty basis. "The dresses were very successful," Schlumberger recalls. *"Harper's Bazaar* gave a full page to them. They sold very well and I made a lot of money."

During the thirties, partner-to-be Bongard did some jewelry designing and was a cameraman for Twentieth Century-Fox. He and Schlumberger became friends when they both had summer houses in Saint-Tropez. When the war began, Bongard was called up, and was also a corporal. On a short furlough, he married his fiancée, Mary (Molly) Roby King, a Detroit girl who had been living in France with her mother, and now was being forced to return to the United States. Bongard rejoined the army, and when it fell apart, was captured by the Nazis. On his way to a prison in Germany he escaped and made his way to Marseilles and thence to America. Bongard arrived in New York broke, and without business connections. For a time he tried making clay buttons, painting them and hawking them to dressmakers along Seventh Avenue. Then occurred one of those coincidences found in fiction which, of course, almost never happen in real life. Bongard was walking along Fifth Avenue one day and stopped at a corner for a red light. There was Schlumberger also waiting at the light. The two rented small quarters at 745 Fifth Avenue, only a stone's throw—say, a stone the size of the Tiffany diamond—from Tiffany's.

This venture was short-lived. When the United States entered the

Nicolas Bongard.

*Trophee of Diana
Vreeland.*

war, the two young men immediately enlisted with the Free French.
Schlumberger was sent to London, Bongard to Libya. Again they lost
track of each other. Then came coincidence number two. Bongard
was forwarded to Beirut. Once more he was walking down a street.
He heard his name called: ''Hello, Nico.'' It was Schlumberger. As
Bongard says, ''There is nothing like a war to help you keep up with
old friends.'' War's end found them back in New York, partners in
designing jewelry in a shop at 21 East Sixty-third Street.

Their first customer was Diana Vreeland, later to be editor of
Vogue, and for her, Schlumberger made a brooch, calling it ''Trophée.'' The background is a shield, displaying a suit of chain mail;
from behind the shield extend the ends of a bow and arrows, the whole
worked in diamonds, amethysts, rubies and transparent blue enamel.

It is the sort of symbolism which seems easy to understand, but
it sent one critic soaring into the wild blue wonder on a flight of very
purple prose. Schlumberger dismisses such recherché analysis with
an amused ''Nonsense,'' but it is great for business.

At first, Schlumberger designed only for the small ''in'' group of
elegant New Yorkers who either had known him in Paris or had heard
about him from friends. The group kept getting bigger and bigger,
and the firm was soon on its way to fame and the fortune which ac-
companies it.

Schlumberger and Bongard are a perfect team. Both are charming.
Schlumberger is slight, five feet nine, and so soft-voiced he almost
whispers. With customers, the relationship is more a meeting of old
friends; they entertain him in their homes, and he entertains them.
Bongard is athletic, tall (six feet one), full of suppressed energy, and
speaks, in the Gallic manner, as much with his hands as with words.

Schlumberger is a bachelor and leads an untypical bachelor's life. In Manhattan, where he spends only three months of the year, he lives in a small gem of a house almost as rare as a black diamond: a white frame house, with a tiny front yard and a porch with four pillars, which the New York Historical Society would have liked to put on its list. (Schlumberger said "No.") The house is simply furnished, but in the basement is a well-stocked wine cellar, which includes a bottle of Cheval Blanc, St. Emilion '55, a present from Jacqueline Kennedy Onassis. The gift came after an exhibition of Schlumberger's work at the Wildenstein Art Galleries in 1961, for the benefit of the Newport Preservation Society—the only time a living jewelry designer has been so honored. The then Mrs. Kennedy opened the exhibit. Afterward, the First Lady and her friends went to Schlumberger's for supper. Schlumberger, who is well known to his friends as a cook, cooked the supper himself. In return, Jackie sent him the wine.

For three months of the year, he lives in Paris, where he and Bongard have their own company, independent of Tiffany's. The other six months he spends mainly in his house on Guadeloupe, in the French Antilles, where he does most of his work: "New York has become too distracting."

His house is, primarily, a workshop, and his day begins at 7 A.M. and continues until one in the afternoon. At his board he wears a midnight-blue smock, designed for him by Balenciaga. The master of sophistication keeps his radio on all the time, tuned to soap operas.

Schlumberger, like other designers, finds much of his inspiration in nature, notably the sea. He has done gold powder boxes shaped like scallops, and a prickly sea urchin containing an Accutron clock. His gold copy of the giant South Sea clam in the American Museum of Natural History is a marvel of miniaturization; the lines on the clam are marked with green garnets and turquoises or sapphires.

In his combining of precious stones with semiprecious stones to get the desired color pattern, Schlumberger again revives the old Tiffany tradition of Louis Comfort who had the same ideal. Schlumberger was also the first contemporary designer to combine enamel with precious stones. Enamel had been used before, notably by Fabergé, but the secret of working with it had been lost. When Schlumberger first began experimenting, the enamel cracked, or was opaque or otherwise unusable. But he persisted until he achieved the transparent effect he wanted, with no cracks.

Schlumberger has heard some complaints from customers in regard to his type of work, that "the mounting costs more than the stones." He reminds buyers of Fabergé pieces, of which the same has been said. "Fabergé is becoming more and more expensive all the time. If you drop any Fabergé piece and break it, the whole value is lost, even though you save the stones."

The more important Schlumberger creations are all three-dimensional, instead of flat as jewelry was heretofore. For all their seeming fragility they are very strong. Actually, the articles are what Schlumberger rightly calls "erected," more like a suspension bridge than a piece of jewelry. If an engineer should turn over a handsome domed clip, he could admire its construction, its fastenings, its architectural integrity. What appear to be exquisite little knobs of gold and platinum are in truth tiny bolts, nuts and screws which hold the construction together.

Beyond its functional construction, a Schlumberger piece is made to be admired from the back as well as the front. One of his handsomest creations is a clip, dominated by a huge aquamarine. The stone is wound around with an inch-wide ribbon of diamonds set in gold. Turn it over: the ribbon continues all the way around; there are as many diamonds on the back as on the front. Does it make all that much difference, since no one will really notice (in fact, the casual viewer cannot)? It does to Schlumberger and the owner, who know they are there, adding to the secret satisfaction of perfection, which is shared by all collectors.

Schlumberger has often taken the most popular and banal type of jewelry, such as a bracelet, redesigned it and started a fad. Several years ago he did an enameled bracelet, decorated with small dots of gold, for five thousand dollars. It became so popular he designed a whole series of them for Tiffany's. Hundreds were sold, since every rich woman who had any pretensions to being fashionable had to have one. "It was like a club, the wearers of these bracelets," Schlumberger says, with a smile.

Schlumberger started a trend for boxes which could double as *objets d'art* on a lady's desk or in a living room, or be carried as powder boxes or cigarette cases. Before, such articles were purely utilitarian; the rich playboy with his thin gold cigarette case was a stock character in fiction. The Schlumberger cases—and powder boxes —tend to be at least an inch thick. Nevertheless, a goodly number of people manage to carry them.

Another signature to the initiated is the interior, never finished, but a reverse of the pattern on the outside. If a box has a pattern of diamonds on the top, the inside of the lid shows the base of the stones.

The boxes are so cunningly designed that it is almost impossible to detect where the two sides join or to see the hinges. Besides, they open differently. One box might slide back on its hinges (not being able to see the hinges complicates this operation). On another, a small part of the design may have to be pressed in a certain way. This can have drawbacks. One day a woman came into the shop, slightly embarrassed. She had been given a box by a friend with a sense of humor. He had told her it was a compact, but had neglected to tell her how to open it. This particular box was shaped as a quatre-foil, each corner having a flower design with a sapphire center. Opening it was simple if one knew the trick; one pressed the sapphire opposite the hinge. Finding that perfectly executed hinge again complicated matters. In fact, one woman insisted that the stone to press on her box be a diamond so she would not have to puzzle in company.

Even the shrubs in Guadeloupe are designed.

The boxes are what Schlumberger calls his ''collectors' items.'' Only ten of each design are made and numbered. They cost from three thousand dollars to ten thousand dollars.

Some 30 percent of Schlumberger's sales are special orders. In these cases, he does more than suggest something which appeals only to him. He analyzes the tastes of the customer, and tries to design something which will have meaning to her. ''I have to find out what she likes, what sort of a life she leads,'' he says. ''Maybe she doesn't like green; or maybe she doesn't like flowers or sea shells. She may live in a small town where women do not wear certain jewelry. If she lives in Switzerland she won't wear diamond necklaces, because the women there think they make them look conspicuous. Some people come into our place and look around and say, ''I don't like this or that,'' and that is a great help because it is a guide. Often customers will give me an idea of what they want to spend on a piece, say, ten thousands dollars or between ten thousand dollars and fourteen thousand dollars. But, of course, it could end up costing nine thousand five hundred dollars or fifteen thousand dollars.

Jean Schlumberger in Paris.

1. Diamond and sapphire ear clips.

3. Turban powder case.

2. Diamond slave link bracelet.

4. Jasmine flower necklace.

5. Starfish clip.

6. Emerald and diamond dolphin clip.

7. *Diamond pod and flame ear clips.*

13. *Coral pear clip.*

8. *Pineapple clip.*

9. *Wings cigarette box.*

14. *Shell box.*

10. *Ribbons clip with Tiffany Diamond.*

15. *Black, white pearl bracelet.*

11. *Butterfly clip.*

12. *Petals ring.*

"Sometimes I turn down special orders. I don't like diamond baguettes, because I feel they are a stiff shape, so long and narrow. A man came to me for a clip for his wife and brought some of her jewelry to show me; it had been done by another house. It was not the kind of thing I do. I finally said to him, 'I have no idea why you're coming here. I can't do the type of thing you want, and I think it's much better that you go to the house that did the other things your wife has.' "

Possibly Schlumberger's most historic special order came fifteen years ago when the present Prince Napoleon, pretender to the Imperial Crown of France (to be distinguished from the Comte de Paris, the Bourbon-Orléans royal claimant) asked him to design a ring for his fiancée. Prince Napoleon, who is descended from Napoleon's youngest brother, Jerome, would supply the diamond, which had belonged to his great-great-aunt Josephine.

What could be more fitting than to surround the center diamond with small marquise diamonds in the form of tiny bees, the emblem of the Empire? Prince Napoleon was so pleased that he gave Schlumberger permission to duplicate the setting.

Often customers come in with jewelry and ask him to redesign the settings. Sometimes the diamonds are large and set solely to show off their size, harking back to the days when size counted ("See how rich we are"), not beauty. "If someone has inherited stones and they are big diamonds," says Schlumberger, "I try to make them easy to wear. But if you have a fifteen-carat diamond shining like a headlight, what can you do with it unless you cover half of it with gold? There are very few places now where a woman can wear necklaces with big stones, except to charity balls. You just can't wear them over a sweater because it is six o'clock."

"When Josh Logan produced *The Wisteria Tree* on Broadway," Schlumberger relates, "one of his associates came to me and asked me to make a pair of cuff links as a memento. I did them with tiny wisteria trees on them. That was easy. When Pearl Bailey was in *Hello, Dolly* I made a necklace of black pearls—a rope all twisted together, what we call a torsade—fastened with bands of yellow enamel and a diamond clasp for producer David Merrick to give her.

"Some people think the things I do are too spiky, and they hate spikes. If they don't like them, they shouldn't have them. But for the late Millicent Rogers who was one of my first customers, I did things that were all spikes, almost like a crown of thorns. They tore the linings of her clothes, but she loved them."

Sometimes the vagaries of the customers baffle both Schlumberger and Bongard. One of their most devoted collectors had seen a $30,000 diamond necklace in the display room that he had liked. A week or so later, he phoned from his out-of-town home and asked Bongard to bring it there so he could examine it more closely. The customer met Bongard at the door, looked about in a conspiratorial fashion, and hustled him into the downstairs powder room. There the gentleman examined the necklace, explaining it was to be a surprise and he didn't want his wife to see it yet. A few more weeks went by, and one morning the man's butler appeared in the shop, necklace in hand. It wasn't wanted any more, he said; he left it and departed.

Came the Christmas season and another call from the same customer —Was the necklace still available and could he reexamine it? This time, Bongard picked him up at a club in New York; the customer was in a hurry to get to the airport, so they called a cab and the necklace was appraised for a third time in the taxi, bought for the second.

A whole year went by, and another call came. It was the same man. Again he had turned thumbs down on the necklace and wanted Bongard to buy it back. Bongard agreed, for something under the original thirty thousand dollars. It happened that there was another customer who had admired the necklace and had been quite disappointed when it was sold. Bongard put in a long-distance call to her. Did she still want the necklace? She did indeed. The necklace was resold for thirty thousand dollars.

This was not the end of the story. Weeks went by, and the original buyer appeared in the shop. He wanted his necklace back. He was upset when he was told it had been sold; he *really* had to have it. Would Schlumberger make a duplicate? Bongard told him yes, if the new owner agreed. Another long-distance call. It chanced that the present owner knew the first one well, and since they lived some thousand miles apart, and there was little chance of both necklaces appearing at some fashionable event at the same time, the lady said yes.

So, for one of the few times he has done so, Schlumberger made the duplicate. However, what with inflation and the necessity of finding stones to exactly match those of the first necklace, the new one cost forty-five thousand dollars. As to the "why" of the performance, Bongard can only lift his shoulders in a Gallic shrug.

Schlumberger makes hundreds of pencil sketches to work out ideas. For an individual order, he will make fifteen to twenty sketches. The final pattern is done in watercolor or oils, to see, and show, exactly how the piece will look. The precise color, size and weight of the stones are specified. It is up to his assistants to find them. This can make for some rather tense moments for the help. You ask, ''How do you do it?'' They shrug. ''When Mr. Schlumberger says 'Find them' you find them.''

But even Tiffany's does not have a bottomless *Arabian Nights* chest of gems. In the case of one large brooch, it took two years to assemble the stones. It took over six months to find enough matching small marquise diamonds for a 1970 copy of the Prince Napoleon setting. And if Schlumberger wants six shades of rubies progressing from a delicate pale pink to the deepest red, they are found—in time. For this reason, Schlumberger refuses to be held to a definite date when he is creating to order. Satisfaction only is guaranteed. The customer pays what the piece costs and gets it when Schlumberger is satisfied that it is what he and the customer want. In ordinary cases, Schlumberger takes three or four weeks to design a necklace and it will be from six to eight months in the making.

The customer is never shown more than one design for a piece of jewelry. No fee is charged for making a design, and it is seldom turned down, but when this happens, it is put in the files. It often delights some future customer.

Only very old and very good customers are allowed to take a sketch out of the shop. ''If Mrs. William Paley wanted a design to show her husband, I'd be glad to give it to her,'' Schlumberger says, ''because I know she wouldn't go to any place else to have it made.''

The file of sketches is also useful in case customers are robbed. One eighty-year-old woman had her jewelry, valued in the hundreds of thousands, stolen. She decided that, at her age, it would be silly to replace the lot. Not long after, however, she called Schlumberger and asked him to duplicate a pair of stolen earrings and a clip. ''I feel naked without them,'' she confessed. For $30,000 she was able to feel partly dressed.

Schlumberger is known more for the customers he keeps than for awards, though he is the only jeweler to win the Coty award for fashion, which he did in 1959. Also, he was the subject of a lecture on the art of the jeweler at the Metropolitan Museum.

At his one-man show at the Wildenstein Gallery in New York, forty-one owners from around the globe lent eighty-five pieces. Since all were custom orders it is interesting to see what different people like. Over half of the pieces were clips; Mrs. T. Reed Vreeland loaned her Trophée, and Mrs. DeWitt Wallace her Pegasus. Typical was the ''star flower'' of sapphires and rubies which he made before he came to New York for the Honorable Mrs. Reginald Fellowes, one of his

*Mrs. Jacqueline
Kennedy Onassis.*

early customers. Mrs. Paul Mellon and her sister-in-law, Mrs. Mellon Bruce, preferred all precious stones. Mrs. Mellon has one starfish in rubies, and one in sapphires; her bluet in sapphires and her shell in sapphires and diamonds are all clips. Mrs. Mellon has a matching shell bracelet, and another of butterflies in diamonds, sapphires and amethysts. Mrs. Mellon's necklaces include diamond flowers, and turquoise and diamond leaves. She carries a number of the collectors' cases, one in emeralds, one diamonds, and one with a yellow sapphire. The famous Mellon flower pot as well as other *objets d'art* were also on view at the show. Mrs. Whitney and her sister-in-law, Mrs. Payson, also stay with precious gems. Mrs. Payson exhibited a butterfly, Mrs. Whitney was represented with a flower with one pear-shaped diamond for the center. Mrs. Paley had several pieces on view: her fruit bracelet in gold and diamonds; her famous tulip necklace (each bloom different); another of fringe and tassels of turquoise and diamonds. She, too, collects cases.

In all his long career, Schlumberger has made only one piece that has not sold. When he first joined Tiffany's, he studied the jewelry the store was making and decided to give his customer—in this case, Tiffany's—what it seemed to want. He did not believe that Hoving meant it when he said that Schlumberger was to create what *he* wanted. He designed a necklace in the old Tiffany style, which was precisely what Hoving did not want. Neither did anyone else. After that, Schlumberger went back to his own style.

Chairman Hoving follows none of the routine of the department, but he likes to see the completed pieces. Schlumberger once made a desk ornament, a large irregular chunk of topaz quartz with a tiny, saucy diamond-and-gold cockatoo perched on top. When Hoving saw it, he burst into laughter. "It's funny, Johnny," said Hoving, "but I love it." Schlumberger got the same reaction from the other executives and customers he showed it to. At first he was hurt. "Designing is serious business," he said later, "it is not funny." Funny or serious, everyone fell in love with the little bird on the big rock and Schlumberger now always has one in stock.

Over the years, Hoving has suggested only one design to Schlumberger. He asked if Schlumberger could make an egg for an Easter window display in the spirit of the biggest egg man of them all, Fabergé. Schlumberger produced a slightly larger-than-life egg, made of purple transparent enamel on 18-carat gold, resting on a gold crown of thorns. The egg is studded with chased raised gold crosses of all religions, ancient and modern, and topped by a plain Christian cross, draped with a golden rope. It took only two days for the egg to be sold out of the window—to Mr. and Mrs. Mellon.

G ene Moore who was brought over from Bonwit's to do Tiffany's windows, was given only one instruction by Hoving: "Make the windows beautiful and don't try to sell anything." As the Mellons—and hundreds of customers have proved—Moore could not help selling jewelry because he made the windows beautiful—and talked about. He works on a simple formula: "The first thing you have to do is to stop people. You can't just cram your windows full of expensive gems and expect to generate any excitement. You've got to make them interesting."

Stopping people is what the windows do—from the Manhattanite to the Iowa couple in town for New York's summer festival. As *Show Magazine* wrote: "Everyone enjoys Tiffany's free side show. It con-

(Above) Gene Moore.

sists of five store windows, five and one half feet wide, thirty-six inches high and twenty-two inches deep, filled with—what do you call them? Three-dimensional paintings? Assemblages? Compositions? Arrangements? Sculptural collages? Call them works of art, maybe. There's a lot more art and artistry in them than you'll find in many of the galleries in the neighborhood.''

The art and artistry is often mixed with humor. In the windows may be a ludicrous juxtaposition of materials, such as diamond rings strung about on spaghetti, or on perpendicular bamboo poles; a sedate party of stuffed monkeys, glasses in hand, may be sitting around a huge silver cocktail shaker.

Several years ago, when New Yorkers were being taught to walk again, courtesy of a strike by subway workers, Moore thought that ''something ought to be done, but it had to be amusing, because when you get too serious, people don't pay too much attention.'' In one window, Moore put a pair of skates, a pogo stick and other forms of ''transportation.'' In another window was a foot bath beside a pair of high-heeled shoes kicked into the corner. In the center was a pair of women's loafers. In a third window was the joke: there was a bicycle, with the front wheel running over a feather quill, a reminder that the unpopular strike had been called by union leader Mike Quill.

Moore's best-known windows were the result of another crisis in city life. Moore had created two tableaux of fountains featuring statues of cherubic boys: one standing amid ferns and flowers spilling water from a large oyster shell into a shallow pool, and the other pouring water from a conch shell into another pool. In one pool lay a $35,-000 Schlumberger bracelet and in the other an $80,000 diamond ring, both resting on invisible plastic stands so that they appeared to be floating on the water.

The displays had hardly been installed when the city, which had been muttering about a water shortage, suddenly decided that there really was one; City Hall decreed that all fountains were to be shut down. Moore's tiny waterfalls scarcely qualified under the ban, but it gave him a wonderful idea. The fountains were kept in operation, and in a corner of each window Moore put a small sign: ''No, this is not precious water. It is unprecious gin.'' People jammed the sidewalks as if they had never seen gin before. Furthermore, Moore did not even have to supply the gin; Seagram's was glad to—thirteen cases to get the tanks full and operating and an extra case a day for the ten days of the exhibit to make up for evaporation.

There was a spot of trouble with the fire department when it heard about the gin. An inspector called on Moore and told him he had to

Drumming up business.

Reclining figure.

Bicycle on Quill.

Ice cream cones.

Ice tongs holding diamond.

Heart cash register.

stop the flow because it was "inflammable." But Moore knew the windows had adequate ventilation. As they stood beside a window, Moore casually took out a book of matches. "Don't strike that match," cried the inspector. But Moore already had, and waved it inside the window and said, "We're still here, aren't we?"

Moore's great success is due to the fact that he sees displays as pictures; he studied at the Chicago Academy of Fine Arts hoping to be a painter. A slight, lean man, who always seems to be in a hurry (and usually is), he gave painting a fair trial for several years until he decided that he would never be more than a Sunday-afternoon dauber. During the Depression, Moore was working in an artificial-flower shop for ten dollars a week when his arrangements caught the eye of a free-lance window-display man named Jim Buckley. Buckley obtained a job as display director at I. Miller's and hired Moore as his assistant at thirty dollars a week. From there, Moore went to Bergdorf's, to Bonwit's and finally to Tiffany's.

Moore has gone about as far as anyone can go in creative design in window display, especially in the use of materials, such as artificial cobwebs, chunks of coal with diamonds mixed in with them; planks bristling with nails (a diamond necklace lying on top); a plot of real grass strewn with diamonds; peacock feathers, stuffed animals and birds. However, his most successful windows have been basically simple; he uses props made in his own shop on the seventh floor, with the help of his assistant, Ronald Smith. Moore's favorite display was also his simplest; it consisted of a huge cake of ice (plastic) and, leaning against it, a large pair of tongs holding a $125,000 diamond.

Moore enjoys holidays, any holiday. For Valentine's Day, he is apt to show a sweet tooth. He has used a cash register on which everything comes up candy hearts, with a few ruby ones interspersed; another display was gumdrops that spelled out "Love" in one window beside the Fifth Avenue door, "You" in the other. He has used an electrocardiograph showing the fluctuations of a heartbeat, with the tape scrawling "I Love You" over and over again, and strewn with diamonds.

Easter means eggs to Moore, as much as to any small child—whole eggs, broken eggs or half eggs, all carefully glued to boards to surround or curtain a window with eggs. Once, he made an Easter bonnet of eggs—a large picture hat with a small bird's nest (holding a bird and a few diamonds) perched on the side. Before the eggs can be used, they must be blown out and washed inside. But one year, Moore took a short cut and hard-boiled his eggs. Unfortunately he did not notice that a few of the shells became cracked. "After a few days," Moore remembers, "the stink got so tremendous in the store we had to throw out the display."

Around income tax time, the windows may comment on that fact of life. One year, a window showed a tax form, surrounded with a bottle of aspirin, an ice bag, a bunch of red pencils tangled in red tape, and off to one side what the taxes had *not* bought—a diamond necklace. Another window showed an open purse on a tax form spilling out the jewelry that had been bought, and containing only a few cents left for taxes; a noose hung in the next window; another displayed a classified telephone directory open to pawnshop listings, and a handful of jewelry. All of the tax forms were worked out correctly, because lookers like to check them for mistakes. Sometimes mistakes are deliberate. Moore once did a window containing six ice cream cones: on five were rings matching the color of the ice cream; the sixth was ringless. Passers-by took the trouble to come into the store to inform the clerks that "someone" had forgotten to top the last cone.

One spring all the windows contained piles of coal, with geraniums, poppies, marigolds and other flowers growing in the midst of the lumps. "I just wanted to make the point that, despite the filth of New York, spring will come here too," Moore explained.

Perhaps the most amusing winter window was a snow scene. In one corner was the head of a St. Bernard carrying around his neck a bottle of champagne. In the center, a woman's arm thrust gracefully up through the snow; around the wrist was a diamond bracelet and the hand seemed to be beckoning with an empty champagne glass tilted in the direction of the dog.

Only once has Moore used the Tiffany diamond, and that was in his very first windows. In the center of one floated an angel made of gold wire, holding in her outstretched hands the great canary diamond. Even the store was amazed to find that the gem could be seen clearly all the way across the avenue. At that time, Moore could use any jewelry in the store in displays, no matter how expensive. The smash-and-grab robbery put an end to that practice. Now Moore has a limit of a hundred and fifty thousand dollars for all windows, with a maximum of fifty thousand dollars in any one window.

Moore's talents have occasionally led him into what might seem unrelated fields. One night, he received a phone call from London. The voice at the other end said, "My name is John Gielgud. I don't know if you've heard of me."

"Yes, I've heard of you."

"I'm coming to New York and I'd like to have lunch with you."

276*The Tiffany Touch*

Gielgud gave Moore the name of his agent, and asked Moore to call him. When he did, the mystery was cleared up. The agent read Moore a letter from Gielgud, saying, "I don't know who does the Tiffany windows, but that's the person I want to do the sets for my next play."

At lunch, Gielgud told Moore that he always "caught" the Tiffany windows when in New York. Now he wanted Moore to do the sets for his London production of Thornton Wilder's *The Ides of March*. Moore agreed; he also agreed to do the costumes, since he had done some clothes designing at Bonwit Teller. When he told a man in the theatrical business about the project, the friend scoffed. What made Moore think he could do the sets and costumes when he had never worked in the theater?

"Sets are nothing but window displays blown up to a large scale," Moore replied. "He became furious because he thought I was belittling his profession. But I wasn't. I had done one off-Broadway show and knew something about it." On opening night in London, Moore received a cable from his friend: "Congratulations on your mammoth window display."

One Christmas window contained only a small gold reindeer in the snow, his antlers decorated with diamonds. A couple came in and asked to buy the reindeer. Since it was the only object in the window, the clerk phoned Moore to come down.

"You know," the man told Moore, "that deer is the only thing my wife has seen in seven years that she feels she must have. Would you mind if we took it now? We're from out-of-town."

"I'm glad she likes it so much," Moore told him. "I'll get it out of the window and do another."

"I really am delighted when things like that happen," Moore says. "Maybe it sounds commercial, but of course Tiffany's is commercial. Only, while you're being commercial, you have to give people the best of everything."

The windows are a magnet which bring people into the store. They are the first step in "seeing Tiffany's," and quite often tourists ask when breakfast is served. Such nonreaders of Truman Capote's novel are not aware that the heroine, Holly Golightly, had her "breakfast at Tiffany's" by walking among the cases on the first floor to nourish her spirits, and not her stomach, with pleasure at the sight of the magnificent gems. The windows have contributed their own share to the Tiffany legend. One day, as songwriter Jimmy McHugh and his lyricist, Dorothy Fields, were admiring a beautiful diamond bracelet in one of the windows, a young man and his girl stopped beside them.

The girl murmured something to her boyfriend, too low for McHugh to hear. But his reply was plain. "I wish I could too, baby," the young man said. "But I can't give you anything but love." And so the song was born.

In addition to window displays, Moore is director of design development in the gold jewelry department. As in his windows, Moore is often inspired by commonplace objects.

"I love to go into hardware stores," Moore says. "I was in a store in Southampton, and while I was waiting I was playing with a nut and bolt. I unscrewed the nut and slipped it on my finger and thought, 'My God! What a wonderful man's ring that would be.' It was a square nut, so I designed a ring that had a stone on two sides of it. I did a similar octagonal one in plain gold. I even did a woman's ring in platinum, with diamonds pavé for ten thousand dollars, and we sold two of them the first month. Imagine."

The customer who has not been in Tiffany's for thirty years would notice little change in the physical appearance of the first floor. The teak floor, badly marred by the fashionable spike heels of women customers, was a casualty of the sixties, and was carpeted in a brilliant emerald-green. Entering the store from Fifth Avenue, diamond jewelry and all the expensive gems are to the left, as is the Tiffany diamond in its case in the wall. To see and try on the very expensive diamond rings, the customer or browser must continue around the counter, nearer the wall, and the very-present guards.

Scene from Breakfast at Tiffany's.

Donald Claflin.

One long display case is devoted to the works of Donald Claflin, a handsome man whose tight black curls looks like a design in themselves. His liking for larger, bolder, chunkier pieces of precious jewelry has made him, so *The Wall Street Journal* found, a "favorite with the jet set." In the fall of 1970 Claflin received what may be considered his most important commission from the store; he conceived a new Tiffany setting. Instead of the historic single band, this setting consists of two crossed bands (plain gold, platinum or with tiny diamonds) the center diamond set within the intersection. The crossed bands are designed to make the ring—and the stone—look more important.

The jewelry created by Donald Claflin is displayed in front of a selection from the designs of Jean Schlumberger, a few of whose pieces can be seen without the trip to the mezzanine shop. The most crowded spot always is before a short counter, to the right of the Fifth Avenue entrance. This is the department for plain wedding bands, pins and small bracelets. Even on a rainy Thursday morning in April the customers are two and three deep. On Saturdays and the days between October and Christmas and in May and June the buyers are lined up five and six deep. The buyers are young—mostly couples, some men on their own, a few single girls. The sales are cash.

As to the expensive jewelry, more men tend to buy and choose on their own. A surprising number pay cash (women usually charge). Sixty percent of the business is done in the eight weeks before Christmas, 35 percent of it coming from out-of-town. If a customer wishes to examine high-priced pieces in privacy, he may use one of the small rooms along the Fifty-seventh Street wall, accompanied by his salesman and, of course, a guard. Customers sometimes impress even the guards with their lack of concern about cash. A few months ago, a guard was called to take a purchase and the money to the wrapping desk for a customer from Korea. He peeled off twenty-two $500 bills and handed them to the guard, who reported, "There were twice that many left in his wallet."

Some of the browsers have a mission not involved with buying. One morning two ladies from the suburbs, in slacks and car coats, went directly to the case where the colored stones are on display. They leaned over the counter. "See," said one, "it is just like my emerald ring. I thought he was kidding, but I guess he really did get it from Tiffany's." The clerk said nothing but beamed at them as they walked happily away. The clerk felt it was not in his province to inform the ladies that the stone they saw was jade.

Before leaving the store, nearly every person, long-time customer or tourist, will stop to take one look at the Tiffany diamond. Children enjoy the experience most since they do not have to pretend they are impressed. (Some are disappointed: "Shouldn't it be white?") The stone is the subject of a story now current. "What would I get if I sold the Tiffany diamond?" an eager new salesman asked. "Fired," replied Boss Hoving.

The diamond still is "worth a visit," even if one knows how cunningly it is lit from every angle in its shadow box so that it appears larger, more yellow and more dazzling than life.

Little boys often ask whether the diamond can be stolen. The answer is no; that glass shadow box is a very secure safe wired to alarms. Inevitably the boys' attention is diverted to the hatted detectives, whom they admire more than the diamond. The children supply one of the few diversions for the detectives, who consider themselves as much a part of the friendly Tiffany legend as the oldest clerk.

It was a guard who objected most vehemently when the emerald carpeting went down; he did not consider it dignified enough. Nor were the guards pleased when Schlumberger had the dark paneling in his department painted white. "They'll be doing it down here next," one of them said, looking around him with the air of a member of the City Commission to Preserve Old Landmarks.

The salesmen are even more proprietary, if possible. Their long service (twenty-five years is not unusual) has taught them to be unfailingly obliging; they not only have an encyclopedic knowledge of gems, but they have learned that it is impossible to tell a buyer from a tourist, or the tourist who may turn into a buyer. While many of those who peer into showcases and ask questions are merely "getting a course in gemology," as the salesmen say, there can be unexpected rewards.

Five women came into the store one noon and began to tour, occasionally asking to try on a particular piece. They seemed to have nothing more on their minds than killing time before the matinée. When they reached the diamond counter, they began to examine rings with more excitement. Patiently the clerk brought out a number to try on. Finally, all agreed that the best-looking was the marquise diamond which one woman had on her finger. As the woman took it off she said to the salesman, "Please put this aside. My husband will be in later to see it."

Delighted that the "lookers" had turned into possible buyers, the clerk tagged the ring. The next day the husband appeared. He turned out to be William Keck, then the multimillionaire head of Superior Oil. He wanted to buy his wife a ring, but he did not like her selection. So the salesman brought out his stock again. Keck inspected them all, and decided that his favorite was a 17-carat emerald-cut diamond, costing around $100,000, more expensive than the marquise. "My wife will be in again," Keck told the clerk, "but, remember, I don't like marquise diamonds."

A few days later, Mrs. Keck reappeared. She did not like the emerald-cut; she still wanted the marquise. "I'm sorry, Mrs. Keck," the salesman told her, "your husband is pretty firm. If you want a diamond ring, I think you'll have to take the emerald-cut."

The Kecks were about to take off for Europe, and for a less ingenious salesman, this might have ended the matter. But this salesman had a suggestion: Why didn't Mrs. Keck take the emerald-cut ring with her on the trip and see whether wearing it would change her mind? A reasonable woman, Mrs. Keck left with the ring. When the head of the diamond department heard about this he took the salesman to task.

"What's wrong with the idea?" the salesman asked. "The Kecks agreed to pay for the insurance policy while the ring is out of the store, so there is no risk. Besides, they'll be looking at jewels in Europe. If they don't take the ring along, they'll probably buy one over there."

The boss was somewhat mollified. He was even more mollified when the Kecks came home and kept the ring. Keck was so pleased with the way Tiffany's had handled the affair that he bought a two-strand pearl necklace, pearl earrings, a pin, a diamond flower brooch and matching earrings. The total: more than $175,000.

Not always has a difference in opinions about rings turned out so well for the would-be wearer. A wealthy out-of-town customer came in with a young woman one day to purchase a ring. They selected a sapphire ring for $27,000, but after some discussion, the man handed it back to the clerk, saying, "She wants a diamond ring. I'll be back later to select one." Two days later he returned alone and chose a diamond ring. The price: $190,000.

He told the clerk that his lady friend was having her hair done at Elizabeth Arden's, just a block from Tiffany's, and to call her there. "Tell her to come right over," the man said. "I can't wait, but if she likes the ring, give it to her and charge it to me."

The sales clerk called Arden's, but the woman had already left, saying she was going shopping the rest of the day. That night the man died. And although the woman tried to persuade Tiffany's that he had actually ordered the ring for her, she never got it.

Sometimes even the old salesmen goof. Everyone at Tiffany's remembers the unshaven man in wrinkled chinos, well-worn sports jacket and sneakers. As he approached the diamond counter, the regular salesmen took one look at his shabby appearance and devoted themselves to more likely-looking buyers. Chino Pants was left to a young woman, one of the temporary employees hired during busy seasons. She had not yet made a sale but she had been told to be helpful to everybody, no matter how unprepossessing, as long as they were well behaved.

Chino Pants leaned over the counter, pointed to a necklace and said, "I'll take that." The girl was so flustered that she broke all the rules, picked up the necklace, and took it to the back of the room to her supervisor. "That man," she pointed, "wants to buy this. Should I have it wrapped?"

Who was the customer? She didn't know. The supervisor, after one look, took over. He went back to the counter with the girl. "The necklace is seventy-five thousand dollars," he said. "I know," said Chino Pants, "I saw it before." He identified himself (he was a movie producer), wrote out a check and went out with his necklace. The salesgirl's commission was thirteen hundred dollars.

All the salespeople have stories in what might be termed the paper-bag tradition à la Hetty Green. One tells about the elderly man who came in one afternoon and asked for the men's ring department. He was carrying a bundle under his arm wrapped in the *Daily News*. He finally picked out a ring tagged at thirty-five hundred dollars, and unwrapped the bundle—it was full of small bills. He explained that he was in the policy business. What did he want engraved on the ring?

"I don't think I'll have anything engraved on it," he replied, "because I may not keep it long. But I'm going to be a big man in Harlem tonight.''

On another occasion the customer was a poorly dressed old woman, carrying a paper shopping bag. She looked at rings, complaining all the while that none of them fit her finger. Gradually the price went up as she fussed about the fit. Finally the salesman brought out a ring for thirty-five thousand dollars. This was her size. The woman lifted her shopping bag to the counter, counted out thirty-five thousand dollars and walked out with the ring on her hand.

While the salesmen are occasionally fooled by the unkempt, they have also been taken aback by the kempt. One day a man came into the store whom the clerk recognized as one of the world's wealthiest men. He wanted an engagement ring. Dreaming of a huge commission, the salesman brought out $75,000 and $100,000 diamonds as a start.

The customer stopped him. The clerk feared he had insulted the man by starting too low. ''No, no,'' the customer protested, ''those rings are too expensive. I want something more modest.'' The more modest rings were eight thousand to ten thousand dollars. The customer took two to show his fiancée.

A few days later, the customer's butler came into the store to return the rings. The only trouble was, they were in Cartier boxes. After some confusion, the butler got the Tiffany rings and the Cartier rings in the proper boxes. The rich lover had been shopping around, just like poor folk, and had found a better bargain than either Tiffany's or Cartier's offered.

The staff may play it cool with the poorly dressed, but what impresses it least is flashiness, either in clothes or manner. Sometime ago a flamboyantly dressed man came in near closing time. His talk and actions made him quite conspicuous as he looked over the stock. He finally settled on a ring for ten thousand dollars, while announcing that he was a West Coast member of a well-known family. However, when asked to show some identification, it was as meager as he was florid in manner. The supervisor was called and backed up the clerk and cashier: Tiffany's really would like to have more references.

The would-be customer then proceeded to put on quite a show. He was a very important man in Hollywood; he had just given a check for three thousand dollars to Saks Fifth and one for five thousand dollars to Bonwit Teller—both had been happy to have his business. Why didn't Tiffany's call the other stores? The man looked at his watch impatiently.

He demanded to see one of the officers of the store and created such a scene that the salesman called Ellsworth P. Hyde, a vice president

Farnham Lefferts,
president of
Tiffany & Co.

and treasurer of the company, and asked if he would come down to the first floor. Hyde looked at the identification and he, too, most politely said no. The would-be customer became even more excited, and said he was catching a plane within an hour—he must have the ring to take with him. He demanded to see the president of Tiffany's. By happy chance, Farnham Lefferts at that moment passed by on his way home, and Hyde called him over. Lefferts also said no. The man flounced out as the doors locked behind him.

When Tiffany's checked later with Bonwit's and Saks, it found that the man had bought everything he said he had and paid with checks—of the purest rubber. Tiffany's gives the man G for Guts, however. A year later, he entered the store again while the salesman he had tried to hoodwink before was out to lunch, and went to work on a new salesman. He was doing fine until the first salesman returned from lunch—and the con man ran from the store.

At Tiffany's a great deal of the selling skill lies in what a salesman calls that "intuitive feeling." An old hand recalls that he was approached one day by a woman, quiet in manner and plainly dressed, who wanted an aquamarine ring. She made her choice quickly; but while she was studying the stock the salesman was studying her. As she waited to have her purchase wrapped, the clerk suggested casually, "You impress me as a person with a taste for beautiful things. Would you like to see some of our new pieces?"

"Yes, I think I'd like to see some of the earrings," the customer said, and with scarcely more fuss than she had made over the aquamarine, she bought a pair of pearl earrings.

"Here are some necklaces that have just come in," the salesman went on, taking two strings from the case. Holding one up to her throat, she smiled. "I've always wanted a necklace with pearls as big as mothballs." The salesman reached in the case again. "Here's our mothball special," he said. The customer tried on the string, identified herself, and asked if she could take the string home to show her husband.

The next day, the husband called the salesman to say he did not like the color of the pearls. The salesman, who had investigated, had learned that the husband's hobby was horticulture. He told him: "You know, there are differences in the colors of pearls just as there are differences in the colors of roses. May I come out and show you the difference?"

The salesman was invited for lunch at the Long Island home. Tiffany's supplied a limousine and liveried chauffeur for the occasion. After lunch, the salesman gave his host a dissertation on pearls, ending the lecture by taking out of his pocket a string of beautiful Burmese pearls with a pinkish sheen. Held next to the flat-white necklace the wife had selected, there was no comparison. The husband was enchanted with his lesson as well as with the Burmese pearls. The string, with the lesson thrown in, cost him $130,000. (Unfortunately, since the nationalization of the pearl fisheries in Burma, the pearls are so poor that they are unsalable.)

The wife has since become one of the salesman's best clients; she has not only purchased over eight hundred thousand dollars in jewelry, but has helped the salesman sell more to her friends, including a $250,000 pink diamond that changed hands at another Long Island lunch.

For many Tiffany customers, it is always "Be kind to animals" week. There was Zita, a small French poodle, who had a platinum collar, set with an emerald, and her own engraved calling cards. One day her master brought Zita into the store after she had finished a horrid session at the dentist. She had been a good patient and deserved a present, maybe something nice in a new collar. It was a simple matter to clasp around her neck a gold-and-pearl bracelet, a solution which Tiffany's had found useful before. Another poodle was even more resplendent; she had her ears pierced and trotted out wearing diamond earrings and a matching collar.

Tiffany's learned Thai etiquette from another customer. He came into the store carrying a good-sized box and made for the earring counter. Could he buy just one diamond earring? Tiffany's does not break pairs, but the man was so insistent that the clerk called over the manager to handle the situation. Why *did* the man want only one earring? At this point the customer reached into the box, lifted out a Siamese cat and placed her on the counter. "This is my wife's cat," he explained, "and it's my wife's birthday and I want to give her a present. You know, of course, that a Siamese cat wears only one earring; that is the correct thing." Always keen to do the correct thing, Tiffany's sold the earring.

A beetle proved more of a problem. In 1965 Mrs. Gene Stephenson, of Altamonte Springs, Florida, made her first visit to New York. With her came Black Elvis, a small, live Mexican beetle, encrusted with rhinestones and pearls, which she wore on the lapel of her suit, attached by a small gold chain. (Tiffany's had sold such beetles in the last century.) The chain broke and the only jewelry store Mrs. Stephenson knew about in New York was Tiffany's, so there she went. The repair department told her that the chain would take two weeks to fix. Back she went to the first floor, where a manager became so interested in the dilemma of Elvis that he found some tools and made the repair himself.

Mrs. Stephenson was delighted. "But what do I owe you?"

"Nothing," replied the manager, "compliments of Tiffany's . . . but could we take a picture of the beetle?" Up to the studio on the sixth floor they went, and Elvis was photographed for the benefit of the press.

"We spent the rest of the afternoon at Tiffany's," Mrs. Stephenson recalled, when she returned home. "It was really fun."

A salesman's service to a customer does not end when the sale is made. Each piece of jewelry carries an identifying number as well as the Tiffany stamp. All salesmen keep track of the numbers in their books, so that jewelry can be easily identified if necessary. From this practice arose the most incredible tale of identification in the history of the store—and a pretty interesting bit of detective work as well.

The story begins in the waters off Pink Beach in Bermuda, in 1968, where Horton S. Spitzer of Fairfield, Connecticut, was skin-diving. Spitzer found a man's ring, wedged in the rocks. On shore, he noticed the Tiffany trademark, and sent the ring to the store to see if it could be identified. It had been sold to a Mr. Brooke Cadwallader. Unfortunately Cadwallader was no longer at his New York address. The salesman did not stop there; he had an old friend named Mrs. Aiken Cadwalader Reese, of Princeton, and he phoned her, even though she did not spell the name the same. It was a lucky shot. Mrs. Reese's mother turned out to be a distant cousin of the customer; both had descended from two brothers who had come to this country from Wales in the seventeenth century, and after a quarrel of some sort, one had dissociated himself from the other by changing the spelling of his name.

Both the store and Mrs. Reese set to work to track down the cousin. He was eventually located in Cuernavaca, Mexico, and he remembered all about losing the ring. It had happened back in 1940 in Clearwater, Florida, where he was visiting his mother and sister. While fishing in a small boat, he had trouble starting the outboard motor. On one of his hard jerks on the cord the ring flew from his finger and was lost.

The big mystery is: How had the ring journeyed from Florida to Bermuda? Had someone found the ring and lost it again? Or, as Tiffany's likes to think, had a fish swallowed the ring off Florida and, like Jonah's whale, spewed it out in Bermuda? Like many tales of Tiffaniana, there is no one to say that this is not true.

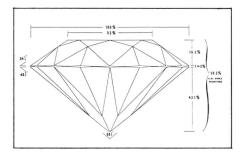

T

he heart of Tiffany's—and
the store that sells more engagement rings than any other single establishment in the world must have a heart—is the diamond office.
Here all precious stones—diamonds, rubies, sapphires and emeralds—
are purchased, graded and priced. Since millions of dollars in gems
are stored in the safe at any given time, it is the most closely guarded
area of the store. Yet the atmosphere is casual; a million dollars'
worth of emeralds can lie for hours in an open box on somebody's
desk, waiting to be appraised and perhaps bought. The attitude would
seem offhand to an outsider; but an outsider, in any case, has little
chance of entering the office. There are only twelve employees in the
department and only one of them has the keys; the others must be let

(Above) Diagram of perfect diamond cut.

in and out through locked doors. Furthermore, each door has two locks and two keys; one key is used to enter and the second is needed to leave. Only one other person in the store carries these keys. To most Tiffany employees, the diamond office is only a name; they have never been there and have only a vague idea of its location.

The elevator to the diamond office opens not into a corridor, but into a small, heavy cage, where every employee is held until he can be certified. The office itself consists of one large room, where most of the work is done, and two smaller rooms. Dealers are not allowed in the office; they must deliver their gems through an opening, really a small chute, in the back wall. It is long enough so that a person inserting a package cannot grab the arm of an employee and force him to open the office door. Any such attempt, of course, would start the alarm bells ringing all over the store.

The busiest machines in the office are the diamond scopes, binocular microscopes especially designed to inspect diamonds, and to determine whether rubies, sapphires and emeralds are natural or synthetic. Before the scopes were purchased about seven years ago, Tiffany's used specially constructed binocular microscopes with dark field illumination, although some old-timers continued to grade with a jewelers' loupe. Down the years there had been no standard way of grading diamonds. Usually, they have been described in terms most appealing to potential customers; "flawless, blue-white stone" was a popular description. But in 1938 the Federal Trade Commission brought down to earth the flights of fancy that diamond descriptions had become. The FTC decreed that a diamond could be sold as flawless if no imperfection could be seen in ordinary daylight with a ten-power magnification of a jewelers' loupe. This is far from complete protection for the customer. One expert will find flaws which another, equally honest, may miss entirely. This can be highly embarrassing, as Tiffany's found out.

An out-of-town customer bought a "flawless" diamond ring for sixty thousand dollars. Back home in Dallas, she could not resist visiting Neiman-Marcus, where she normally bought her jewelry, to show off her Tiffany diamond to the salesman who always waited on her.

"Tiffany's said it was flawless," she told the man, with the implication that she could not have found so fine a stone in Dallas.

"It is a beautiful ring," the salesman told her admiringly, "may I see it, please?"

The customer handed it over. The salesman screwed his loupe into his eye and studied the stone as he had never studied a diamond before. After several minutes of intense concentration, checking the stone from every angle, a pleased look came over his face. He handed back the ring.

"You're quite right," he said "it *is* a beautiful stone, one of Tiffany's best." And then he added with false regret, "It's too bad it has a slight flaw."

"Impossible," the woman retorted.

"It's only a slight flaw," the salesman consoled her, "so what does it matter."

He knew how much it did matter, so much so that the woman flew to New York and called on the Tiffany clerk who had sold her the ring.

"It has a flaw," she told him flatly.

"Impossible," replied Tiffany's man. "It's marked flawless." (Every ring has a tag which tells the salesman the grade of the diamond, the size and price so that the stone cannot be misrepresented.) The ring was sent up to the diamond office for another inspection. This disclosed what appeared to be a flaw near one of the prongs, so the stone was removed from the setting and cleaned. The "flaw" disappeared; it had been caused by the reflection of a bit of jewelers' rouge caught under the prong. To be on the safe side, Tiffany's then sent the stone to an outside expert, the Gemological Institute of America, generally known as GIA. This is the laboratory of the American Gem Society, to which most reputable jewelers belong, and which makes its own objective tests and issues a certificate specifying exactly the grade of a gem.

Tiffany's was dismayed to learn that there was indeed a flaw in the stone which its grader had missed. Naturally, Tiffany's told the customer that it would take back the ring or reduce the price. Impressed by the admission of error, and the price reduction, the customer thought things over and said, "It really is a beautiful ring; I'm going to keep it anyway."

The grading of diamonds is a minor art, takes excellent eyesight, long practice and, in the case of Tiffany's, predetermined standards which it had set long before the FTC stepped into the picture. In judging diamonds as to color, i.e., whiteness, the firm has used four "grading stones," each of two carats, for the past forty years. The stones are of varying shades of whiteness. Color is one of the four C's by which diamonds are graded: the others are Clarity, Cutting and Carat weight. (The matter of flaws is classified under Clarity.)

The top Tiffany color is "Extra River," the term "River" coming from the fact that in the early days of African mining the best stones were found in the alluvial wash of rivers. The second grade is

"River," the third "Fine White." (No reputable jeweler still uses the term "blue-white"; all white diamonds throw off blue flashes.) Tiffany's grades its stones for color by how closely they match the grading stones. Occasionally the firm will acquire a gem whose color is better than its finest grading stone. Such a diamond will be termed "Extra Extra River," or even "Extra, Extra, Extra River." These gems are rare and becoming rarer.

If a stone shows no flaws when viewed through the scope at ten power, it is designated "Perfect." If there is only a slight flaw, the stone becomes M1 or M2 ("M" for microscopic), depending on the size of the blemish, which can be a tiny crystal spot. The third class is VSI, "Very Slight Inclusion"; the fourth class is SI, or "Slight Inclusion"; and the bottom class, "Imperfect," if the flaw can be seen with the naked eye.

Next in importance to the beauty and value of the stone is the cut. Because of the diamond's great power to refract light, a properly cut modern stone will catch rays of light and direct them toward the center of the stone, from which they will be reflected back through the top, the "table," to give the greatest brilliance.

For centuries the cutting of diamonds was avoided. In India, where all diamonds were mined until the discoveries in Brazil in the eighteenth century, the stones were simply polished and rough points smoothed off, leaving them as near their original size as possible. Sometime before the first travelers from the West appeared, a workman had found a stone that was flat on both top and bottom and polished it crudely with diamond dust to create the ancestor of the table cut. Diamonds still were not as impressive as the great colored stones. In some period before the fifteenth century an unknown genius in India began to shape diamonds by cutting facets, for the first time bringing out their brilliance. Eventually, the idea of faceting crossed to Venice and moved north.

Like most stories in diamond history, there are as many conflicting tales as there are facets about who faceted the first stones in Europe. There is an anecdote about a certain Louis de Berquem, who supposedly lived in Belgium in the fifteenth century and is credited with being the first to cut diamonds to a geometric pattern. While a statue has been erected in his honor in Antwerp, some diamond experts say that the great pioneer never existed at all.

Later sources agree that it was Cardinal Mazarin (who collected the gems which became the nucleus for the French crown jewels) who gave the impetus in Europe toward the daring innovation of cutting. For it did take daring and some knowledge of diamond cleavage to

split or facet a stone correctly, when any error would shatter the gem
and leave only a worthless heap of diamond dust. At any rate, the
Cardinal permitted one of his stones to be put to the test, a cut of 24
facets which is now called Old Rose. Before many years there were im-
provements; the Dutch cutters raised the facets to 36, the Dutch Rose;
then 48, the Brabant Rose; and then the full glory of the 58 facets *
as we know diamond cutting today.

In the last cut, there are 32 facets on the Crown or Bezel, the portion above the Girdle, the widest part of the stone, and 24 on the lower
half, called the Pavilion. To make 58, add the Table, the widest clear
part of the stone on the top, and Culet or tip at the bottom. All facets
have quaint or romantic names: Star, Templet, Quoin, Lozenge,
Spew. The trap brilliant has 72 facets and the Tiffany diamond has
90, the greatest number of all.

All this romance was reduced to cold science in 1919, when a physi-
cist by the name of Marcel Tolkowsky mathematically determined the
precise, most advantageous placing of each of the facets, which until
then was arranged at the whim of the cutter. The Tolkowsky Cut was
so superior that all cutters were glad to adopt it. Even the emerald-
cut diamond gets its brilliance from faceting: 24 above the girdle, 8
comprising the Girdle itself and 24 below.

The cutting of a diamond is the only way by which man can enhance the value of a stone; the other three "C's" are either there or
they are not. But cutting can make a vast difference in brilliancy as
well as in retail price. There is an ideal cut for diamonds as well as an
ideal number of facets, but the ideal cut often reduces the finished
stone more than the cutter wishes. To compare a stone to the ideal cut
instantly, the diamond office has a "proportion scope," an instrument
which magnifies a diamond onto a small screen where the ideal cut is
outlined. Too shallow a cut will distort the reflections of light so that
they do not flash up through the table properly, but slip away through
the sides or the bottom.

Since more than half the weight of a stone may be lost in faceting
(the Tiffany diamond went from 287.42 carats to 128.51), cutters are
often tempted to sacrifice brilliance for a larger stone. That is why it
is possible to buy a "flat" stone for less than a smaller stone with the
ideal cut. That is also why the unknowing buyer thinks she is getting
a bargain when she finds a larger stone selling for the same price as a

---

* When the Regent, the greatest of the French crown jewels, was cut in 1719, it was given
the full 58 facets to show its perfection, but the size of the stone decreased from 410 to
140.5 carats. Diamond experts consider the Regent the greatest brilliant of them all, even
though it has a slight flaw. It was last on view when the French crown jewels were displayed
in 1962; if shown again, it might be worth a trip to Paris.

smaller stone at Tiffany's or another top jeweler's.

The last "C" in judging stones is the weight, the carats, so named from the seeds of the carob tree which were used to balance the scales in ancient Oriental bazaars. About 142 carats weigh an ounce; stones of less than a carat are called "pointers" (100 points equal one carat).

Unlike most products, the value of diamonds does not go up in arithmetical progression but in geometric progression. A two-carat diamond costs more than twice a one-carat diamond of the same quality, a four-carat diamond more than four times a one-carat and so on. As of 1971, Tiffany's prices for an ideally cut, flawless River diamond rose like this:

1 carat	$1,750
2 carats	$5,850
3 carats	$12,775
4 carats	$21,500
5 carats	$33,000
6 carats	$43,300
7 carats	$54,800

However, buyers must never forget that all four "C's" are taken into account in the price. A one-carat flawless Extra River will fetch much more than an off-color, flawed or poorly cut stone of much greater weight. With rare exceptions, Tiffany's buys no uncut stones; outside cutters, through long association, know exactly what Tiffany's wants. But even with this, Tiffany's must sometimes make decisions after purchase, and sometimes they are wrong. Tiffany's recently bought a large stone of fine color which it knew had a minor flaw, shown by the diamond scope. (Flaws can be studied under the diamond scope, which can magnify up to forty-five times, to determine if a slight recutting of the stone will eliminate the defect.) The high magnification showed that this flaw was near the surface, so the diamond office decided that the stone could be recut slightly and, as a flawless diamond, become more valuable. The store checked the operation out with both the original cutter and with the GIA; they agreed with Tiffany's. The cutter recut as he was told and returned the stone; there still were traces of the flaw. Back the stone went.

When the stone was returned a second time the flaw had been eliminated, and the diamond was sent to the GIA to be certified as flawless. GIA found that the flaw was gone, but . . . it was a big "but": right in the middle of the stone was another flaw, which the cutter, Tiffany's and the GIA had all missed on two inspections. This flaw could not be taken out. The stone, smaller and now classified, M1, was worth less after the "improvement."

Tiffany's does not think that minor flaws should unduly influence the purchaser. The diamond office estimates that 85 percent of the diamonds sold in the country as "flawless" are not. In Europe the term is not used at all, and there are no regulations similar to the FTC's. There, stones are "pure" or "eye perfect"; and a European certificate that a diamond is perfect is often a considerable distance from the truth. Tiffany's considers color more important than clarity in choosing a diamond. A stone of good color, though flawed, is more beautiful than a flawless stone of poor color—and is easier to resell.

Hoarding has always been a favorite form of hedge against disaster in unstable countries. Diamonds are not only the most portable form of wealth but have a stable universal market, as opposed to the currency of any one country. Many Jews were able to flee Hitler's Germany with enough capital in diamonds sewn in a coat lining to start a new life in a safe refuge. The price of diamonds fluctuates less than that of anything else precious, such as gold, in the free market, for the simple reason that there is no free market in diamonds. The market is controlled by the De Beers Syndicate. Even the United States trust busters know that they can do nothing about this. The federal government once brought suit against De Beers, but after a considerable waste of money and loss of face, dropped the case. Dealers thought that the United States was lucky that De Beers did not take offense and cut off the sale of diamonds to this country. Women can do without diamonds, but industry, and the explorers of space and the oceans, cannot.

De Beers is also the reason why diamonds are considered a better investment than stocks by many people. From 1960 through 1969, wholesale prices of diamonds over a carat rose almost twice as much as the Dow-Jones industrial average. There is small chance prices will go down, not only because of the cartel, but because the supply of diamonds has not increased at a time when the custom of giving an engagement ring, once chiefly popular only in the Western world, has spread around the globe. Also, the market in the United States has gradually changed; the once popular one-quarter carat diamond ring is too small; most young people now want a half carat or larger.

As it has for eighty years, De Beers keeps the supply remarkably in line with demand. Lest the news that large alluvial deposits have been found in Russia cheer the diamond-minded with the thought of competition, the sad fact is that even Russia markets most of her diamonds through De Beers. It is more profitable that way. In all, 85

percent of the world's diamonds are parceled out at the ten sights
(sales) a year in London, where De Beers sells its wares. "Parceled
out" is the correct term. Each dealer is handed a package of stones;
he cannot pick or choose, whether he is buying twenty-five thousand
dollars' worth or the nine-million-dollar sight which Harry Winston
takes as his share. Tiffany's does not attend; it depends on the dealers.
If a dealer refuses to take what he is dealt, he probably will not be
invited to the next party. Dealers are usually amazed at how perfectly their individual packages meet the requirements in their markets. (It has been suggested that De Beers has its own espionage
system to keep tab on the world's retail markets.) Furthermore, the
packages are remarkably uniform in quality and price.

The Tiffany diamond office also buys and grades what it refers to
as the "colored stones"—rubies, emeralds and sapphires. There are
no FTC standards for these, and since most of them are flawed,
grading and value depend largely on color. Jewelers speak of pigeon-
blood rubies, cornflower-blue sapphires, and the subtle shadings of
yellow-green or blue-green that give depth to the emerald. The employees who do the grading have to keep in mind the innumerable
nuances of color that increase or decrease the value of a stone. There
is also the matter of size, but here the problem is simplified because
some colored precious stones are not as large as diamonds. A ten-carat
gem ruby is a rarity.

In recent years the creation of synthetic stones has afforded competition for natural ones, and has created an occasional problem for
Tiffany's. The store not only will not sell synthetic stones, it will not
reset or handle them in any way.

There are synthetic diamonds and imitation diamonds. Imitation
diamonds have nothing in common with synthetics because they are
made not from carbon but from a variety of different materials, and
are very low-priced. To Tiffany's diamond experts, the imitation stone
does not look like a diamond, does not have the brilliance and often
has strange flashes of colors which do not resemble the colors in
natural diamonds. Moreover, there is no imitation diamond that
comes even close to a diamond in hardness.

Imitation diamonds have been widely advertised since the rise in
jewelry robberies and difficulty of obtaining insurance. Yet the fad
is encountering most resistance where one would expect the least—
among those who might consider it the better part of valor to wear
imitations instead of the valuable jewels put away in a bank vault.

"In the first place, your friends can always tell the difference,"
one such woman explained. "In the second place, if you are really

afraid, you are the greater fool to go around with a four- or five-carat fake on your finger. It's good enough to pass at a quick glance from a junkie—and who wants to be mugged or killed for a few hundred dollars of junk?''

A few hundred dollars will also buy a fancy colored stone, but these are true synthetics, made of corundum, the same material as rubies and sapphires, and it is not possible to identify them by simply taking a squint through a loupe. They must often be put under high magnification under the diamond scope or, in the case of emeralds, even under the spectroscope before they can be told from natural stones.

The diamond office and the purchase of all precious stones are supervised by Henry B. Platt, whom everyone calls Harry. A handsome, forty-six-year-old bachelor, he is a great-great-grandson of Charles L. Tiffany. Harry Platt was once described by the San Francisco *Chronicle* as a ''gem of an executive in a Tiffany setting.'' Allowing for the exuberance of the press, which dislikes seeing a good phrase go to waste, it is not difficult to see comparable traits in the founder of the store and his descendant. Platt is the only Tiffany of his generation connected with the firm. The description of Charles Tiffany at approximately the same age, when he bought out his partners and stayed on himself because that was what he enjoyed most doing, applies to his great-great-grandson. It is impossible to talk with Harry Platt and not realize that he finds his job great fun. Like Charles, the thing he likes next best is people and he too dines—as well as skis, swims, sails, jets and shoots—with his customers.

There is no doubt that Platt grew up in a Tiffany setting on Long Island, where his parents, Mr. and Mrs. Collier Platt, have their

Henry B. Platt.

(Top) Tanzanite winning at Churchill Downs, 1970.
(Bottom) W. L. Lyons Brown, owner (fourth from left),
with Tanzanite and Jockey D. Crump.

home. Harry well remembers his great-grandfather, whom he confused with Santa Claus, and the last great days of Laurelton Hall. Platt says candidly, "The society I grew up with was the carriage trade. Now society is based on money and *the* families don't have the influence they had in the twenties and thirties."

Platt has made the transition smoothly from Carriage Trade to Jet Set. A graduate of Yale, he had first thought of law, but took his degree in international history and economics. His youthful interest in international affairs has served him well in the world of precious gems which is still an international diplomatic enclave, with its own rules, and occasionally rule breakers, as it was when Charles was secretly picking up the French crown jewels.

In international circles, Platt has acquired the title "Mr. Tanzanite" as a result of a diamond-buying trip to Europe early in 1968. While in Idar-Oberstein, Germany, the lapidary capital of the world, he was shown a tray of gems, among which were some blue stones, beautiful and clear as sapphires. Platt was immediately fascinated and remained so, even when he was told that the stones were zoisite, a common, grayish-green and normally opaque mineral hitherto useful only for knick-knacks, such as the ash tray on his desk back in New York. No one had ever before seen zoisite like these deep-blue gems with their flashes of purple, green and red. Platt was told that they had been discovered in 1967 in Tanzania by a long-time prospector, Manuel D'Souza, who had been led to the stones by a Masai tribesman.

The stones, found only in Tanzania near Mt. Kilimanjaro are freaks of nature, formed by a combination of heat and gases under tremendous pressure a billion years ago, deep in the earth.

A stone as rare as this—no transparent blue gem stone had been found in the past two thousand years—was obviously valuable, but its exact worth could not be established until the jewelers of the world began to bid for it. Platt envisioned enormous possibilities for the stone if a market could be created. After all, how many Americans had really wanted genuine pieces of the Atlantic cable until Charles Tiffany had sold them the idea?

The first thing to do was to give the stone a name of its own. ''When you come to think of it,'' as Platt said, ''what man would give his girl something called a blue zoisite?'' The name he chose now seems the only possible one. The blue zoisite became the tanzanite, a tribute to and an identification with the land which gave it to the world. The next step was to make the world aware of the tanzanite. The best method would be to let the gem speak for itself. The task of designing the collection was turned over to Donald Claflin. He worked through the summer of 1968 to complete his collection, which ranged in price from five thousand to fifty thousand dollars. The grand premiere was to be handled like a Broadway show: open out-of-town and bring it to New York.

The tanzanite was launched in October in San Francisco, where Tiffany's had opened its first branch store and where both the store and Platt had many friends. The opening was a great success: pictures, stories and a pride of the best San Francisco names to meet the new beauty from Africa. At the same time. the rest of the country was given a hint of what it was to see. Eugenia Sheppard carried the story in her syndicated column under the headline ''Beautiful New Freak,'' with all the details but the price: ''less than a sapphire, more than an aquamarine.'' Something had to be kept for New York. (The price was set at four hundred dollars a carat, compared with as much as twenty-five hundred dollars for the best Kashmiri sapphire.)

In New York the tanzanite was introduced at ''Harry Platt's little cocktail party in the St. Regis,'' as the press dutifully reported. Columnist Sheppard noted that many of the guests outsparkled the guest of honor, i.e., the tanzanite. ''Tiny Dewi Sukarno, wife of the former dictator, was wearing a magnificent pair of emerald drop earrings . . . Mrs. Robert Gardiner had on her thirty-nine carat diamond and her sapphire earrings. Robert Gardiner, a dedicated collector who always carries a pet gem around with him, had a spare fifty-carat sapphire tucked into his vest pocket that evening and was worried about the rise of tanzanite at Tiffany's.''

Shortly after, an advertising campaign was undertaken to make the tanzanite synonymous with the beauty and mystery of Africa. Full-page ads featured snow-capped Kilimanjaro towering over the Tanzanian plain, where zebras and wildebeest grazed.

The quick popularity of the tanzanite soon made it the biggest selling stone (after diamonds) at Tiffany's—an indication of how valuable the right to market the stone would be. Unfortunately, mining in Tanzania was chaotic, with claim jumping, smuggling and all manner of skulduggery going on. To insure a supply of stones, Platt decided to go to Africa.

Tanzanite ring.

There he found that order was being restored to the mining of tanzanite by an operator named Theodore Wolff and his two sons, who were delighted to make an agreement with Tiffany's to supply all the stones needed. Also on the scene were a reporter and photographer from *Life,* working on a story which was bound to further publicize the new stone. (*Life*'s interest was aroused, somewhat incestuously, by a story in its sister publication, *Time.*)

With his supply of tanzanites seemingly assured, Platt flew back to New York, where, in May of 1969, *Life* ran a seven-page story with the headline ''Tanzania to Tiffany's,'' giving full credit to Platt for naming the gem.

The warmth of self-congratulation which Platt experienced was cooled suddenly before the month was over. Tiffany's carefully negotiated source of tanzanites was abruptly cut off. The Tanzanian government had refused to renew the export license of the Wolffs, along with those of several smaller operators, thus cutting off Tiffany's gem supply, and extending permits to only two firms, neither of which did business with Tiffany's.

The clue to what was going on in Tanzania turned up in the waiting room of Tiffany's diamond office when a salesman mentioned that his firm was going to acquire sole rights to mining and distributing tanzanites. The word was phoned upstairs to Platt, who called in the salesman, found out all he knew, and set up a meeting with his boss, the New York representative of a mining company in Tanzania. The mining representative was tough. He told Platt that his company and another mine operator in Tanzania had made arrangements with the socialist Tanzanian government to market tanzanites throughout the world. Furthermore, they planned to sell no rough stones; they would have the cutting done by their own firms and sell only the finished product, controlling the gem from mine to the retail counter. In other words, his manner said plainly, Who needs Tiffany's?

Platt winced on more than one account. He knew the difficulties the most experienced lapidaries had had in cutting the stones, and he knew that the cutters named had no connections with top gem cutters. He realized that in such hands the chances were all too real that all his promotion would be wasted, that the tanzanite would fail and disappear from the gem market. It would remain a freak of nature, on display only at the Smithsonian, or the American Museum of Natural History.

The mining representative had one final insult: If Tiffany's wanted to give him the name of its cutters . . . ?

Platt picked up the telephone. Before the mining representative reached the elevators, Platt had the Tanzanian ambassador to Washington on the wire. Armed with a book of clippings and display ads featuring Mt. Kilimanjaro, Platt conferred with the ambassadors of Tanzania, both to the United States and to the United Nations. He found that they, too, had been reading the ads and were pleased with what they had read. Nevertheless, Platt decided he should go back to Tanzania and see what more could be done on the spot.

On his arrival, he saw that the obvious next move was to go to the top and arrange for a meeting with George Kahama, manager of Tanzania's National Development Corporation. Kahama told Platt, "My country wants Tiffany & Co. to distribute our tanzanites." Impressed with the way in which Tiffany's had created a market for the Masai's blue stones, Kahama had a proposition for the firm: How would Tiffany's like to become partners with the government in mining and marketing the tanzanite? Platt jumped at the chance.

Months passed without final confirmation of the deal, and as in a Hollywood scenario, spring came around once more. Hearing that Kahama was in Geneva, and beginning to feel like a shuttlecock, Platt took off after him. Kahama explained at once that his government had decided it would be more correct if they considered several bids.

1. Diamond necklace.

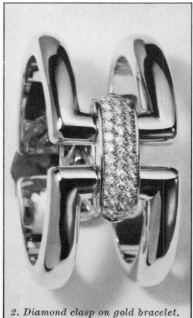

2. Diamond clasp on gold bracelet.

3. Onyx and jade clip with yellow sapphire.

5. Emerald and diamond earrings.

4. Diamond frog with emerald eyes.

6. Emerald, diamond and coral zodiac clip.

7. *Diamond criss-cross ring in platinum and gold.*

8. *17-carat tanzanite link ring.*

9. *Diamond and sapphire pendant.*

10. *Bracelet with carved coral strawberries and emerald-studded leaves.*

11. *Sapphire and diamond clip.*

12. *Pearl necklace with 87-carat tanzanite.*

Zebras roam the foothills of Kilimanjaro where tanzanites were discovered.

Jack Block, owner of famed Treetops, and Platt in East Africa.

Emerald, actual size.   *Platt (center) with North Carolina rock hounds.*

Africa and North Carolina are close together, as the jets fly. Back in 1882, Dr. George F. Kunz predicted that Hiddenite, North Carolina, would become the finest source of emeralds in the United States. Since then, amateur miners, called rock hounds, have found many stones. In 1970 a rock hound named Wayne Anthony discovered a 59-carat emerald which was cut to 13.14 carats, the largest and finest cut emerald found in North America. Platt went to Hiddenite and negotiated the purchase of the emerald for Tiffany's in 1971.

Kahama suggested that Platt come to Tanzania in July. It was then the end of May.

Came the Fourth of July, and Platt was spending the holiday with friends in Southampton. A cable was telephoned; Tanzania suggested that he cancel the trip. In the atmosphere of intrigue which had surrounded the business from the start, Platt translated this to mean that he should make the trip soonest. The next day he was in Africa. There Kahama told him that Tiffany's "had the deal."

But a private agreement was a long way from a public contract. Again, months went by as Tiffany's waited for some official announcement. Finally it came—at the place where it counted most, the gemstone fair at Frankfort, Germany, the most prestigious gathering of jewelers in the world. Fair officials had designated the tanzanite as the "gem of the year." Officiating at the opening, George Kahama told the gathering: "I would like to pay tribute to Mr. Harry Platt and the Tiffany Company for all it has done to introduce and enhance what they decided to christen tanzanite. My government has always chosen the best partners and therefore we have chosen to work jointly with Tiffany's to make this stone available to the world." The showstopper of the fair was a Claflin design of tanzanites, inspired by the leather collars worn by Masai warriors.

Under the arrangement, Tanzania has nationalized all of its mines (as it had planned to do for months), except the diamond mine owned by De Beers, and has become partners with Tiffany's. Tiffany will handle the marketing of the gem all over the world. If the partnership proves as profitable as both sides expect it will, Tiffany's may become the marketing agent for other gems from Tanzania. Thus, the firm whose name for more than 170 years has become synonymous with the

George Kahama (center) opening the Frankfort Fair.

glitter and show of private capital has joined hands with a nation whose eventual goal is the abolition of private capital. More important, the partnership will furnish the world with an example of how one of the best-known firms in capitalism can work with one of the newest socialist states for their mutual benefit.

Looking back over the legend of Tiffany's, this partnership should not seem unusual. The whole tenor of the firm's history has been that a paramount factor in Tiffany's success is the ability to change, to adapt and profit from the shifts in the political and economic worlds. If the Revolution of 1848, the year of *The Communist Manifesto,* could create the King of Diamonds at a time when kings were well thought of (but going out of style), it is not surprising that the proletarian ferment in Africa should create its own titles more in keeping with the times. Harry Platt is ''Mr. Tanzanite'' by appointment of a recognized government and not by anointment of the popular press.

When Tiffany's made its coup in diamonds, it was impossible for the ordinary traveler to journey from the store on Broadway to the snows of Kilimanjaro. In this jet age, Charles Tiffany's great-great-grandson can make the trip in far less time than it took Charles—and in far more comfort—to journey to Boston to buy his beautiful Japanese desk and table. This feeling for beauty, this taste, were a portion of the inheritance which Charles left, along with his readiness to change, to throw out the cheap gewgaws from Germany for the better Palais Royale ornaments, and then on to the best in jewelry.

The secret of the Tiffany touch may simply be this talent for adaptability, combined with an appreciation of aesthetic values and the great commercial skill which helped make the country aware of artistic excellence. Inspiration from the art of the American Indian, the glowing colors of a Favrile vase, the delicate tracery of gold and enamel in a diamond necklace and, in the seventies, the bold design from a Masai warrior's collar—all have molded what has come to be regarded as the best in American taste.

ABOUT
THE AUTHOR

———

Joseph Purtell was born in Milwaukee,

Wisconsin, and attended Marquette University and the University of Wisconsin.

He worked as a reporter on the Milwaukee Sentinel and the

Detroit Times and joined Time, Inc., in 1942. He was a senior editor of Time magazine

from 1946 to 1961, when he left to become owner and publisher of

the Town Crier in Westport, Connecticut. He is the author of a mystery,

To a Blindfold Lady, and lives in New York with his wife.